IMAGES
of America

AROUND HARTWICK

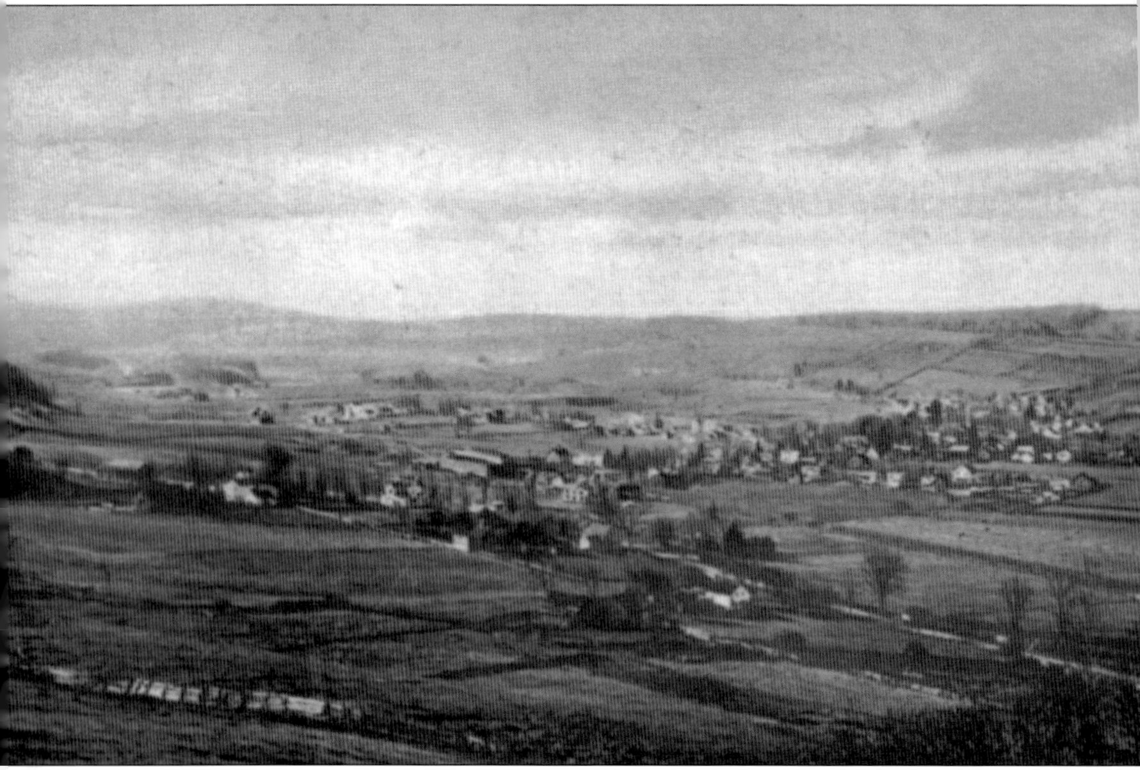

This early-1900s view looks south from Hartwick hamlet toward the Otego Valley. The trolley carbarn is seen at the center, and the powerhouse is in the distance at the top left. Hartwick, a rural township, is at the heart of Otsego County. (Courtesy of Richmond Field.)

On the Cover: Frederick D. Field and an assistant are haying on his farm in Pleasant Valley, Hartwick, New York, in the 1930s. (Courtesy of Richmond Field.)

IMAGES
of America

AROUND HARTWICK

Hartwick Historical Society

ARCADIA
PUBLISHING

ISBN 978-1-4671-2374-7

Published by Arcadia Publishing
Charleston, South Carolina

Printed in the United States of America

Library of Congress Control Number: 2014959795

For all general information, please contact Arcadia Publishing:
Telephone 843-853-2070
Fax 843-853-0044
E-mail sales@arcadiapublishing.com
For customer service and orders:
Toll-Free 1-888-313-2665

Visit us on the Internet at www.arcadiapublishing.com

This book is dedicated to all those who have created our history by living it and leaving records of their lives that we might know, enjoy, and share it with others.

Contents

Acknowledgments

This book came into being as a result of an inquiry from Sharon McAllister of Arcadia Publishing about our interest in producing a history of Hartwick. With enthusiasm, the Hartwick Historical Society agreed to share its collective love of our local history through the images in this book. This project has been a team effort by volunteer members of the society who sought previously unseen "old" pictures from the community, searched through historical society collections, and met together to scan and plan the final publication.

We are especially grateful to Rebekah Ambrose-Dalton, archivist of the Paul F. Cooper, Jr. Archives at Hartwick College (PFCA at HC) for sharing images from the archives with us. Without her knowledge, time, and assistance, the chapter on Hartwick Seminary would not have been possible.

Several photographs are included with permission from the Smith & Telfer Photographic Collection at the Fenimore Art Museum (ST at FAM), Cooperstown, New York, and we are most thankful for each community member who opened up their family treasures of images to share in this book. In particular, we thank Richmond Field (RF), Orlo Burch (OB), Gloria Waro (GW), David Petrie (DP), Daniel Conklin (DC), Charles Buckland (CB), Carol Goodrich (CG), the Stanley Clark family (SC), the Risley family (R), Elaine Harvey (EH), Nancy Mitchell (NM), Lawrence W. Gardner, and Shari Adams (SA). Unless otherwise labeled by these sources, all images are from the collections of the Hartwick Historical Society or town historian files.

INTRODUCTION

Hartwick is a township of small communities, each with its own distinct history but centered today on the hamlet of Hartwick. This community/hamlet is itself the geographic center and the very heart of Otsego County.

Many of the settlers who made up these small, rural communities had moved west from New England in search of opportunities on virgin frontier lands, and much of the early land was leased or purchased from the land patents of John Christopher Hartwick. Settlements reflected pioneer families in name (as in Hinman Hollow, Toddsville, and Christian Hill) or else were named after descriptive geographic markers such as Pleasant Valley, Arnold Lake, or the White House District. These pioneer settlers shared in the ebb and flow of daily life pursuits, in social activities, in agriculture, in business, and even in manufacturing (as with the water-powered woolen, paper, and cotton mills), all within their common geographic locations.

With the formal establishment of the Town of Hartwick in 1802, and through the years that followed, neighborhood communities first prospered before declining in size. Emphasis gradually shifted away from these local entities and toward a more unified and common hub of commerce, government, and transportation in the hamlet of Hartwick. While family neighborhoods still existed, the hamlet became the seat of government and, with the coming of the trolley, a larger commercial center for numerous businesses.

Construction of the trolley/electric railway line, with tracks, rolling stock, carbarns, and a large powerhouse, established Hartwick as both the headquarters and the source of power for the major transportation link between the small communities and large cities to the south of town and north to the Mohawk Valley.

John Christopher Hartwick, the eccentric, itinerant, German-born Lutheran preacher (and namesake for Hartwick Township), purchased land as early as 1754 from the Mohawk Indians. Nearly six years later, in 1761, he finally petitioned for and received the letters and patent giving the right to bring in settlers. But only after 1791, with employment of William Cooper as his land agent, did settlers begin to move in to lease and to purchase land.

Hartwick dreamed of creating a "New Jerusalem" on his land patents. These settlers were to become his congregation, composed of converts from Native Americans and pioneer families. After his death, without fulfilling his larger dreams of a school and a church, Hartwick Seminary came into existence as the first Lutheran Theological Association in America. With time, this expanded into both a seminary and a coeducational academy. In 1927, this school became the foundation for a private liberal arts college, now known as Hartwick College, located in Oneonta, New York.

In over 200 years of Hartwick history, many people and personalities (besides John Christopher Hartwick) have influenced its growth and change. There were the common folk who lived and labored in construction or as farmers, craftsmen, mill workers, or railway employees. Also, there were those who were the mill owners, businessmen, inventors, educators, professional men, or government leaders. Each played a part in shaping Hartwick's history.

The heyday of the railway/trolley has long since past, the Lutheran seminary has closed, and the academy has merged into the private Hartwick College. The mills have closed or moved to other, more promising, economic locations. Neighborhood district schools and Hartwick High School have closed or merged into larger districts made up of adjoining townships or villages. People of the past, whether influential or not, are long gone except in memory.

The hamlet of Hartwick remains the basic hub of the township with some new businesses, but most commerce has now shifted again away from the hamlet. Commercial development has exploded along the eastern border of the township and down the State Route 28–Susquehanna River corridor.

New history is being written, and the town has new growth and vitality. But, along with the new, Hartwick retains a rich and interesting local historical heritage. We invite you to share this with us now, through photographic images, as we travel around Hartwick.

One

Beginnings of a Town

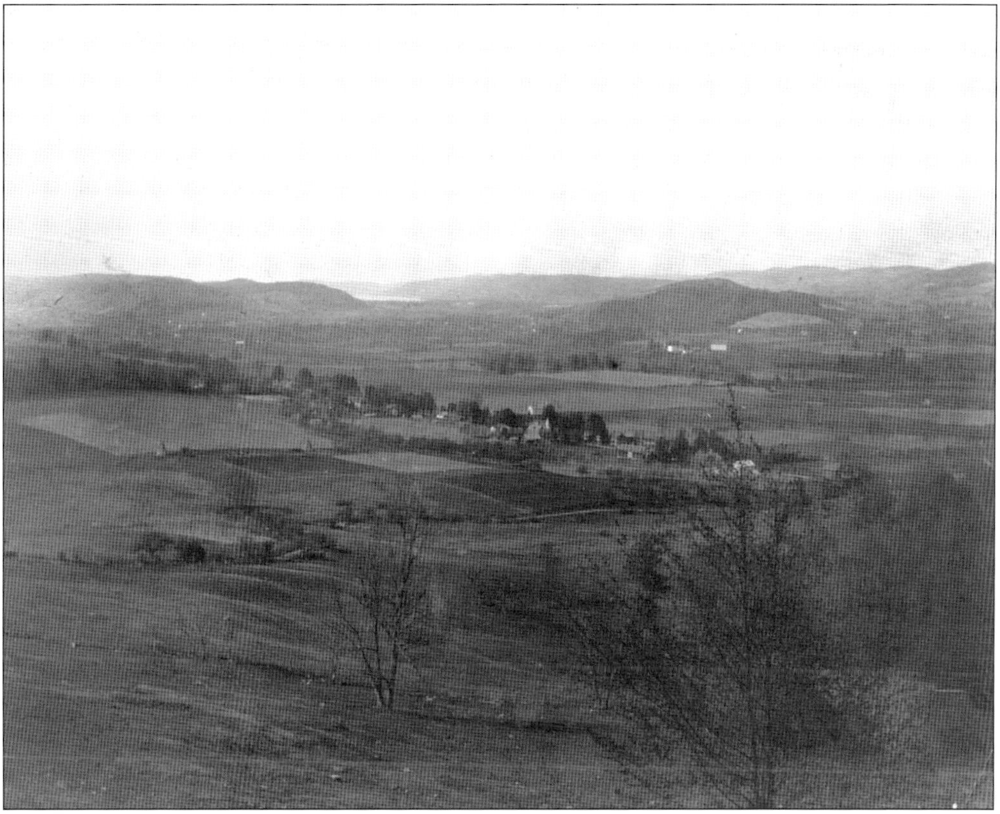

Early settlers moving west from New England likely would have seen a view like this one of Hartwick Seminary from Goewey Pond as they came to this area in search of virgin forest and new farmland. The area then would have been more heavily forested, but Otsego Lake could be seen in the distance to the left, and the Susquehanna River boundary was out of this view to the right.

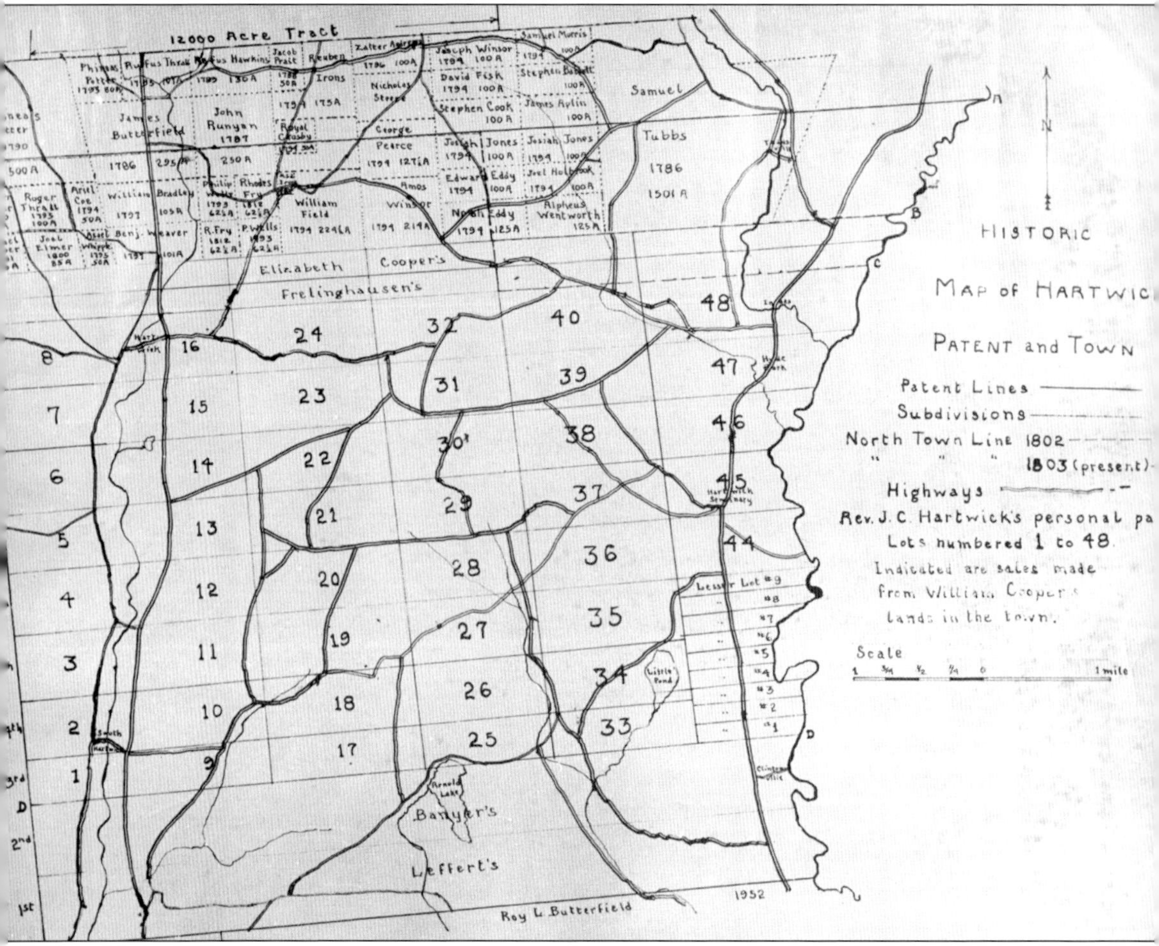

John Christopher Hartwick, as a Lutheran preacher, had a vision of creating a " 'City of God' in the wilderness . . . to bring together the savage Indian and the white settler for peaceful worship . . . community living." With the assistance of superintendent of Indian Affairs Sir William Johnson, the Mohawk Indians deeded Hartwick about 21,500 acres of land in May 1754 for 100 pounds. After much delay, land negotiations, and surveys, a land patent was issued by Acting Colonial Governor C. Golden in April 1761 to Hartwick and his associates. The land remained unsettled until 1791, when William Cooper was employed as a land agent by Hartwick. Cooper's land bordered the Hartwick Patent on the north, and soon both his Otsego Patent and Hartwick's land were divided into lots for lease and sale to settlers. By September 1791, Cooper had disposed of 38 of Hartwick's 48 lots and most of his own land to the north. Leases and sales of land continued after Hartwick's death in July 1796 and Cooper's in 1809, but by 1800 the majority of land that formed the Hartwick Township was fully settled.

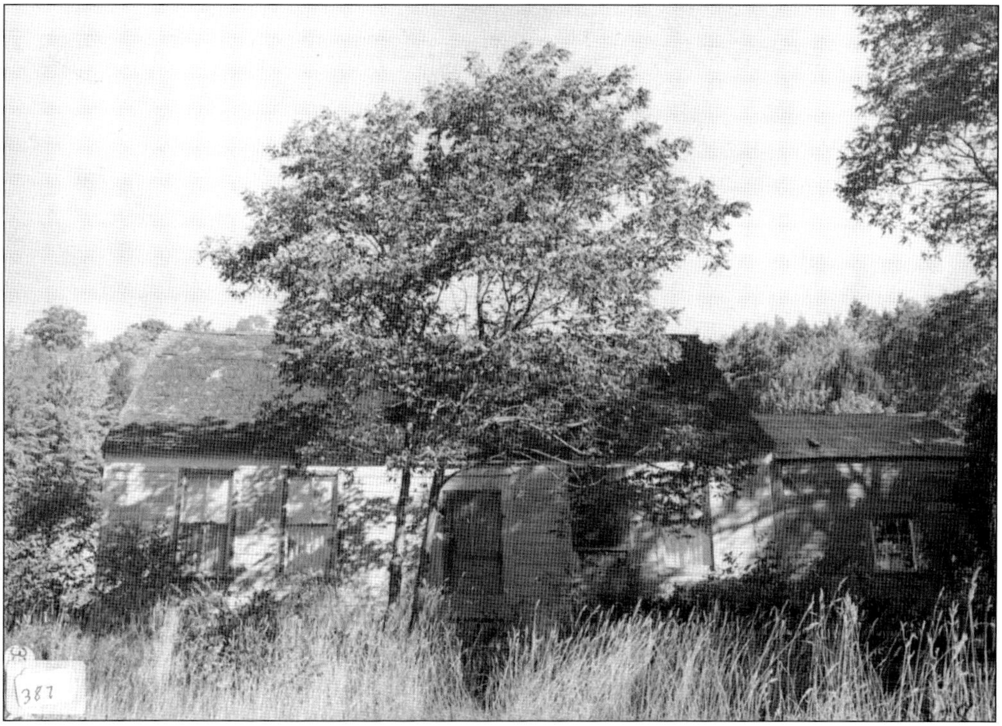

Rhodes Fry was one of many settlers who migrated west from Rhode Island, as early as 1787. By 1793, land had been cleared, and the family had settled in a home on a divided (with brother-in-law Phillip Wells) 250-acre lot leased and purchased from William Cooper on the Otsego Patent. This homestead on a hill northeast of the Hartwick hamlet exists today as a partially restored summer retreat for a New Jersey family.

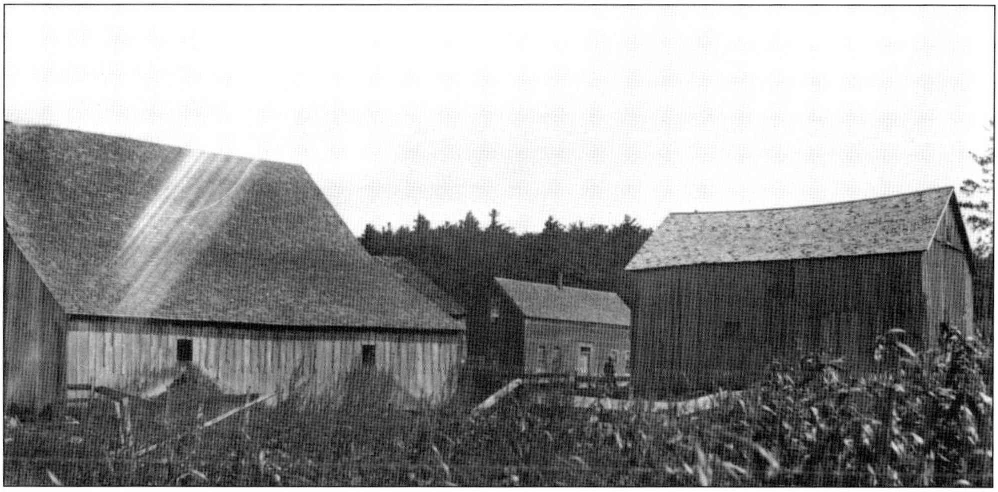

Joseph Lippitt came to Hartwick from Warwick, Rhode Island, in the winter of 1793 with his parents, brother, and five sisters. Other family and friends soon joined them, and by November 1800, Lippitt had leased 128 acres on lot No. 29 of the Hartwick Patent from William Cooper. Rent for the land, totaling $120.62, was paid, and the first Hartwick town organizational meeting was held here in March 1802. The Lippitt farmhouse in this 1908 view was preserved and moved to its present location at the Farmers' Museum in Cooperstown, New York. (ST at FAM.)

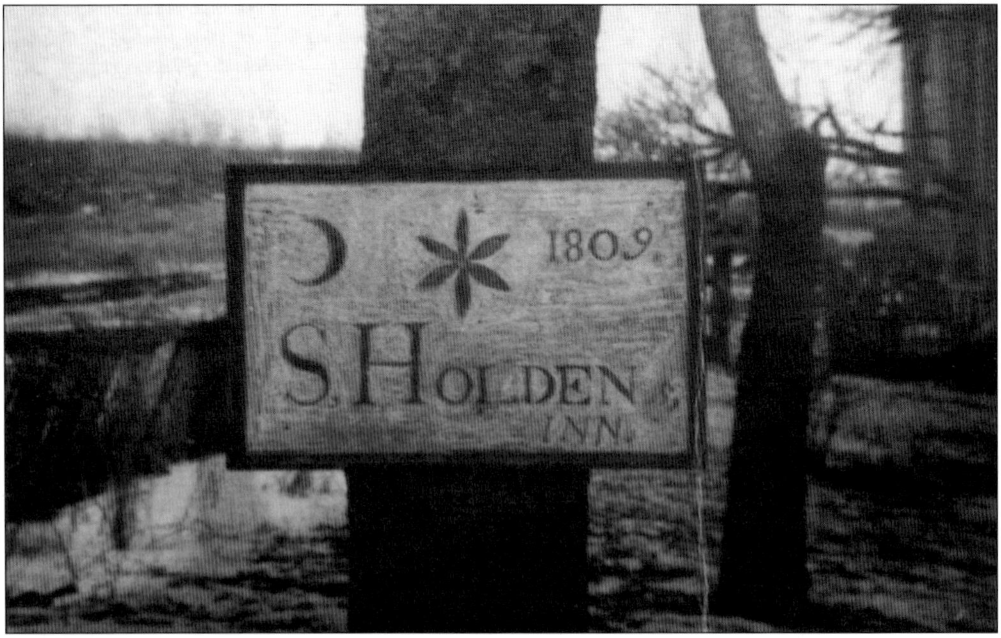

Stephen Holden, neighbor and future brother-in-law to Joseph Lippitt, emigrated from Rhode Island in 1794 and settled on 100 acres in the western portion of Lot No. 30 of Hartwick Patent. The family lived in a log cabin there while land was cleared and the house, Holden Inn, was being built. Holden Inn was a landmark in the Hinman Hollow area, and travelers moving west through the county regularly enjoyed a stop there. The first recorded town meeting in Hartwick was held there in March 1804, and five years later, the original sign in the photograph above appeared. Holden Inn fell into disrepair but was purchased in 1930 by Alfred T. Brown and restored over the next decades. The landmark inn is seen below before its loss to fire in October 1986. (EH.)

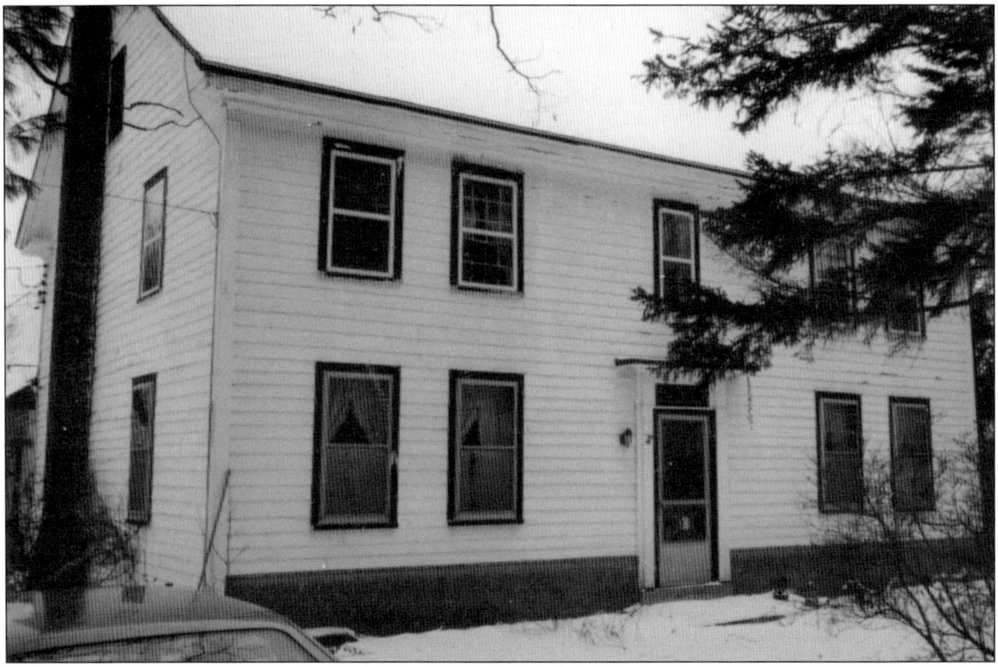

Two

NEIGHBORHOOD COMMUNITIES

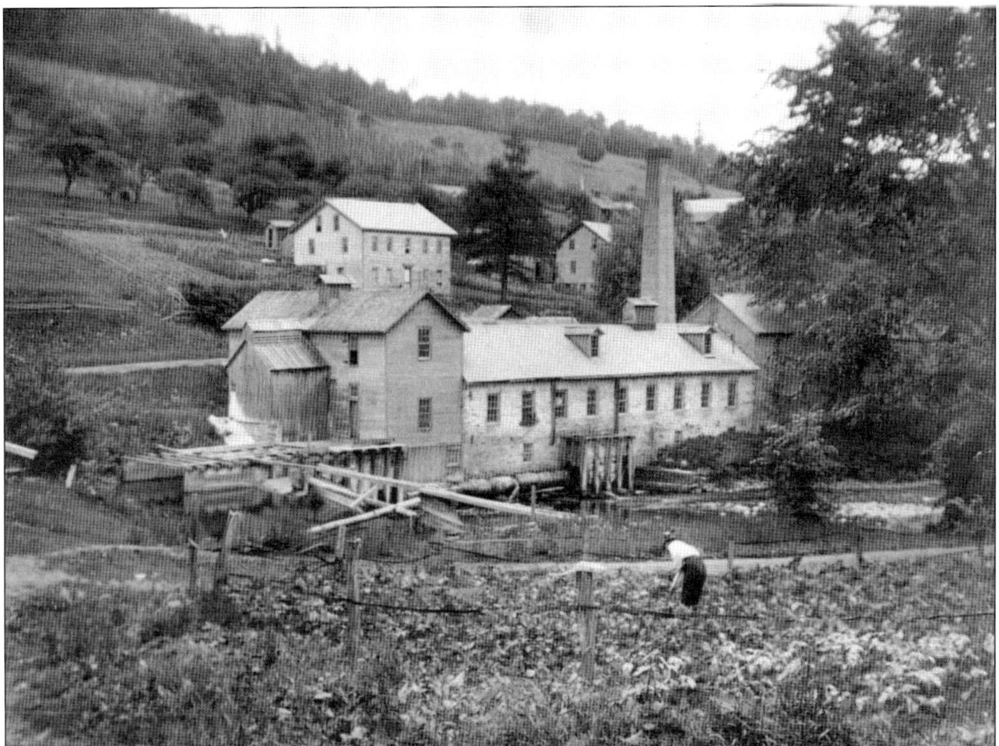

Early settlements first spread along streams and rivers of the Hartwick Township. Samuel Tubbs purchased patent land from Judge Cooper along Oaks Creek in 1788 and erected a log home and gristmill along the Hartwick side of the stream. Joined by the Jehiel Todd family in 1796, Tubbs Mill (later Todds Mill or Toddsville) grew into a thriving mill town, known for manufacturing paper and cotton goods. An early paper mill is pictured here.

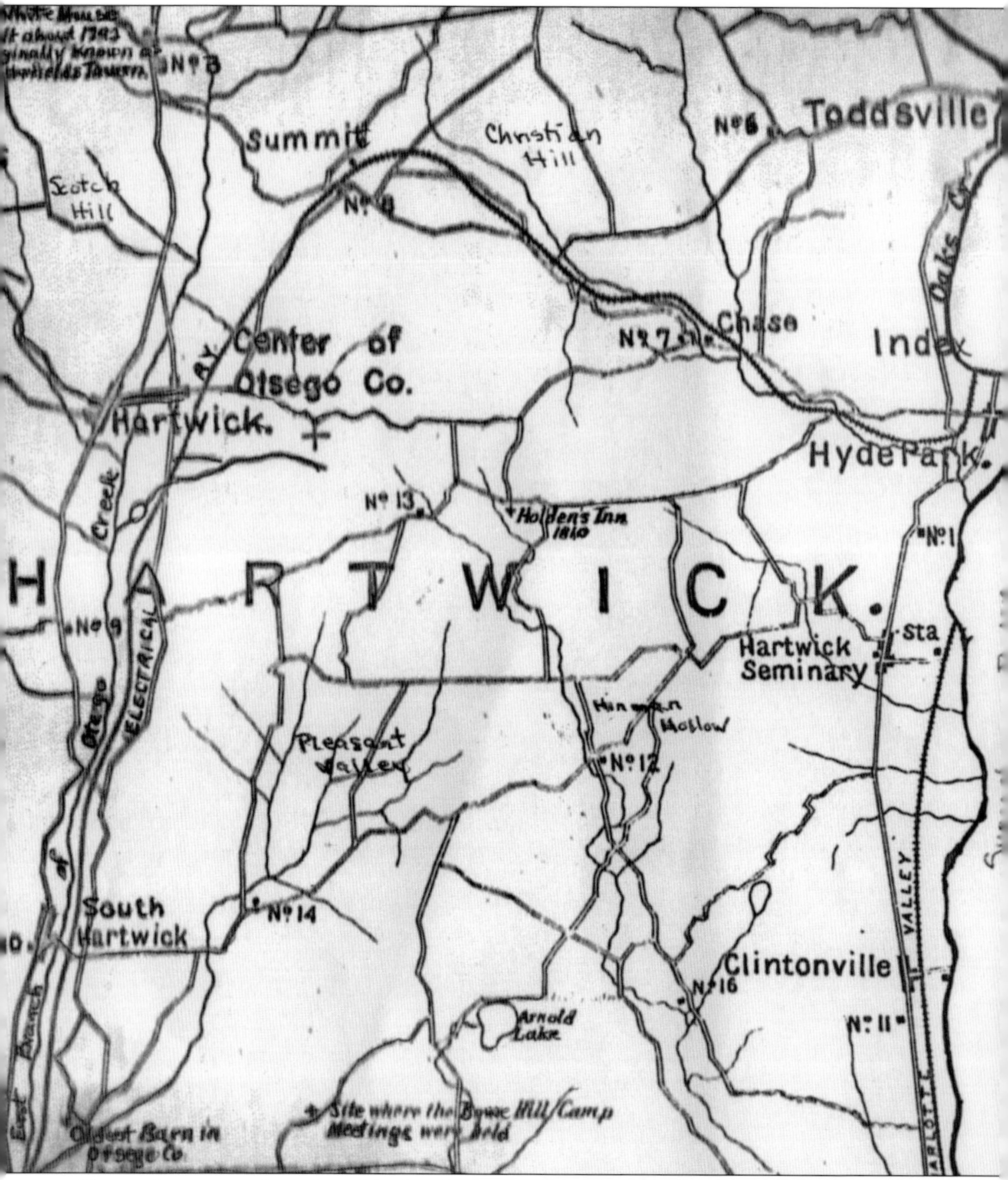

Hartwick is a township of neighborhood communities identified by geographic description or names of early settlers. This early-1900s map shows the location of those small neighborhoods that make up the whole of Hartwick today.

Settlers from Connecticut and Rhode Island came as early as 1789 to southeastern patent land known as "the Hollow." The settlement, later known as Hinman Hollow after the Hinman family, grew to include farms, a brickyard, a school/church, mills, and small businesses. Pictured here is the Augur Homestead, the original home of 1794 settler Martin Luther Comstock.

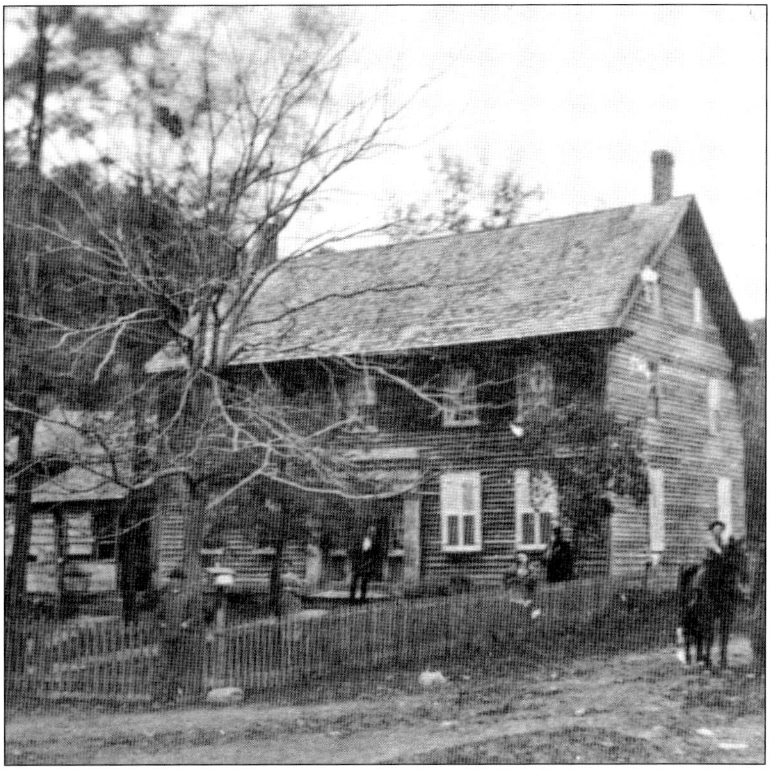

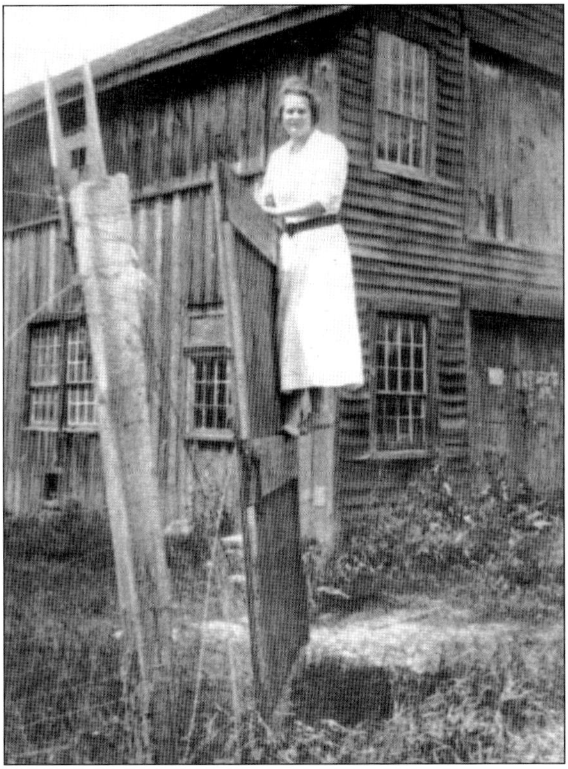

Communities often included cheese factories to make productive use of excess milk before it was profitable to ship milk to distant markets. An 1868 map identifies the Hartwick Union Cheese Factory west of the Hollow. Pictured here is the Hinman Hollow Cheese Factory, built around 1906 and located at the crossroads near the school. Thomas Millard operated the factory for many years. (EH.)

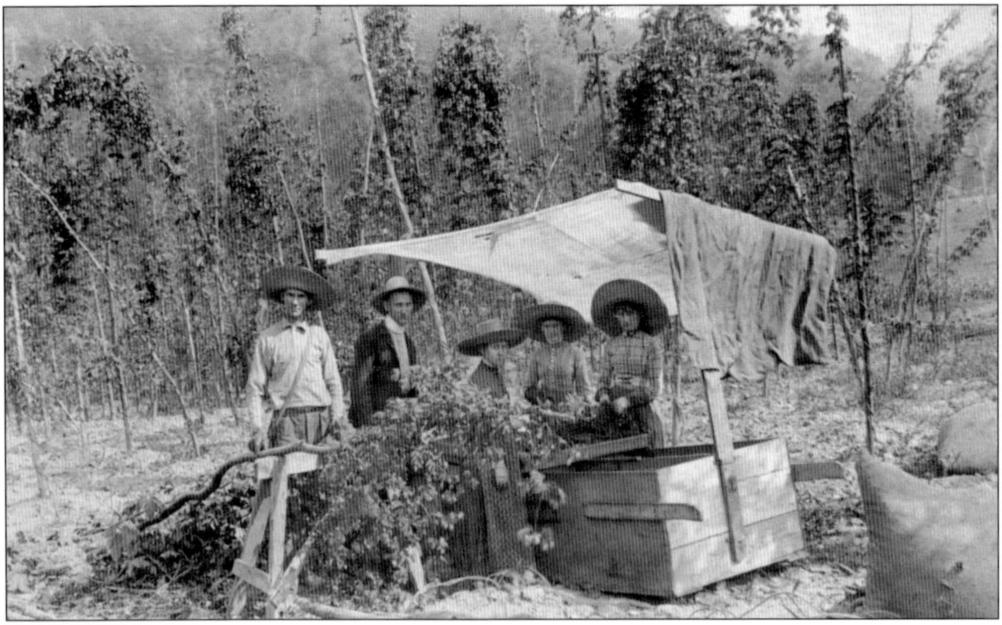

Otsego County, including Hartwick Township, produced the largest quantity (and best quality) of hops in New York and the world. Hops provided a cash crop for farmers. Pictured here are hop pickers on the George Milton Augur East Hill Hartwick farm in 1888.

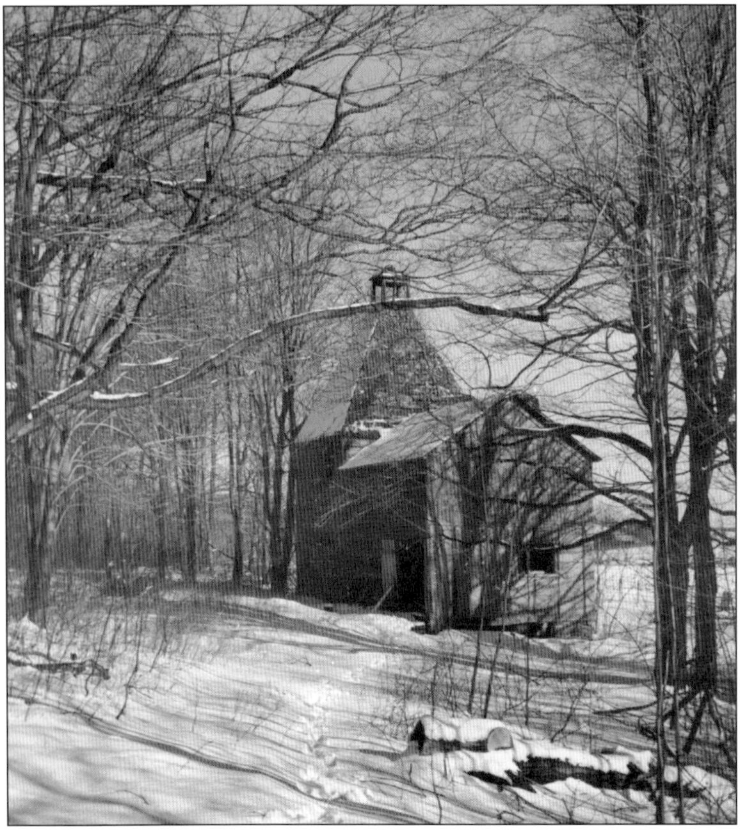

After harvest, hops were dried in local kilns and pressed into bales for market. Many farms had hop kilns, and one is pictured here in the early 1900s on the Maples Farm. (CB.)

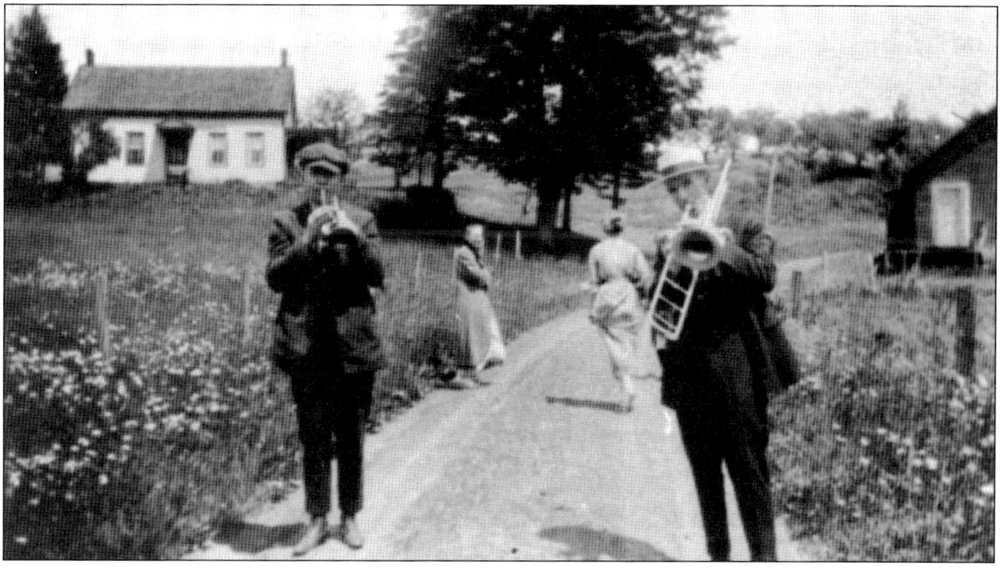

Hinman Hollow was well known for musicians and family production of the Phillips violin. In this parade view, music of a different kind is enjoyed. The Beers home, where Marcus Wells wrote the famous hymn "Holy Spirit, Faithful Guide," is seen in the background to the left, and the Grange Hall is on the right. (EH.)

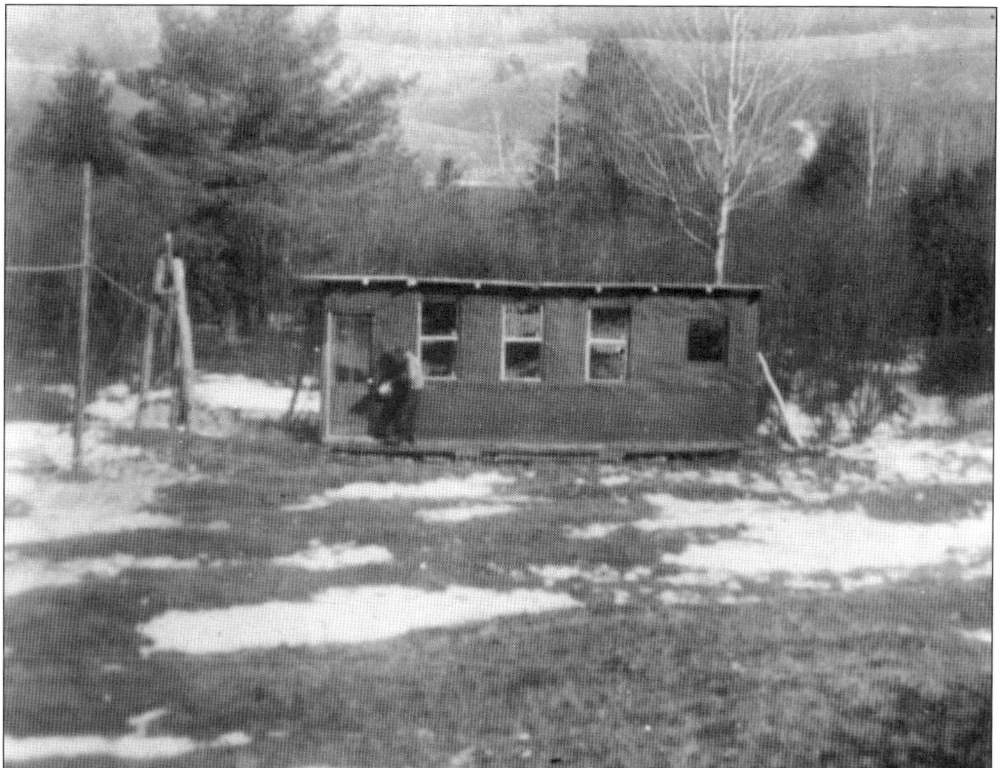

Neighbors in Hinman Hollow shared social and athletic activities. About 1940, William Powers and his father constructed a ski rope tow with this warming shed for a season of winter fun. (EH.)

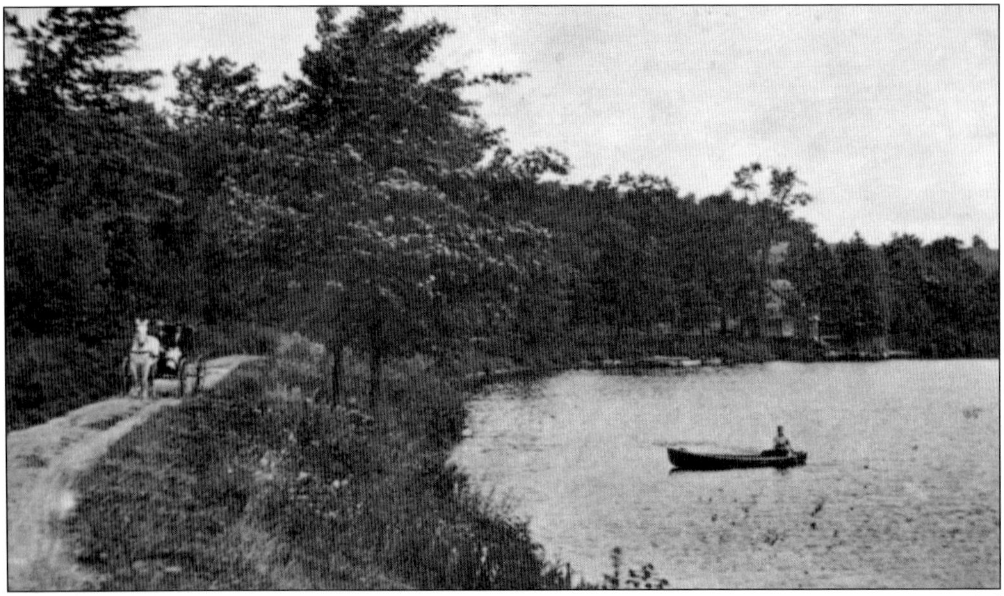

Arnold Lake, described by Rev. John Price in the 1940s as "the best spot on earth," is a spring-fed mountaintop lake covering 64 acres and located just south of Hinman Hollow. It was named after Capt. Josiah Arnold from Rhode Island, who migrated here in 1793 and purchased 112 acres of land at the south end. The lake today is surrounded by seasonal camps and year-round homes.

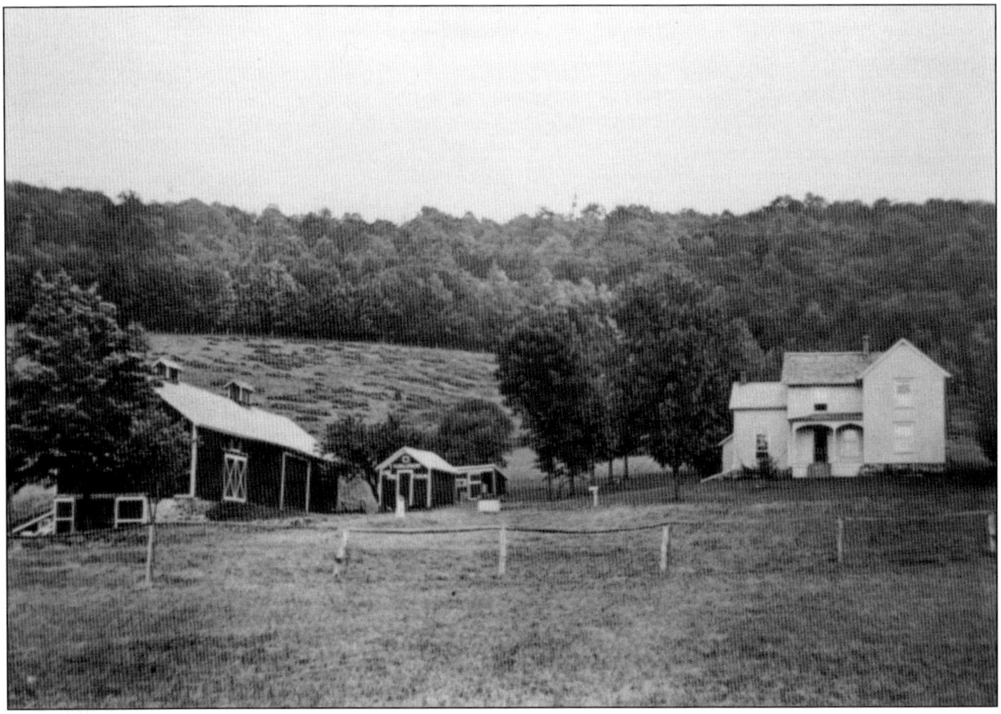

Ida and Edgar Salisbury owned the large farm pictured here at the top of the hill on the northeast end of the lake along with the land bordering the lake's eastern shore. Owners of seasonal camps built there between 1905 and 1922 enjoyed fresh milk and farm produce from the Salisbury farm. (EH.)

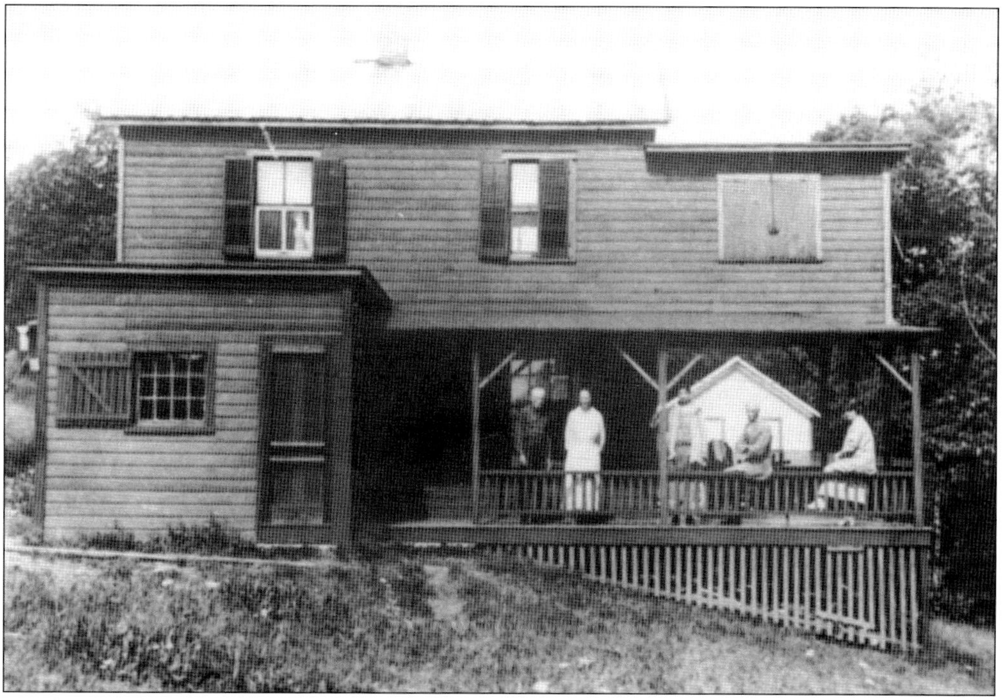

Residents and visitors to this Arnold Lake community could enjoy activities such as group picnics at the picnic grounds, tour boat rides, lakeside walks, fishing, or swimming, followed by light refreshments at the camp store. An increase in the number of camps, from 3 in 1900 to 78 by 2003, brought improvements in basic services like electricity, seasonal mail, and indoor plumbing. The typical early seasonal camp viewed here was an old Mount Vision store moved to the lake for camp use around 1930.

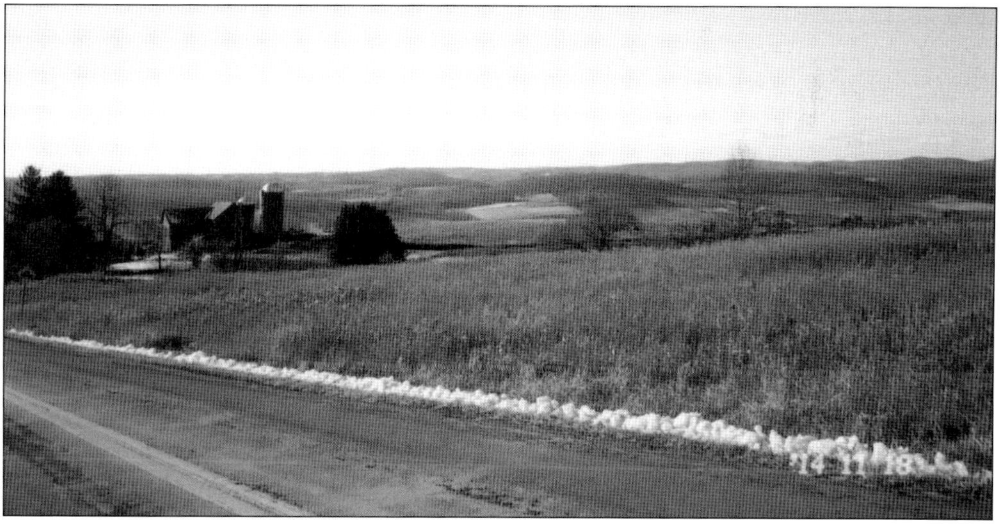

By 1800, Revolutionary War veteran Edward Bowe leased and settled Leffert Division Patent hill land west of Arnold Lake, overlooking the Otego Valley. Other New England families followed, cleared land, and formed a busy farm community along Bowe Hill. Popular camp revival meetings, held between 1805 and 1847 on the hilltop land to the right of this image, brought in large crowds for the annual weeklong events. (CG.)

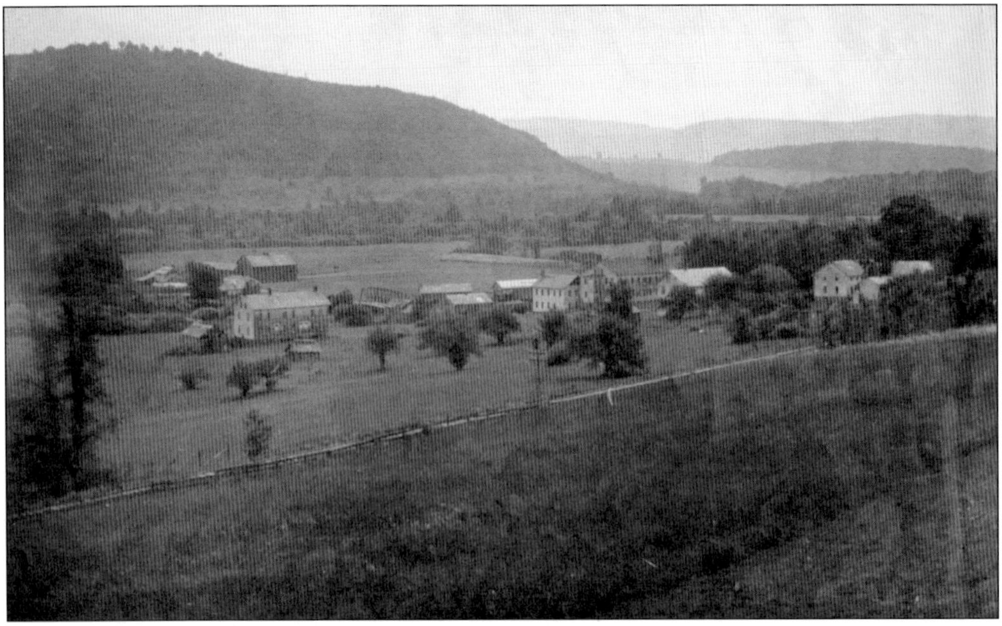

In 1813, Samuel Crafts was given state permission to build a dam across the Susquehanna River, the eastern boundary of Hartwick Township, and a large cotton and woolen mill was constructed. When William Clinton bought the mill in 1840, the community became known as Clintonville. This view shows the growing community with family and boarding homes, church, school, blacksmith shop, cooper shop, and sawmill.

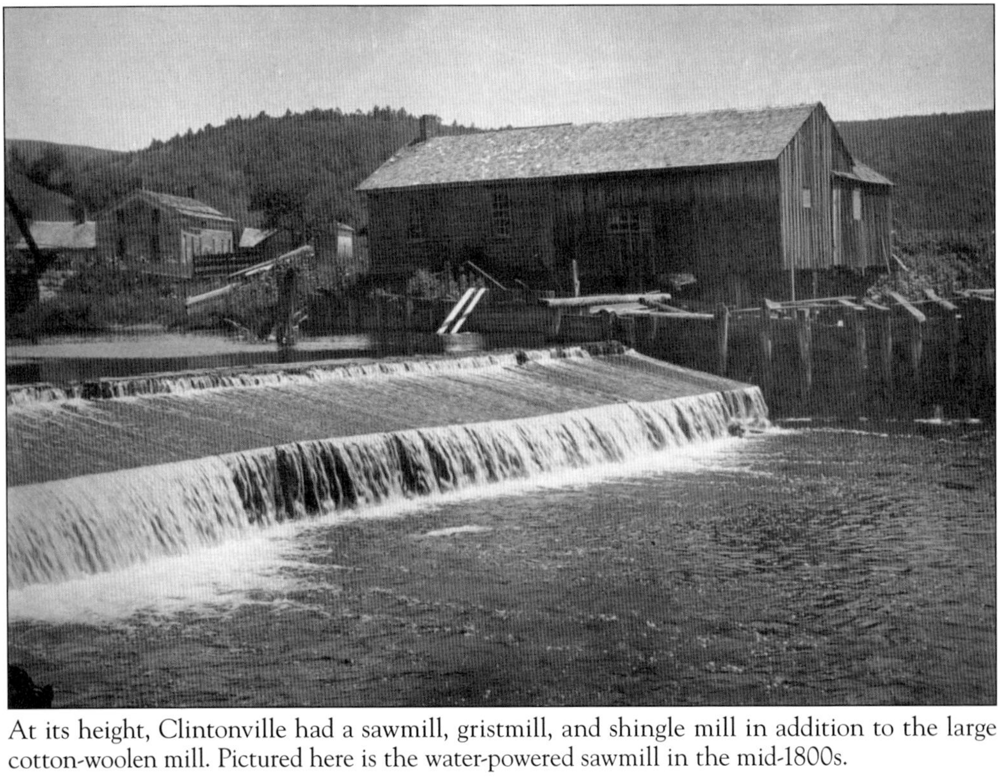

At its height, Clintonville had a sawmill, gristmill, and shingle mill in addition to the large cotton-woolen mill. Pictured here is the water-powered sawmill in the mid-1800s.

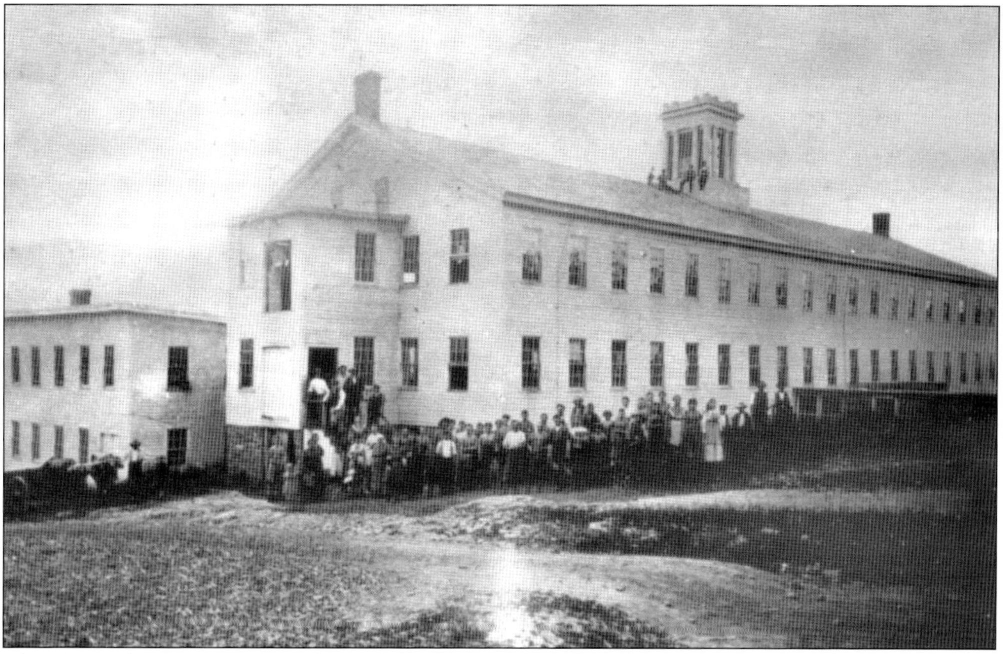

The Susquehanna Cotton and Woolen Manufactory Company Mill constructed in 1814 was the major Clintonville industry, with an annual output in 1855 of 624,000 yards of printed cloth, valued at $24,960. The community thrived, with this mill alone employing a workforce of 35 to 40 people.

This undated poem by John Kisselburgh tells the story of Clinton's Mill (cotton and woolen) both at the height of business and with the decline by the mid-1880s.

Clinton's Mill

A bridge spanned Susquehanna's tide
Where the waters were not too wide,
And nearby on a steep-sloped hill
The houses rose in Clintonville.

The lab'rers came from far and wide
With cart and horse from mountain side,
And labored with a right good will
All making cloth at Clintonville.

And still the pits and stones are seen
And ancient flume where walls are green,
And timbers deeply buried still;
Just ruins of Clinton's cotton mill.

Still stand the arches mossy green,
And still the timbers may be seen,
And still the walls stand straight and true
Where ancient flume comes burr'ing through;

While lazy waters idly lie
Harb'ring the frog and dragon-fly,
And clinging vine and long-plumed fern
Cover the spots where wheels should turn.

Poem by John Kisselburgh

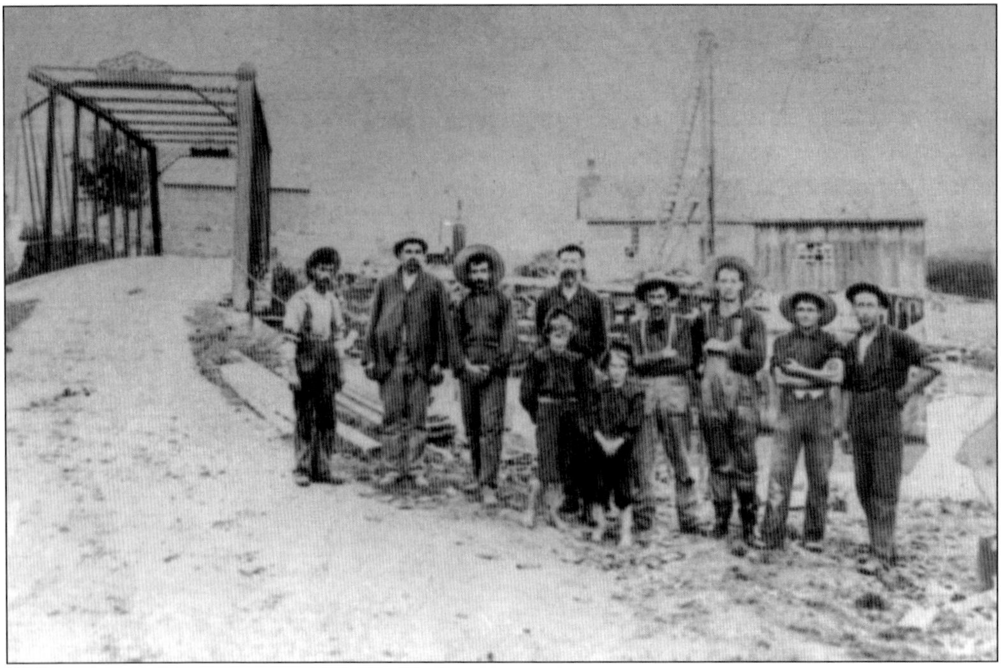

Mid-1880s Clintonville was still an active mill community, though without the manufacture of cotton goods. In 1896, with a new dam completed across the river, a portion of the old knitting mill was demolished, and the basement was roofed over for a powerhouse. The Clinton Mills Power Company, operating 24 hours a day and using three 150-horsepower waterwheels, began supplying electricity in 1897 to county buildings, the Otsego County Home, and the entire village of Cooperstown. Operation continued for 20 years until the dam washed out in the 1914 flood. Pictured here are an early construction crew and the Clinton power plant in operation.

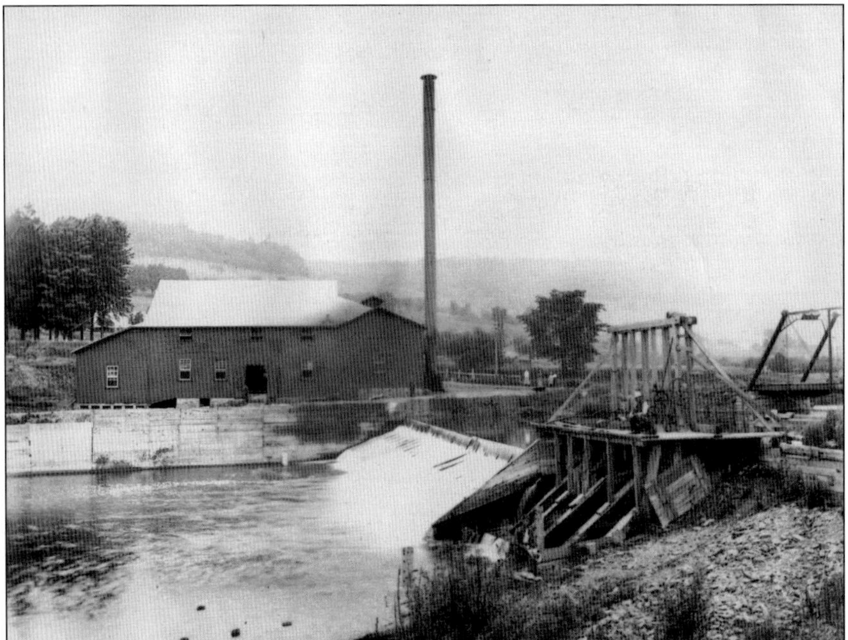

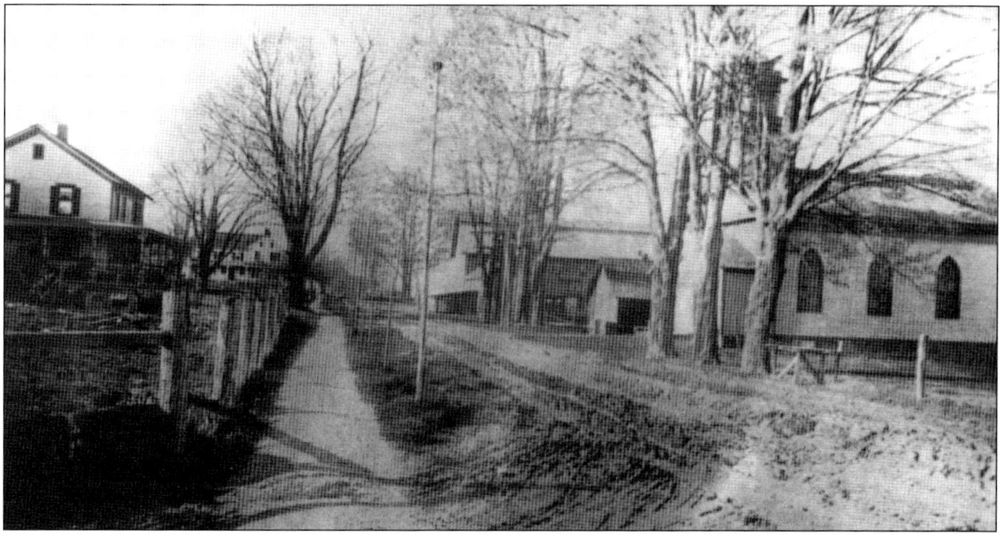

Hartwick Seminary was both an agricultural and academic community. It was home to the first Lutheran theological seminary in America and to a secondary school called "the Academy," and much activity centered on school, church, and student life, but farm families also shared equally in their own work and social events. This 1909 street view shows both farm buildings and the Lutheran church, which had close ties to the seminary.

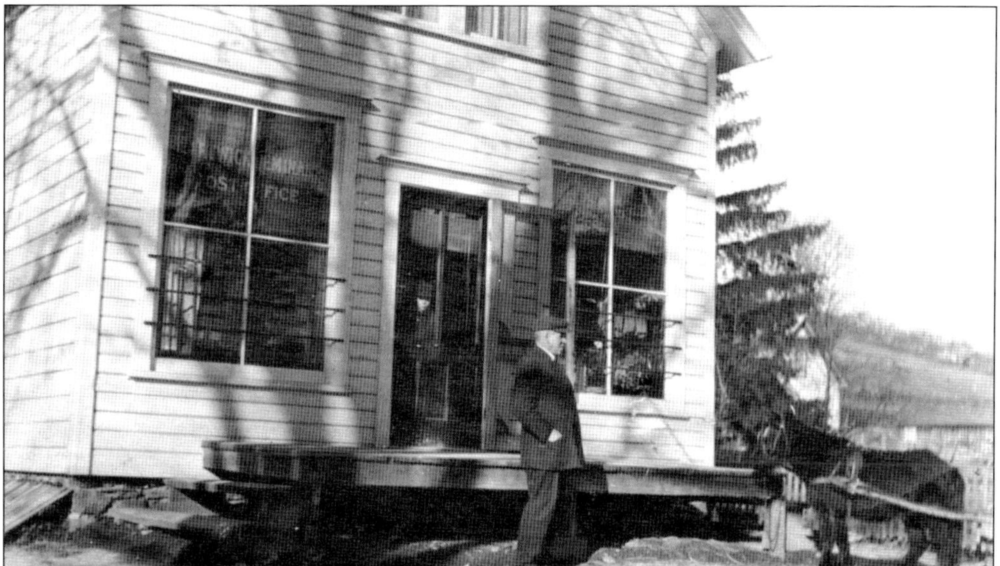

The local store and post office was a daily gathering place for conversation and pickup of mail or supplies.

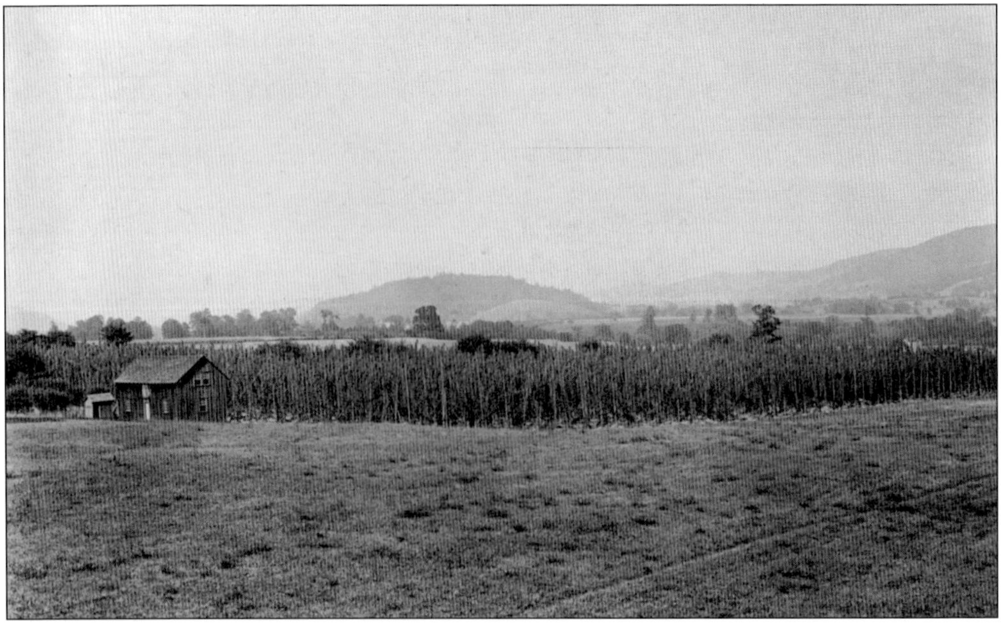

Hartwick Seminary was an active center for hop production in the early 1900s. The Kinne Hop Yard, seen here about 1900, covered many acres of fertile land near the Susquehanna River.

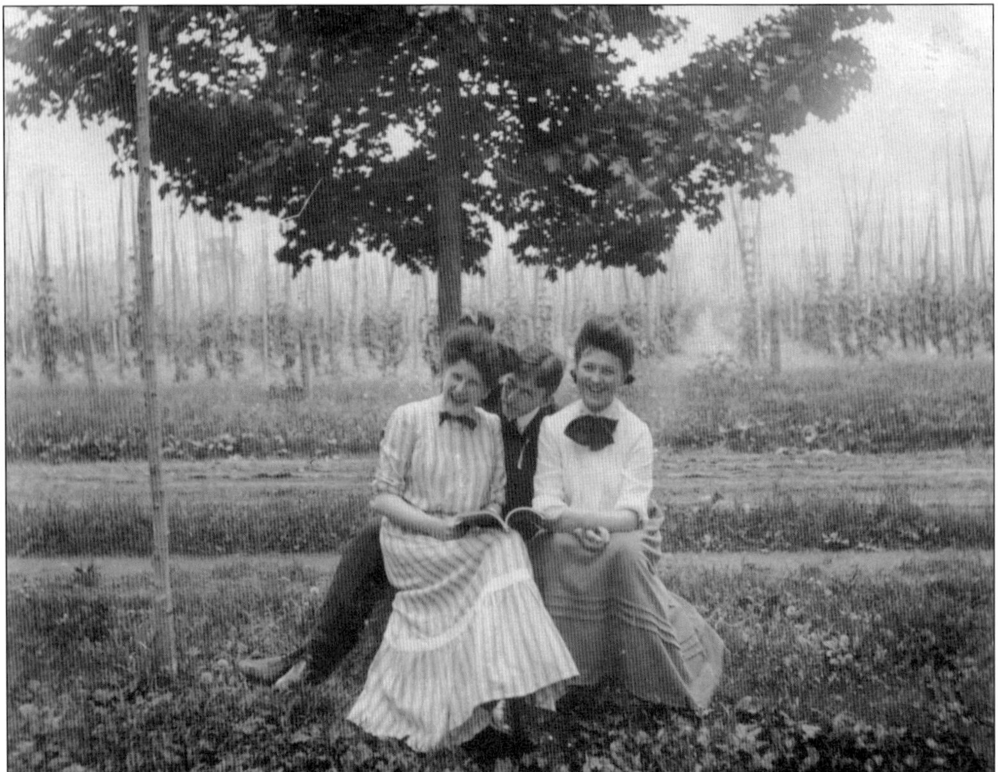

Hartwick Seminary students enjoy some lighter social moments across the road from the hop yard in this early spring image. Notice the hops are beginning to grow up the poles.

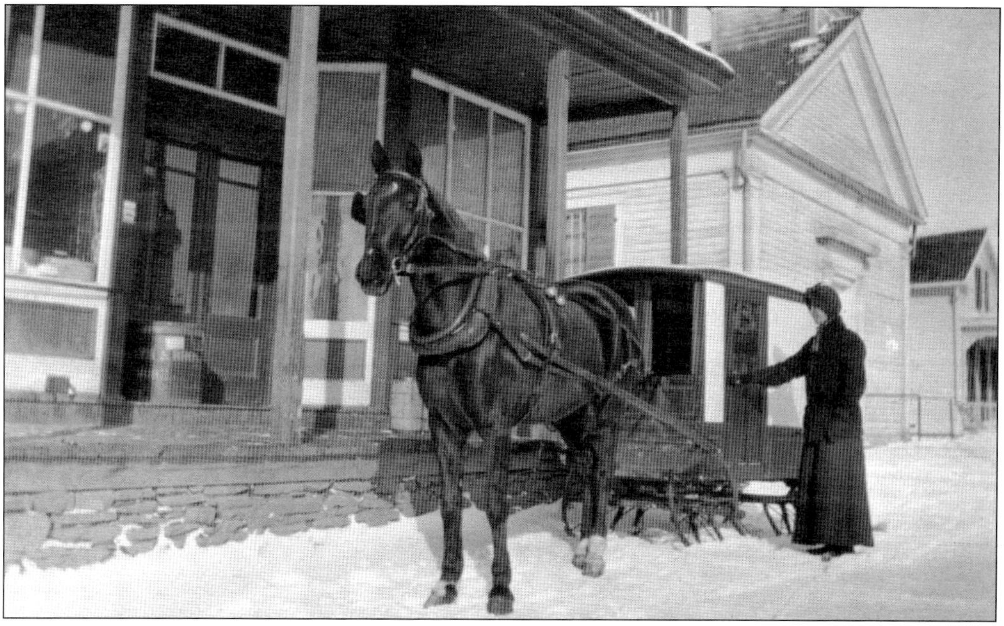

Hyde Park, the neighboring community north of Hartwick Seminary, was named for Abel Hyde, a tanner who settled here in 1801. The 1868 map of the small settlement shows several homes, a cheese factory, a Methodist church, a slaughterhouse, and a hotel. By 1900, a wagon shop, blacksmith, silversmith, and the Hyde Park General Store had been added. Loie Wayman and a delivery cart are seen here by the store in the early 1900s.

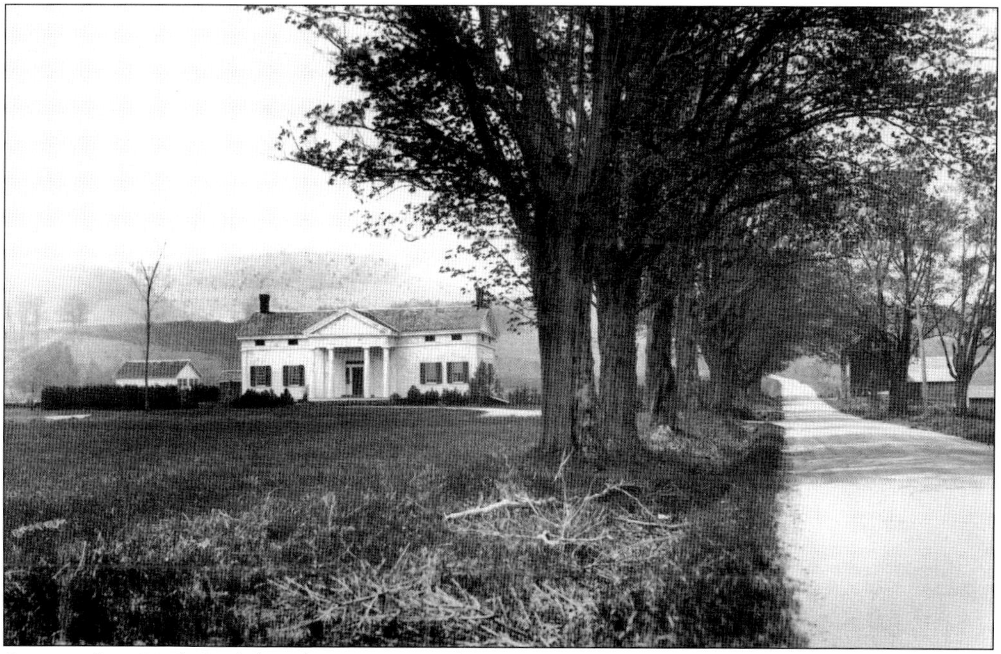

Surrounding Hyde Park hamlet were several dairy farms. One of them, built in 1817 by Clement Miller and viewed here, was later owned by Patrick King, who raised hops along with other farm crops to support his dairy. The story is that this farm was once a station for the Underground Railroad, used to move slaves north toward freedom in free states and Canada.

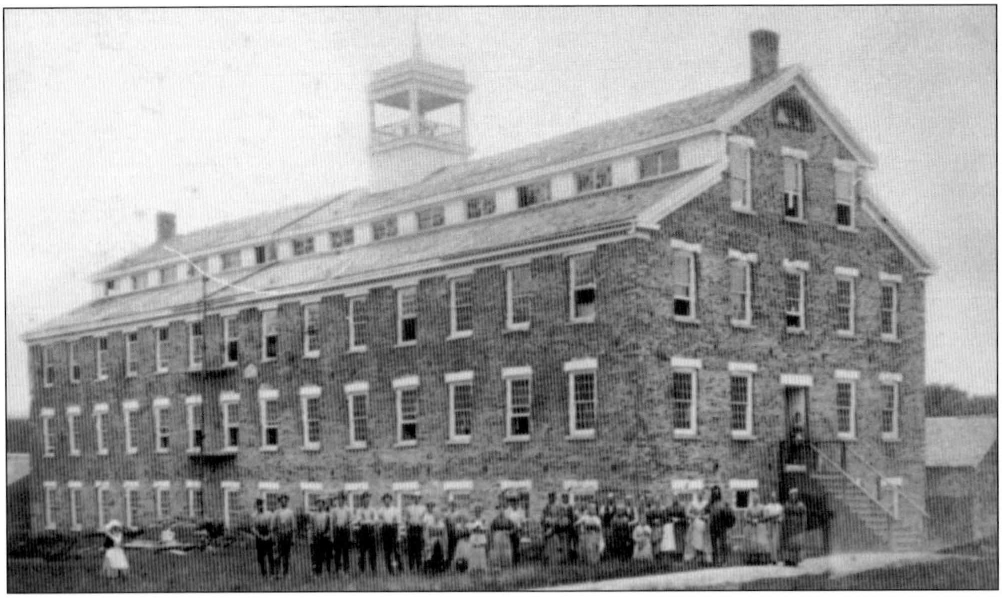

Originally built in 1809, only one year after New York State's first water-powered textile mill was constructed near Utica, the Union Cotton Mill in Toddsville was part of the first wave of industrialization outside of New England. The mill, rebuilt in 1828 after a fire, was served by a large pond and millrace that diverted water from Oaks Creek. Merchants between Philadelphia and Lake Erie purchased cotton goods from the factory.

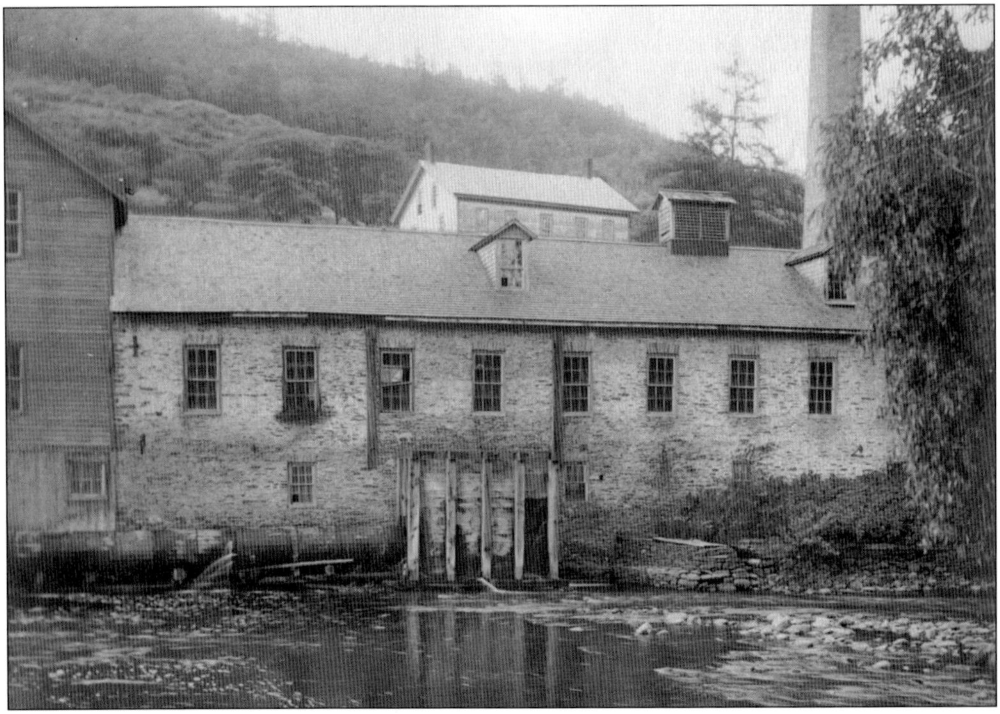

The Otsego Paper Works Mill, located on the Otsego Township side of Oaks Creek, utilized rags to make paper used by newspapers throughout the region. Built in the first decade of the 19th century, this mill was rebuilt three times because of fire.

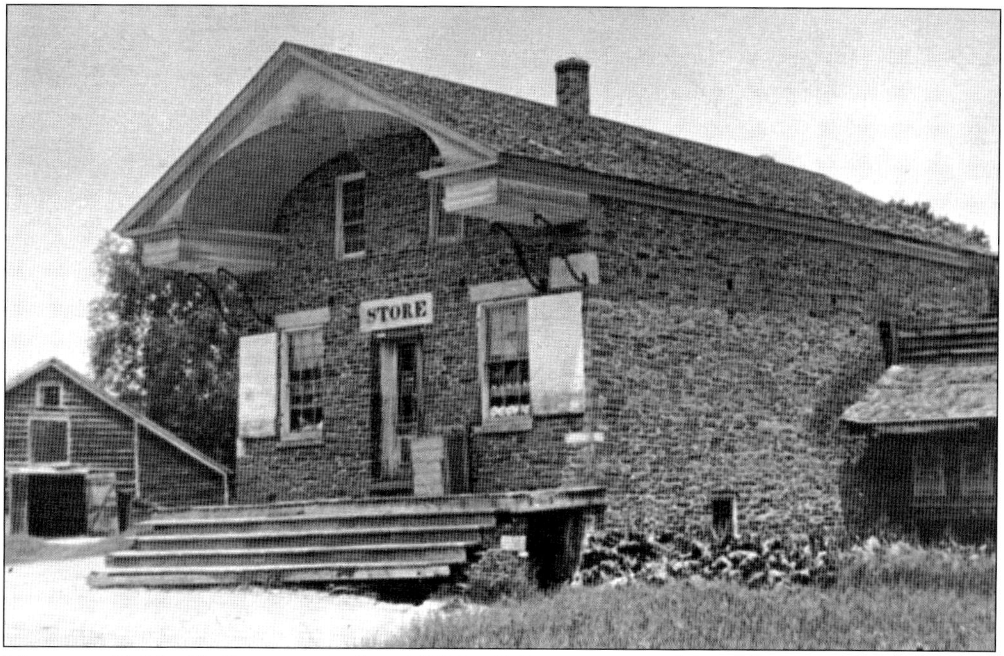

The stone Toddsville Store was built in 1827. In 1944, it was moved, stone by stone, to the Farmer's Museum in Cooperstown, where tourists still buy candy and souvenirs. Employees of the Union Mill were paid in company script, which they could spend in the store.

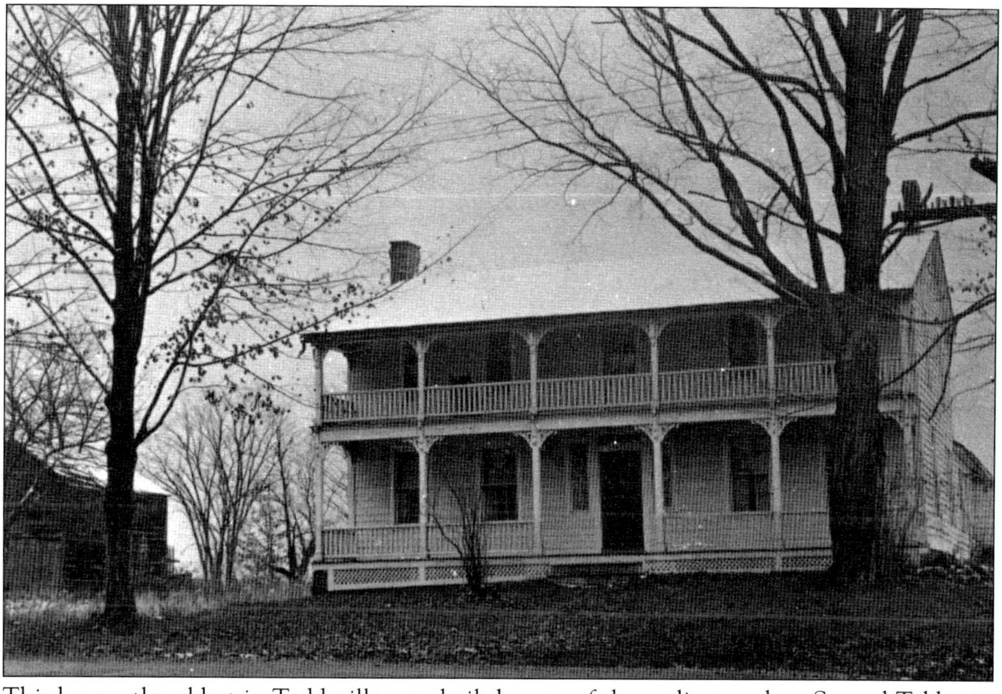

This house, the oldest in Toddsville, was built by one of the earliest settlers, Samuel Tubbs, in 1794 and was later purchased by mill owner Jehiel Todd. Dr. H.H. Clapsaddle made it his home in 1889 and practiced medicine from here (traveling about by horse and buggy) for many years. Today, it is the private home of the William Hayes family.

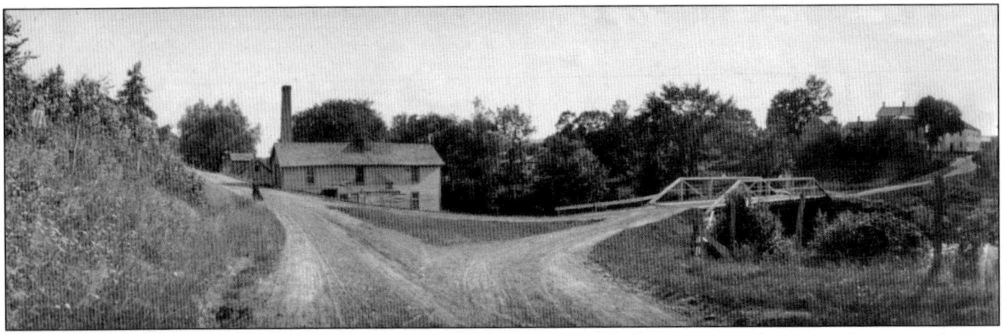

Like many rural towns, manufacturing, housing, and agriculture were often in close proximity. This photograph shows the paper mill on the eastern bank of Oaks Creek and across the street from the hops field. The original road to Cooperstown started near here and ran northeast over the hill to Maple Street in the village.

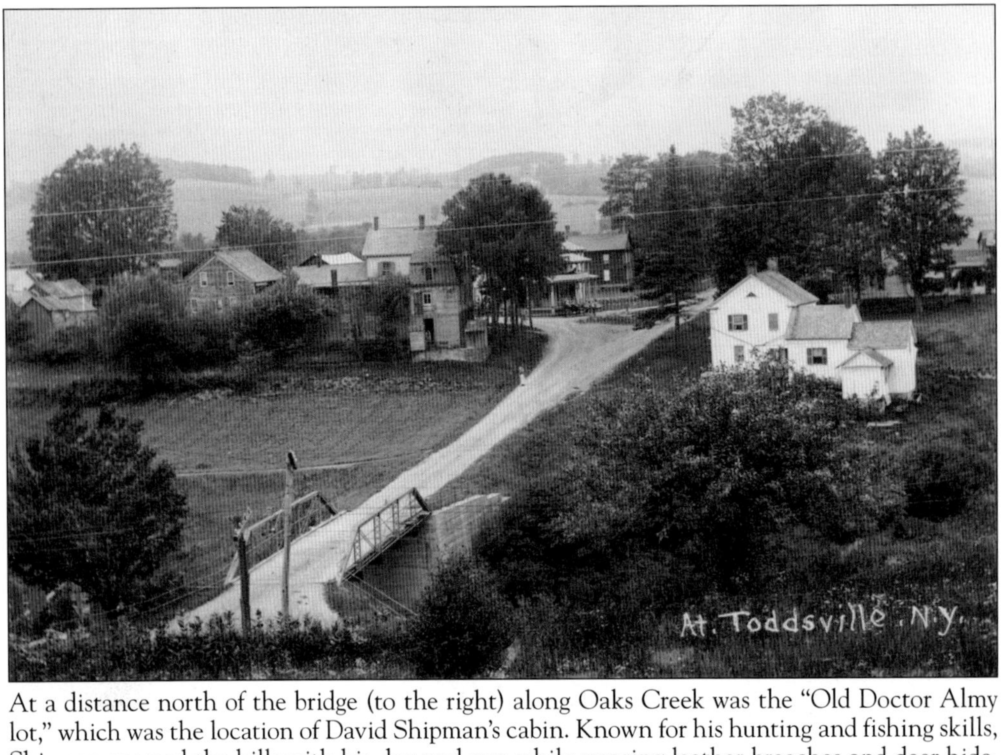

At a distance north of the bridge (to the right) along Oaks Creek was the "Old Doctor Almy lot," which was the location of David Shipman's cabin. Known for his hunting and fishing skills, Shipman roamed the hills with his dog and gun while wearing leather breeches and deer hide. According to legend, Shipman was the original Leatherstocking in James Fenimore Cooper's Leatherstocking Tales. (ST at FAM.)

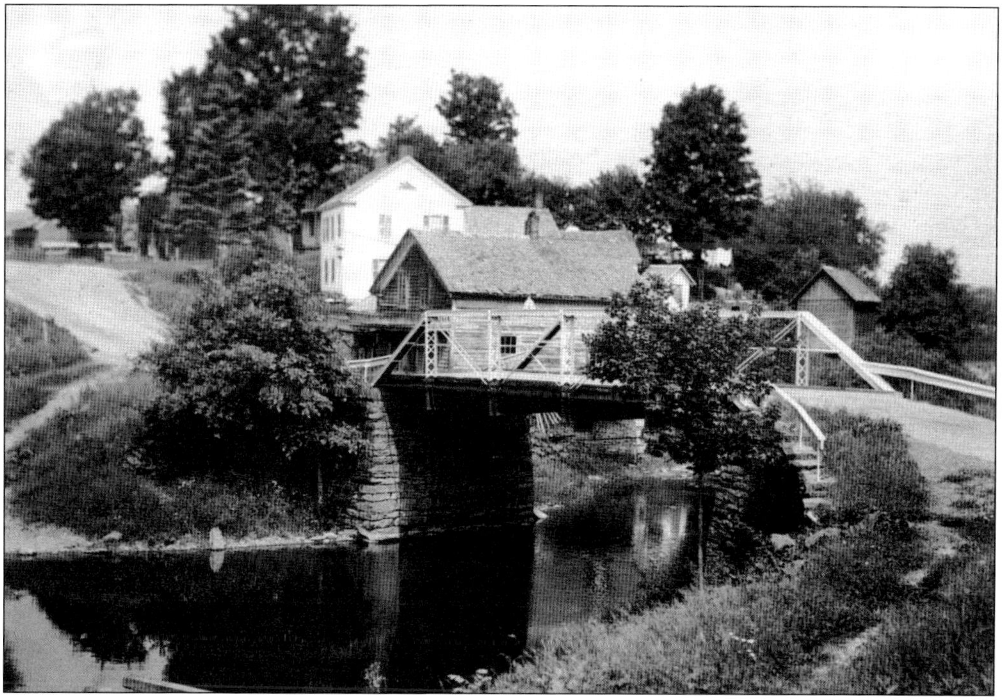

Like other waterways, the creek was the lifeblood of the community. The water from Oaks Creek supplied the power for the Toddsville Mills, and the bridge across the creek led to an ideal place for the store and saloon on the other side.

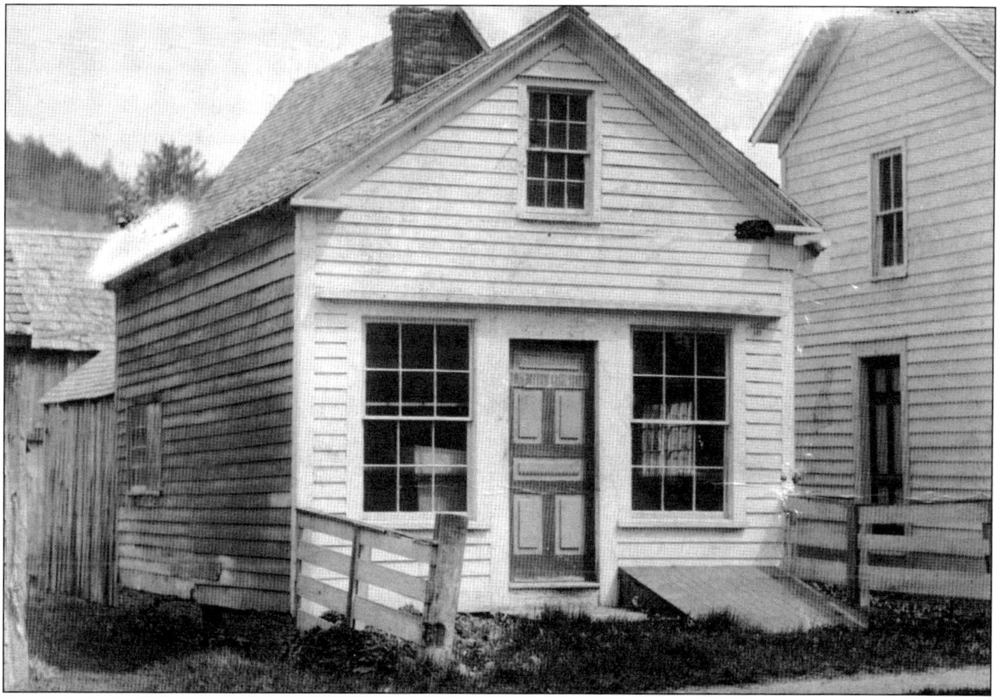

This grocery store was built prior to 1877 across the street from the Wasantha Hotel. Later, Richard Freeman began his mercantile business here before moving to Cooperstown.

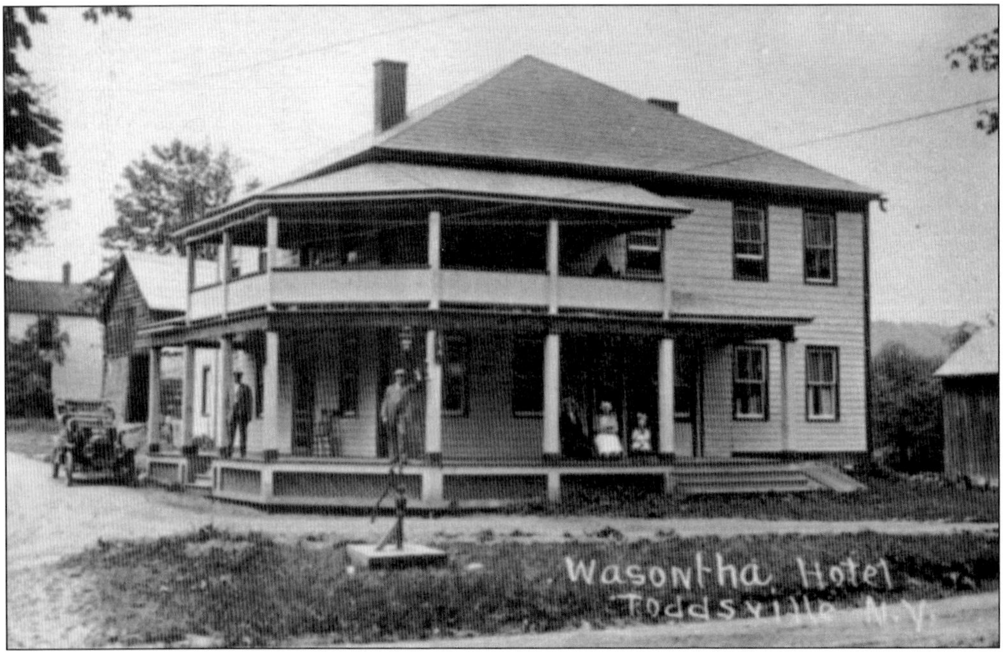

The Wasantha Hotel was built by Caleb Todd in 1827. The community well was in the center of the green in front of the hotel. The upstairs had a "spring floor" for dancing.

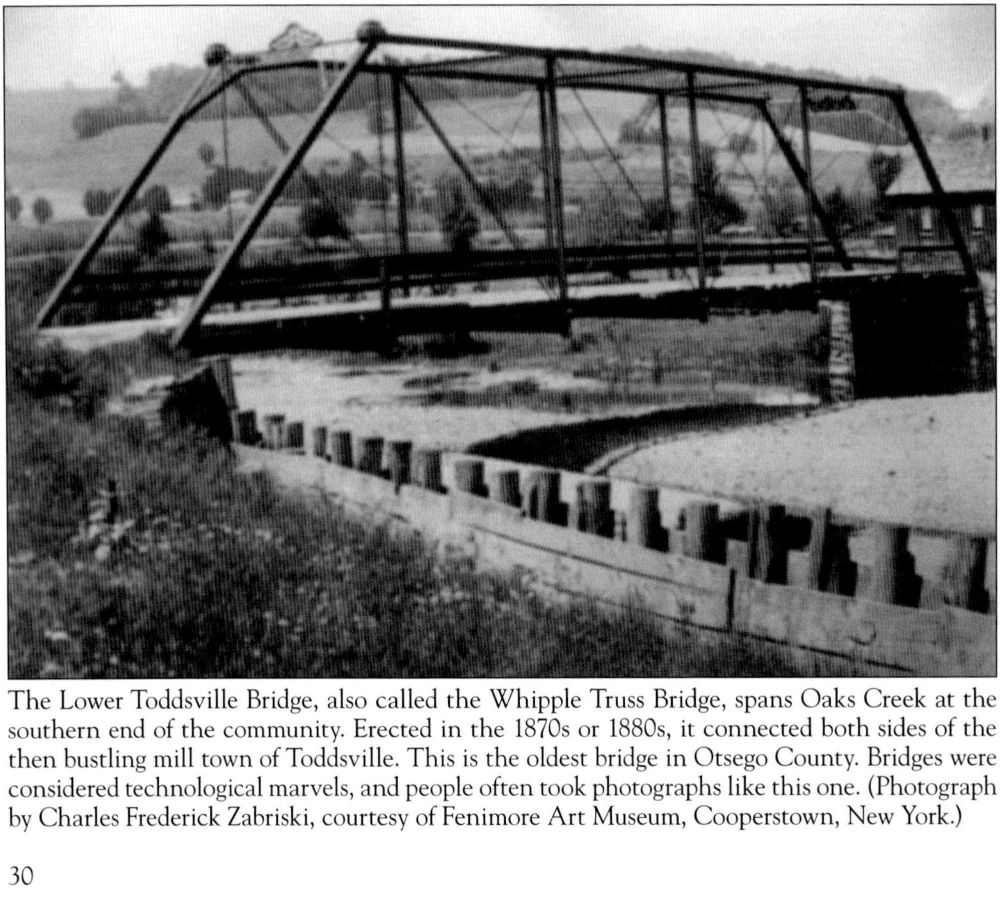
The Lower Toddsville Bridge, also called the Whipple Truss Bridge, spans Oaks Creek at the southern end of the community. Erected in the 1870s or 1880s, it connected both sides of the then bustling mill town of Toddsville. This is the oldest bridge in Otsego County. Bridges were considered technological marvels, and people often took photographs like this one. (Photograph by Charles Frederick Zabriski, courtesy of Fenimore Art Museum, Cooperstown, New York.)

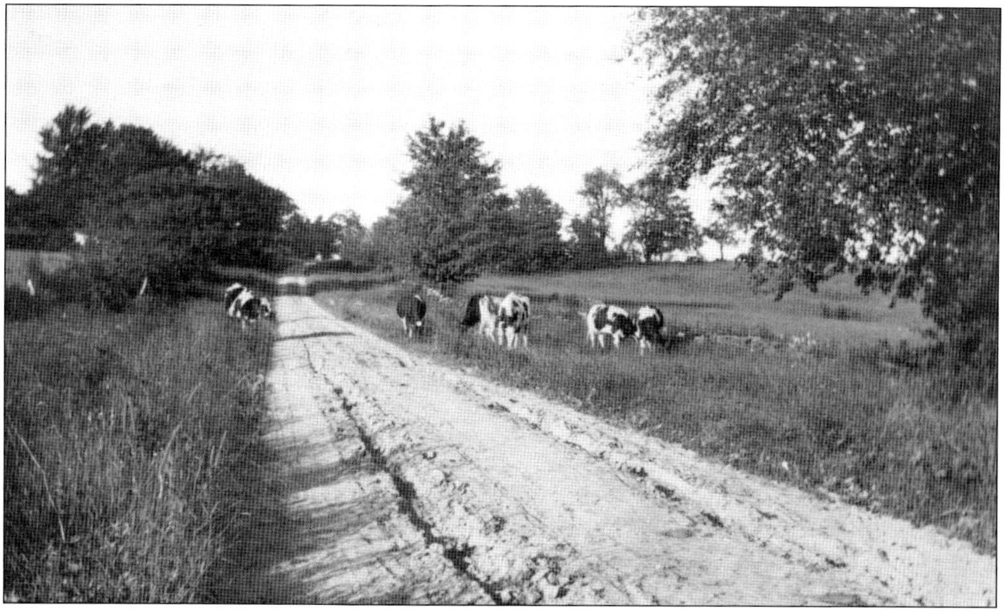

Christian Hill, site of one of the first Christian churches in New York State, was a farm community spread over the hill west of Toddsville. Hops and field crops were produced and horses trained, but poultry and milk were primary income sources in the 1900s. In this view, a group of cows, headed home for milking, is grazing along the road near the Frank (later Jesse) Wells farm. (DP.)

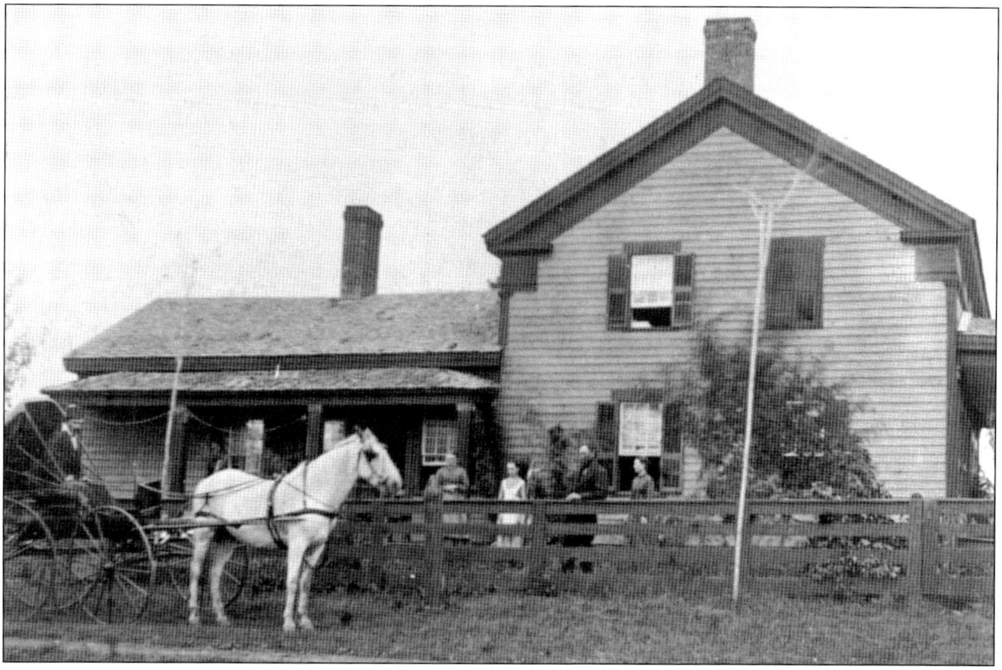

Amos and Frank Wells owned a dairy farm in the 1880s at the top of Christian Hill to the west of Toddsville. The nearby Eddy Schoolhouse was located on land purchased from the Wells family, and the Hartwick Grange was organized in 1891 at the schoolhouse. Seen here around 1886 is the Wells homestead. The people are, from left to right, Frank Wells (in the carriage), Ann Wells, Alice Wells, Amos Wells, and Phoebe Wells. (DP.)

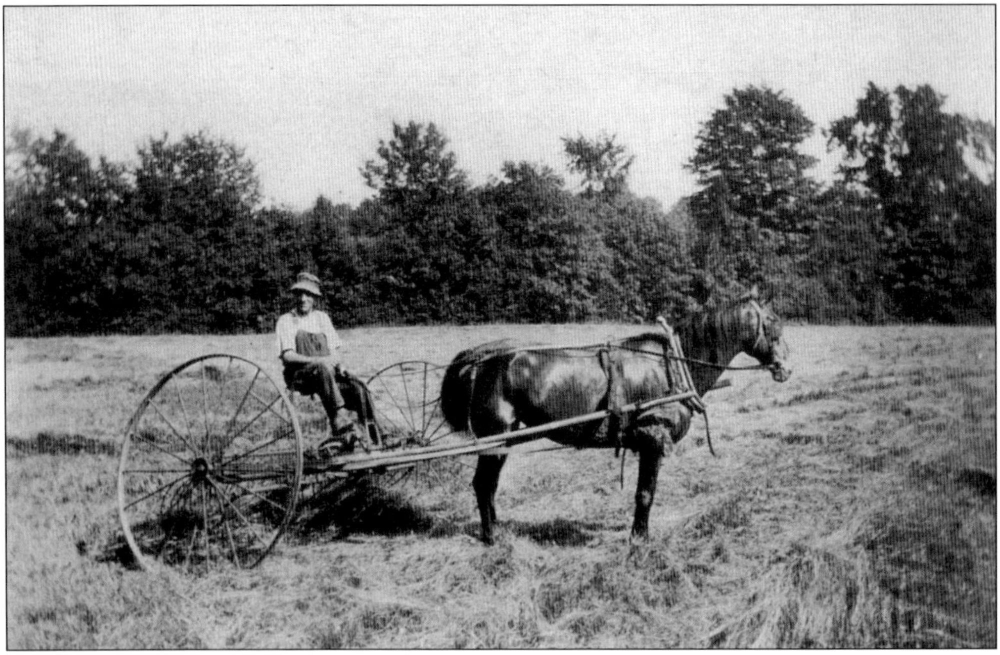

Christian Hill land, part of Cooper's Otsego Patent, was largely leased or purchased by 1794. Daily life and labor, both then and later, centered on small farms with field or garden crops produced to meet family and animal needs. Jessie Wells is seen here (possibly in the 1920s) with a horse-drawn rake during haying season. (DP.)

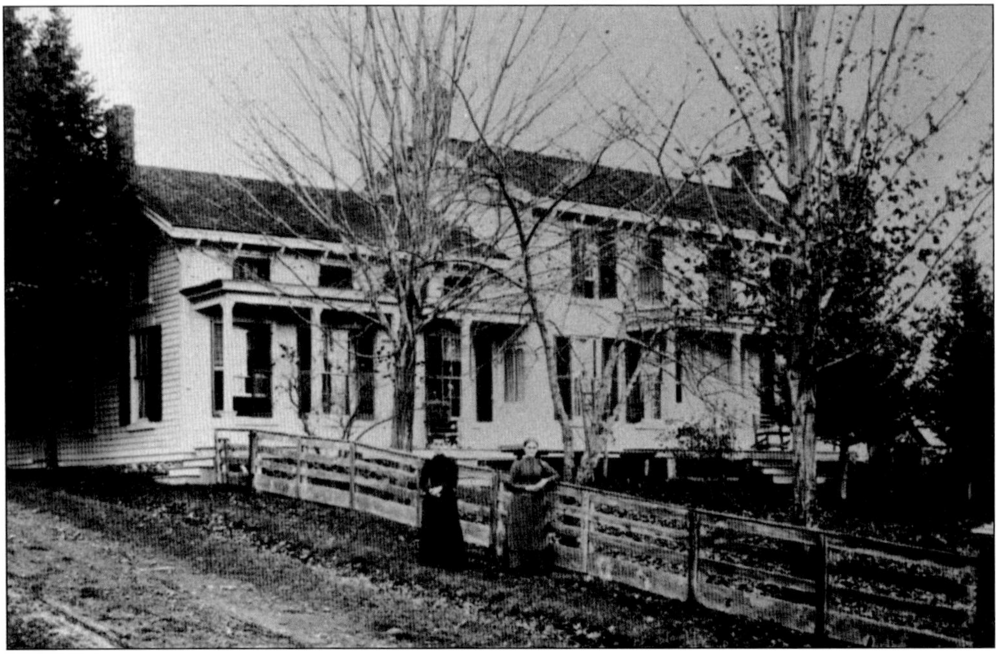

Robert Carr migrated west from Connecticut to settle on land lower on Christian Hill and west of Toddsville. Carr purchased 200 acres in 1796, established a farm, and built a home in 1800. The house viewed here was built by son Ephriam in 1815. Ephriam's granddaughter Mary Carr (left) and daughter-in-law Phoebe Field Carr can be seen in this photograph. (DP.)

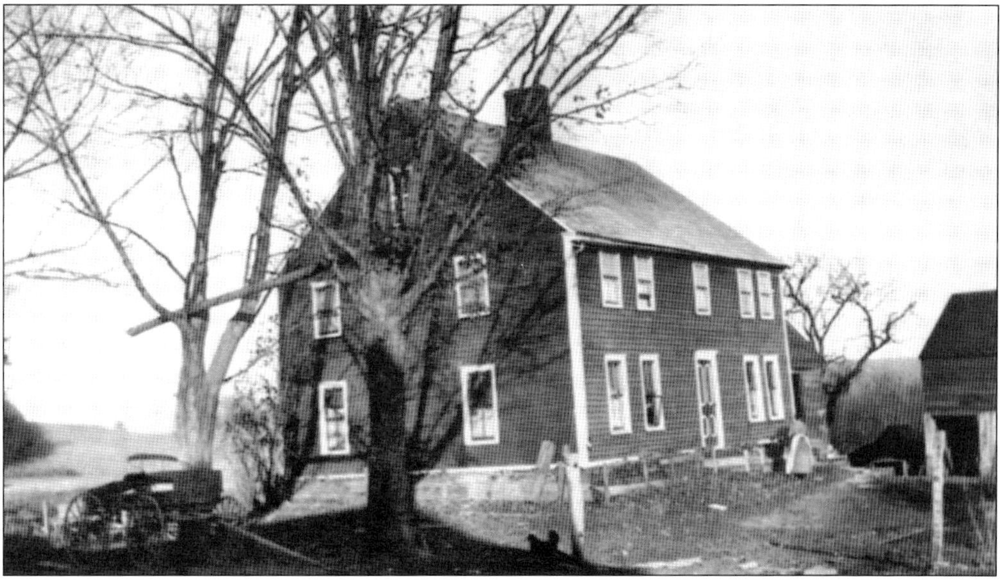

David Matthewson from Rhode Island purchased 125 acres of Otsego Patent land on Christian Hill in 1796. Farms were established and homes were built. The original home pictured here, erected by Amos Matthewson, has been preserved and is now listed in the National Register of Historic Places. Farm families of Christian Hill not only raised dairy cows but also poultry and pigs for family use and occasional sales. Below is a 1920s slaughter-day image of pigs on the Matthewson-Bice farm. (SA.)

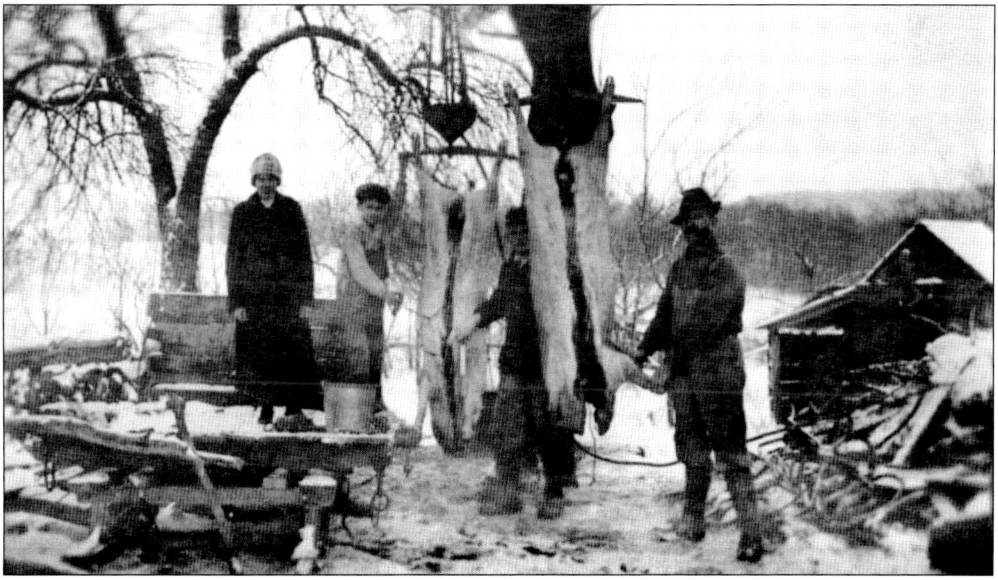

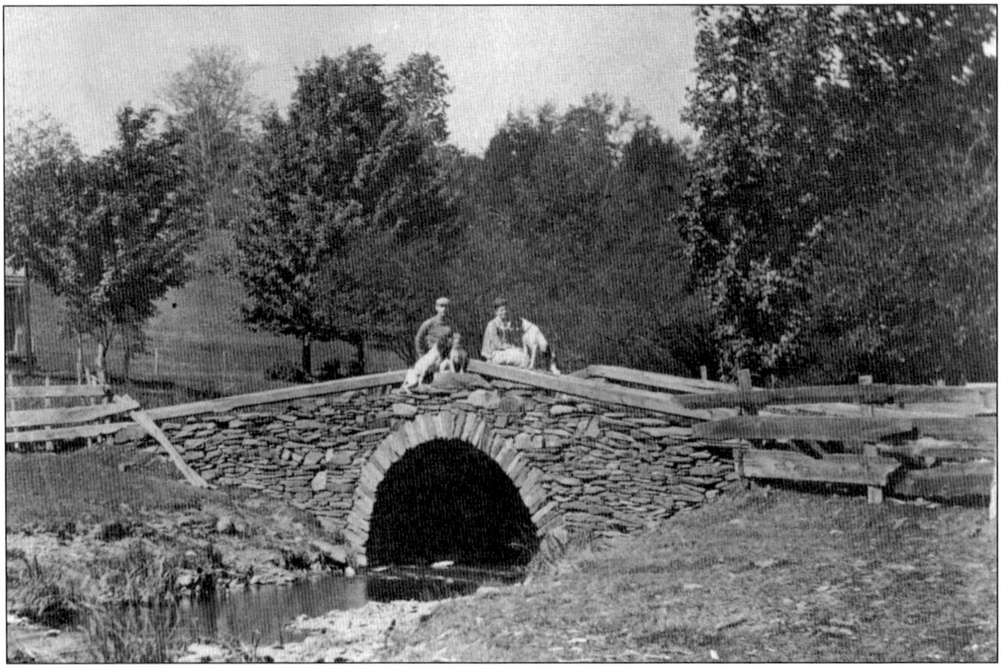

Chase, formerly called Bissell Hollow, was a farm neighborhood on the hill and valley south of Christian Hill. This stone bridge crossed Chase Creek near the Samuel Bissell home. A cooper shop, pottery factory, and sawmill (operated by Comfort Chase and later by son Nathan) were clustered nearby along the creek. (DP.)

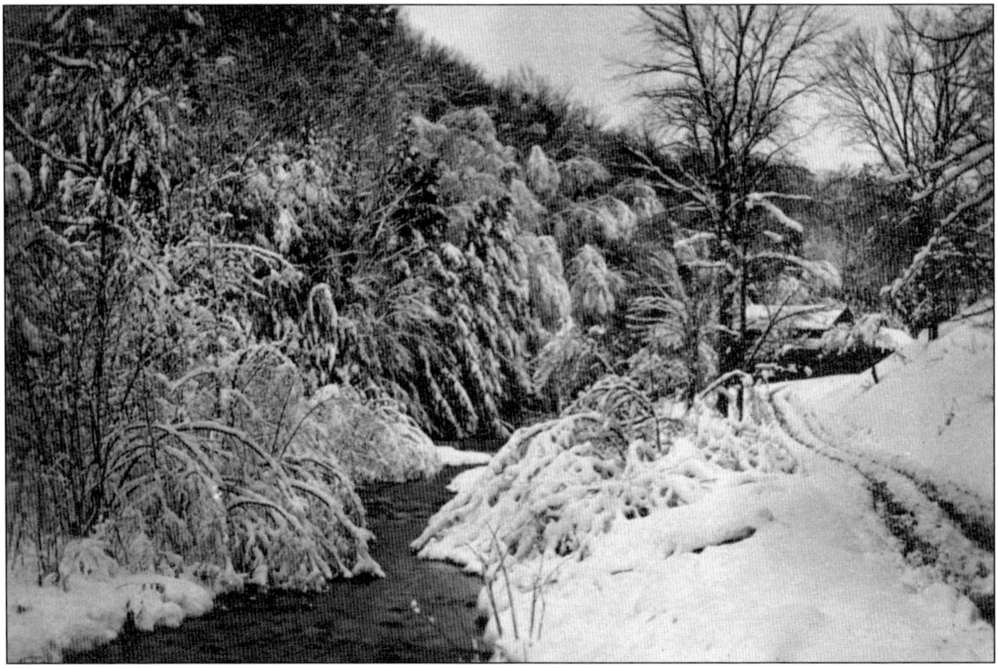

After 1901, the road and trolley line wound through Chase Gorge on the route northeast from Hartwick to Index. A sawmill was located at the sharp bend in the road and creek along Chase Creek Gorge.

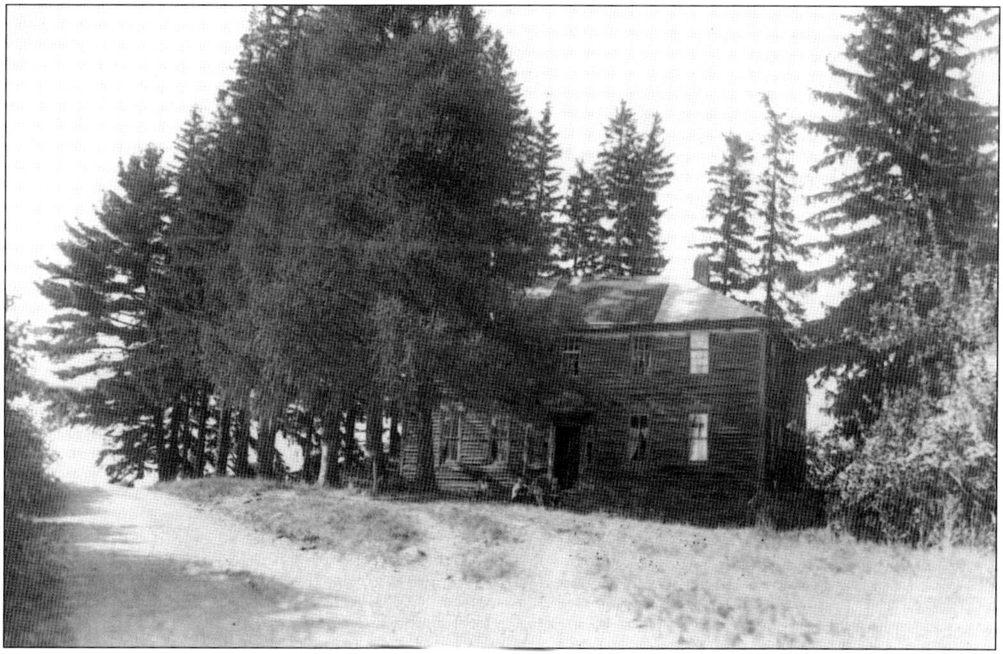

The White House Community north of Hartwick hamlet is named for this central landmark built in 1792 by Revolutionary War veteran Maj. James Butterfield. The building, pictured here before its 1935 restoration, was reported to be the first house painted white west of Albany. As a tavern/inn, it sheltered travelers going west as well as some local settlers while they cleared land and built homes. It is now in the National Register of Historic Places.

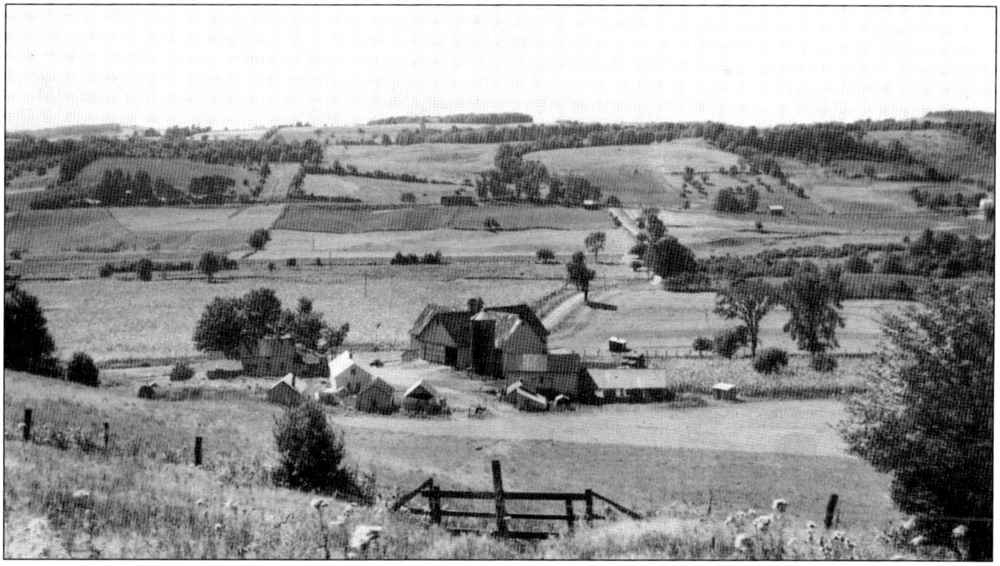

The White House neighborhood extends north of Hartwick hamlet about two miles to the northwest corner of the township. Farmland purchased as early as 1786 from the Otsego Patent spreads across the Otego Creek Valley. The Pierce-Mott dairy farm, seen here in 1940 with a valley view to the west, was purchased by Gordon Pierce (landowner No. 6) in 1850. (CG.)

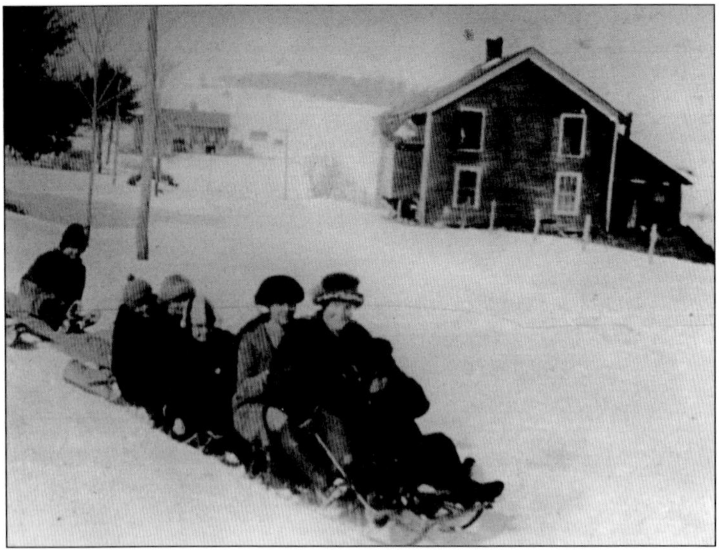

Like many small communities, White House had both a district school and a cheese factory. Both were located across the road from the White House. Delos Lamb operated the White House Cheese Factory, seen here, which produced butter and cheese from excess local farm milk. The factory operated as late as 1921.

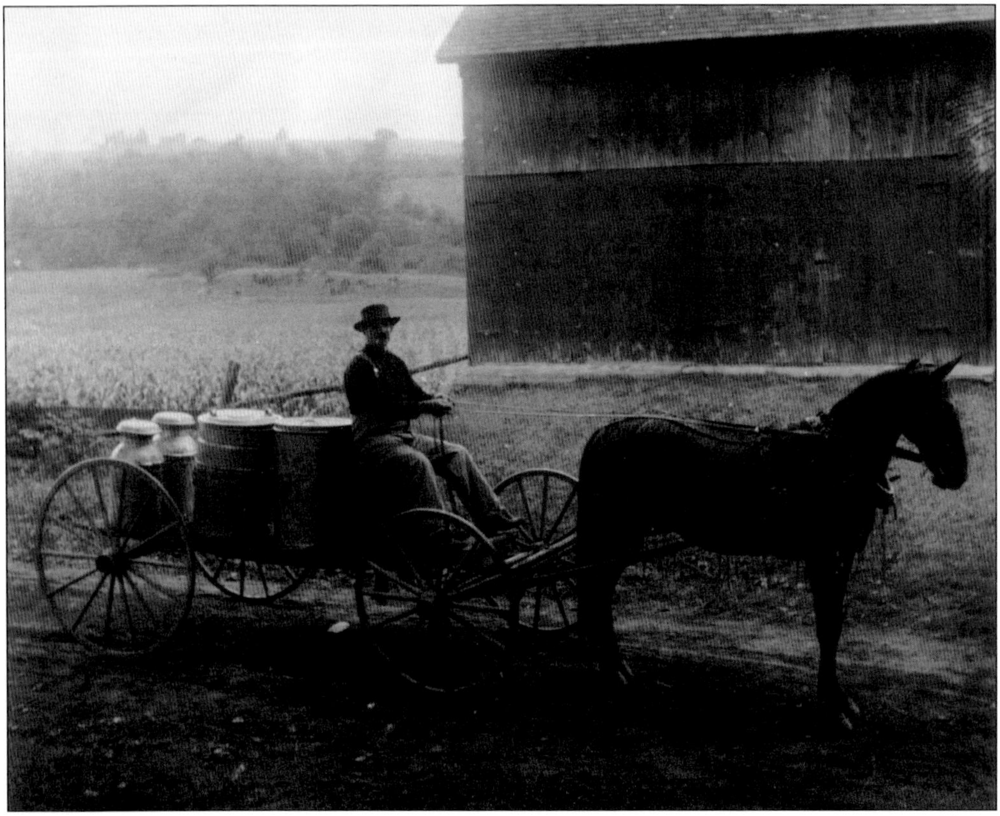

Milk was delivered by horse and wagon to the White House Cheese Factory, as pictured here with Robert Stoller. Butter and cheese produced at the factory were shipped by wagon or trolley (after 1901) to more distant markets. Milk, in 40-quart cans, was hauled by wagon either to trolley platforms for the Cooperstown milk plant or directly to a creamery at Phoenix.

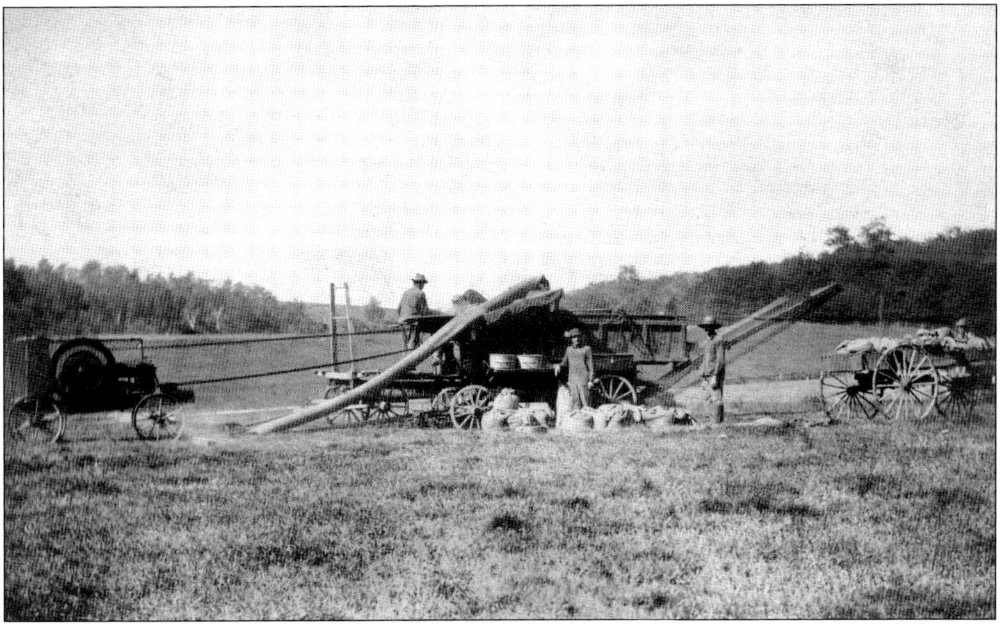

Farming was a year-round, labor-intensive way of life at White House and in other farm communities. Plowing, planting, and harvesting farm crops, along with daily dairy chores, were all essential tasks. Neighbors helped neighbors as needed with shared labor and equipment. As owner of a threshing machine, William Petrie, seen here threshing oats, provided harvest services farm to farm in the White House and Christian Hill area. (DP.)

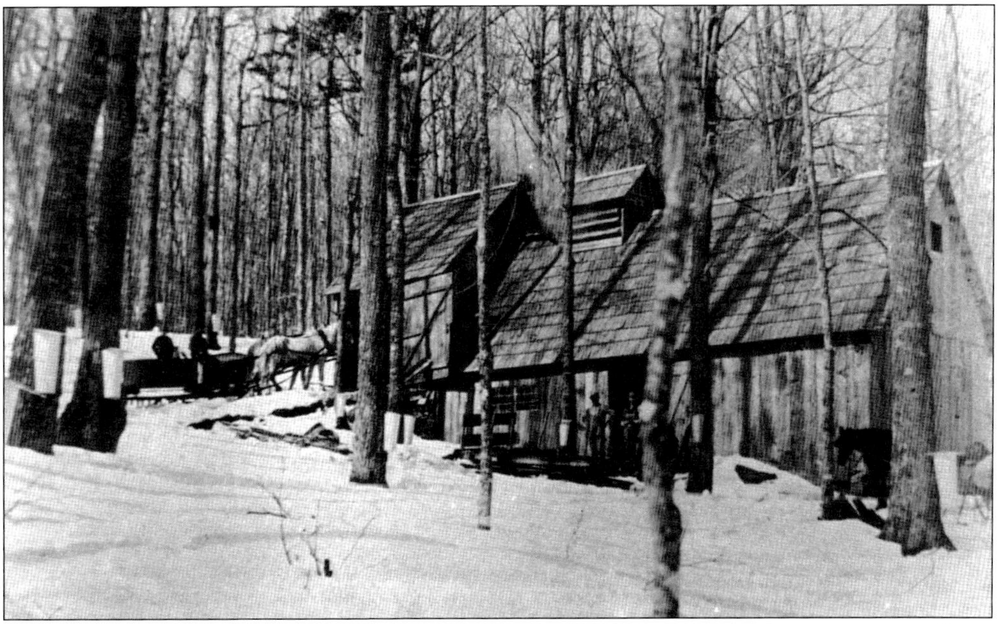

Maple sugar and syrup were the most commonly used early sweeteners. In 1791, Gerritt Boon purchased 265 acres north of Hartwick hamlet as part of a short-lived national plan to supply maple sugar to the world. Otsego County and Hartwick, with the best county sugar bush, led the state in syrup production in 1865. This 1930s photograph (possibly on the Weeks farm) shows the process, with gathered tree sap being transported to the sugarhouse to be boiled down into syrup.

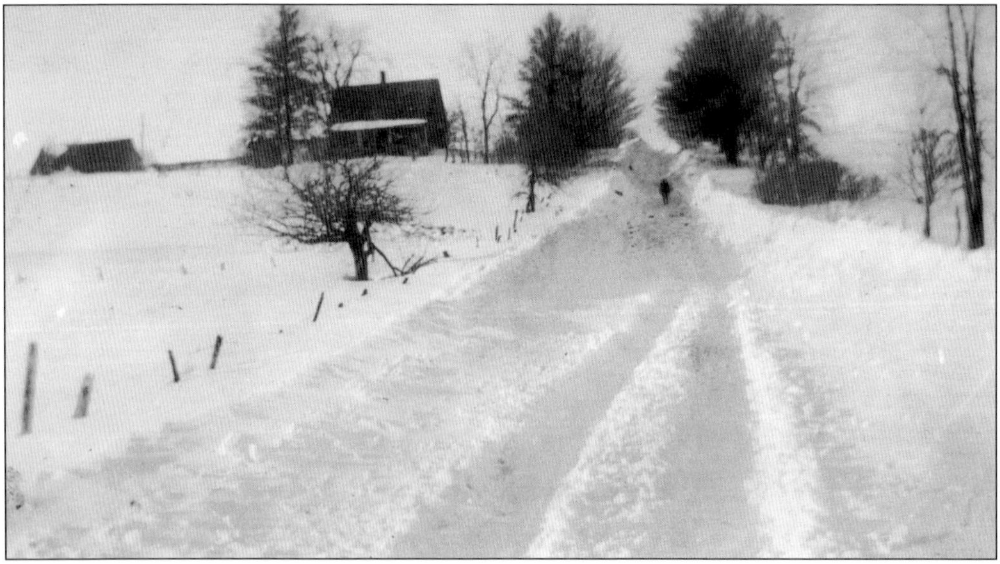

In the 1840s, Scottish immigrant families (the Ainslies, Currys, Loughs, and Potters) settled hill country land west of Otego Creek along the Hartwick township border. Scotch Hill settlers become well-known sheep farmers and breeders with George Lough Sr.'s introduction of the first Cheviot sheep into the United States in 1842. Viewed here is one Scotch Hill farm (Curry/Potter) in an early-1900s winter.

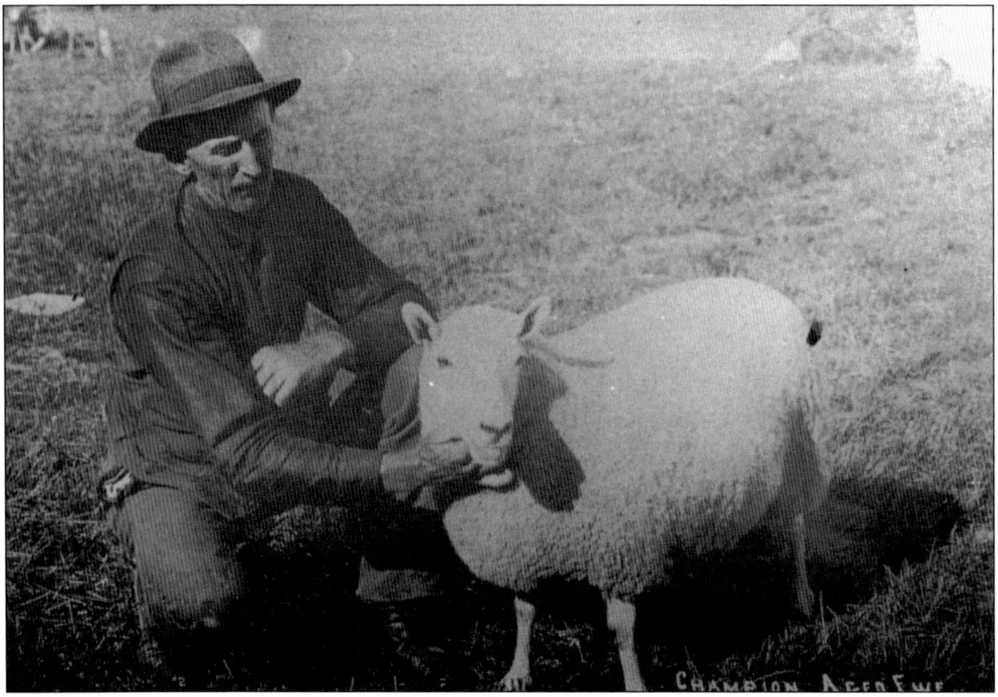

Both Merino and Cheviot sheep were popular in the Hartwick Scotch Hill community, and the Cheviot Sheep Society of America was organized there. One well-known Cheviot breeder, William Curry, exhibited his prize-winning "Gold Medal Flock" at large fairs, including the World's Fair. Curry is pictured here with a champion aged ewe.

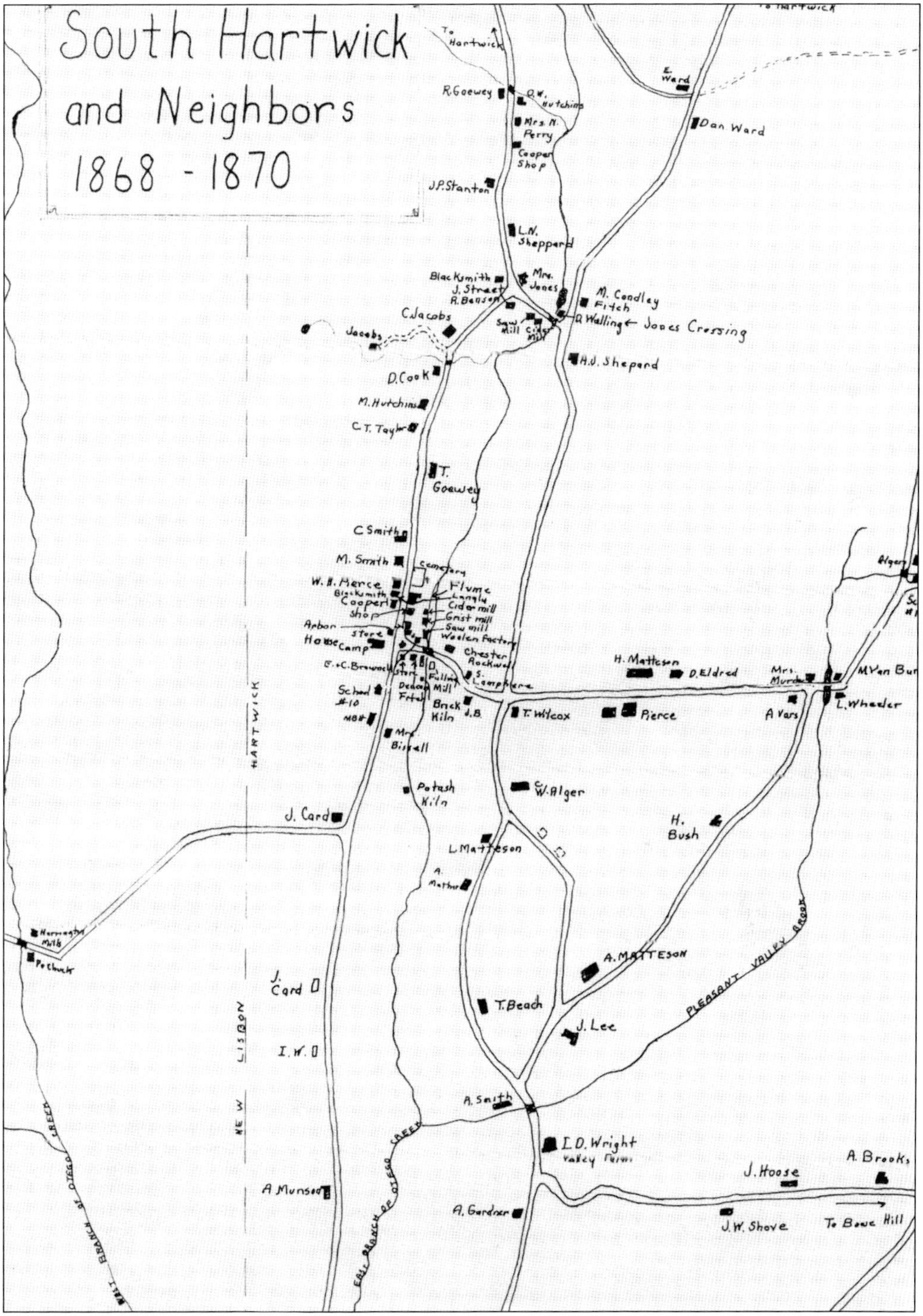

Eva Chamberlin moved to South Hartwick in the early 1950s. She documented South Hartwick's past and present and prepared this map (copied from the 1868 *Atlas of Otsego County*) to show the vibrancy of South Hartwick during the 1800s. Note the mills on Otego Creek powered by the dike that was located near the bridge on County Highway 11D.

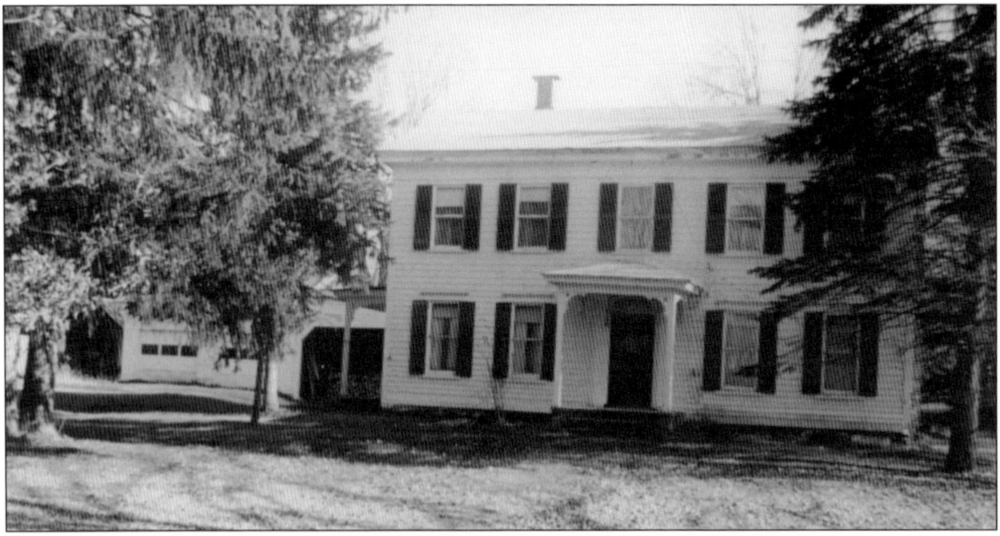

The Rockwell family purchased Lippitt Mills in South Hartwick in 1812. Shortly thereafter, this large family home, similar to early New England mansion houses, was situated on the east side of Otego Creek near the County Highway 11D bridge. The interior hosted a loom room, buttery, and milk and cheese room. Rockwell Woolen Mills burned to the ground in 1861, and Chester W. Rockwell moved his business to his brother's factory in Mount Upton, New York.

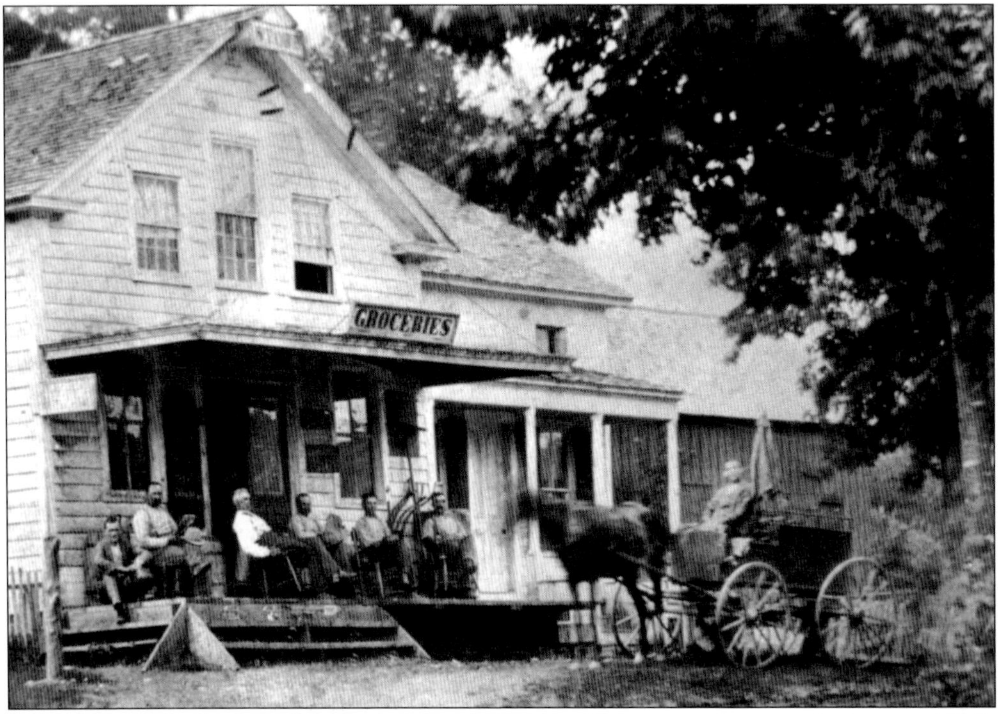

The storefront that launched the future Bresee's Oneonta Department Store was built around 1810. It housed several merchants and the post office prior to housing Frank H. Bresee. Commercial buildings provided social venues for small communities. The store was conveniently located at the corner of what are now County Highways 11 and 11D. The owner, Frank H. Bresee, is seated on the store steps to the far left. (NM.)

Excerpt from 1858 South Hartwick School Paper:

Of Sodom I'll talk so thriving, yet small
The Post Office, South Hartwick, the pride of us all-
so secluded, so snug, yet teaming with life
so active, so bustling with business and strife.

We've a factory, a store, a school house too
filled with masters and misses and rouges-not a few
Of stage lines we've one, a hotel we once had
but that's gone up and we are all glad.

We've a music teacher, dress maker, tailoress too,
and of young ladies we have very few.
We've women of labor and women of leisure
and women who make gossip their principle pleasure.

****

Our Mills
written by C.H. Rockwell, March 24, 1862

I
Not like the burning Phoenix found,
but still we mean to keep around;
although we have removed from ruin,
our motto is, still keep a-doing.
And now Secesh is on the wane;
we hope your patronage to gain.

II
Our cards, revolving, can release
and straighten out a tangled fleece;
but never yet could play or sing
Secession's a tune, "Cotton is King".
They chime with strains of seventy-six;
No cotton with their wool they mix.

III
Our spindles, too, prolong the strain,
when marching out and back again,
in two extended lines they move,
thus stretching out the wooly rove
when marshalled on the iron track,
they show the way to freedom back.

IV
Our looms of course for union run,
our warps thus made, on wool thus spun;
and while the threads are passing there,
swift as our eagle flits the air,
they form a fabric firm and strong-
like Union men assailed by wrong.

V
What through success our efforts crown,
though fortune smile or gold abounds,
our constant prayer shall still ascend
that rebel plans may quickly end;
for country, and for him who fights
for freedom, and for chartered rights.

South Hartwick, previously known as Sodom Point, was appreciated by residents, as noted in this 1858 South Hartwick School (District No. 10) student's poem that appeared in the school paper. The destruction of Rockwell Mills is memorialized by Chester Rockwell in an advertisement in the *Oneonta Herald* on June 18, 1862.

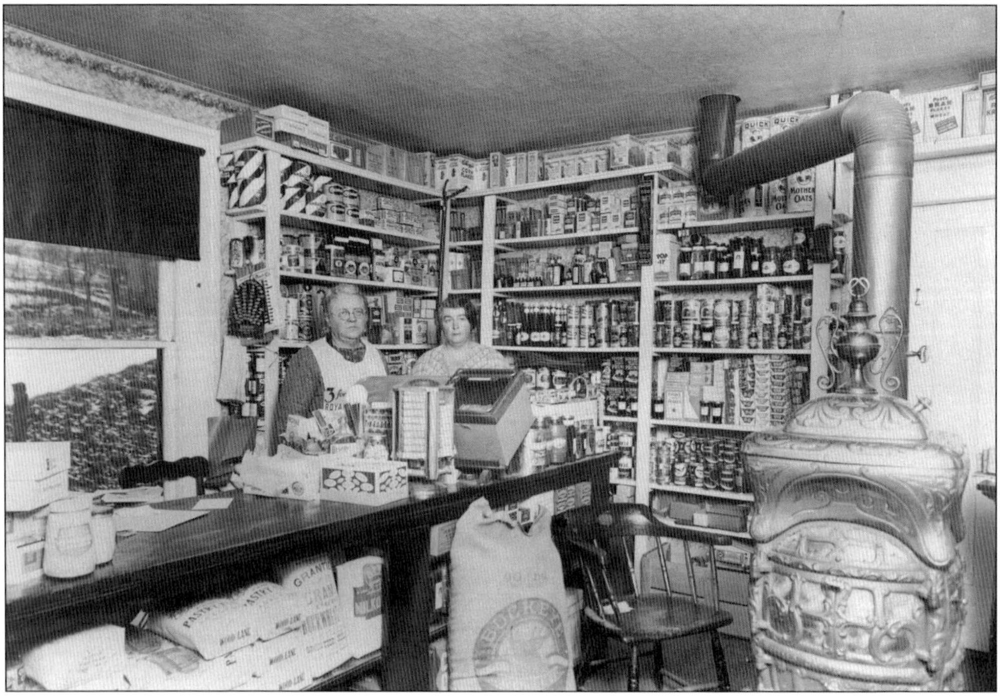

Chester Rockwell had houses built near his woolen mills, and several remain. The home that sits on the west bank of Otego Creek was the South Hartwick Post Office and a general store during the early 1900s. Owner F. Belle Sherman (left) was the proprietor. The current owners possess pieces of the wallpaper as seen near the ceiling, as well as the original metal South Hartwick Post Office sign seen below.

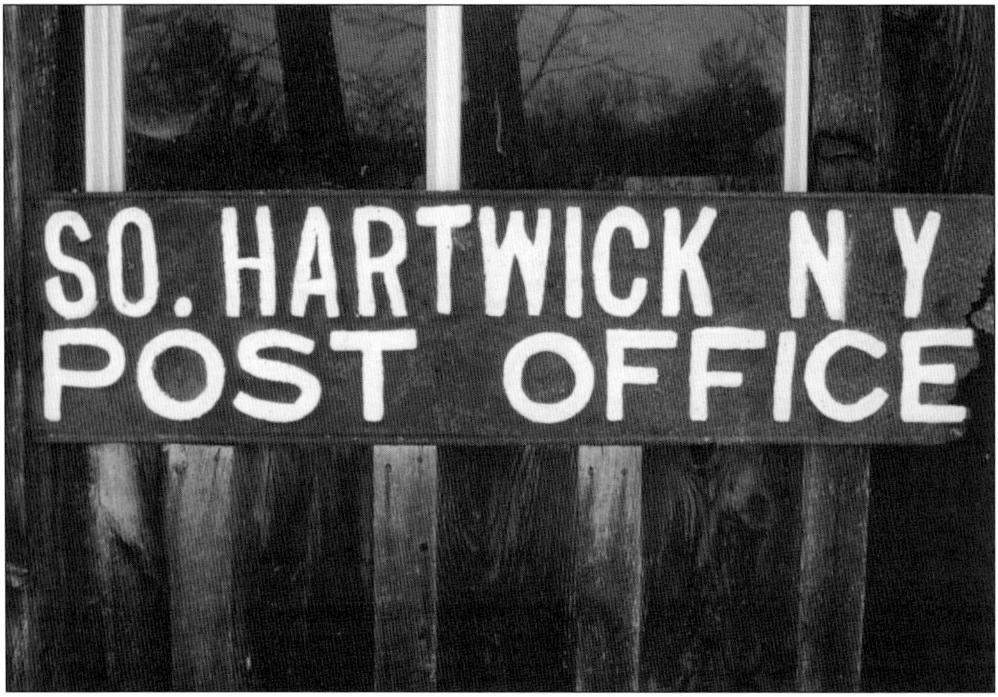

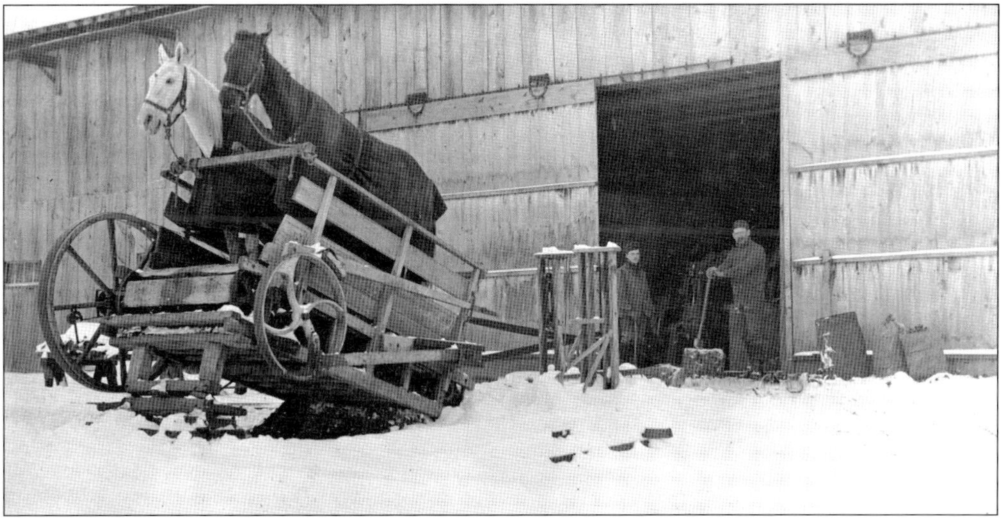

Pleasant Valley, as named by early Connecticut settlers, was a farm community on a hill and valley between South Hartwick and Hinman Hollow. Settled early in 1794, the neighborhood developed along the Pleasant Valley Brook with family dairy farms, a log schoolhouse, and soon a prosperous cheese factory. Marketed cheese gave some cash income, and the by-product, whey, supplemented feed for farm calves and pigs. Lyle and Daniel Burdick are seen here at work with their horses on their Pleasant Valley farm. (EH.)

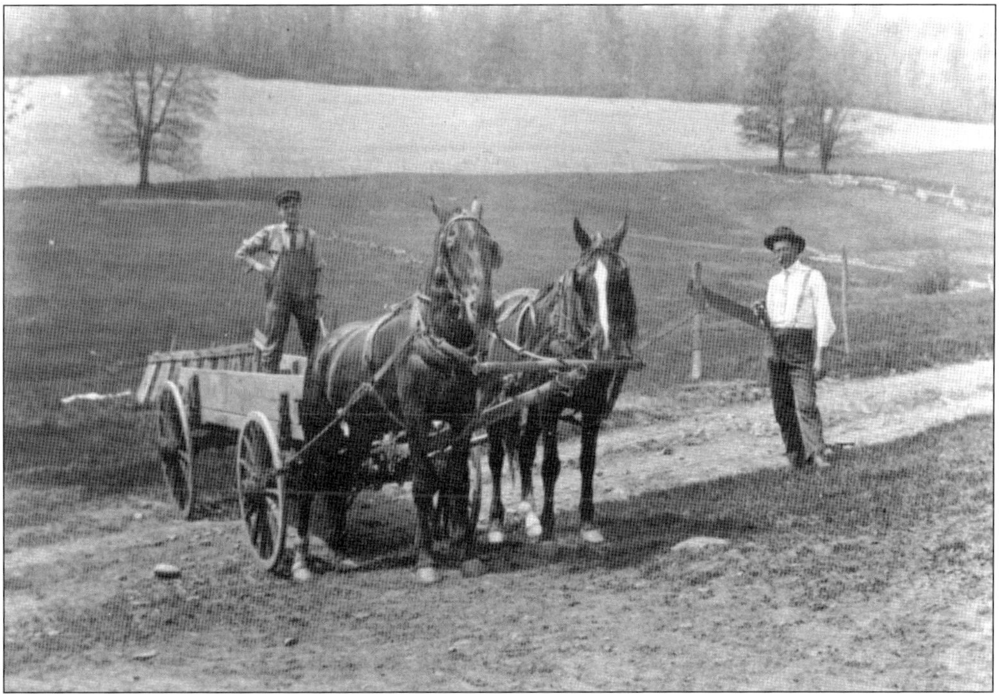

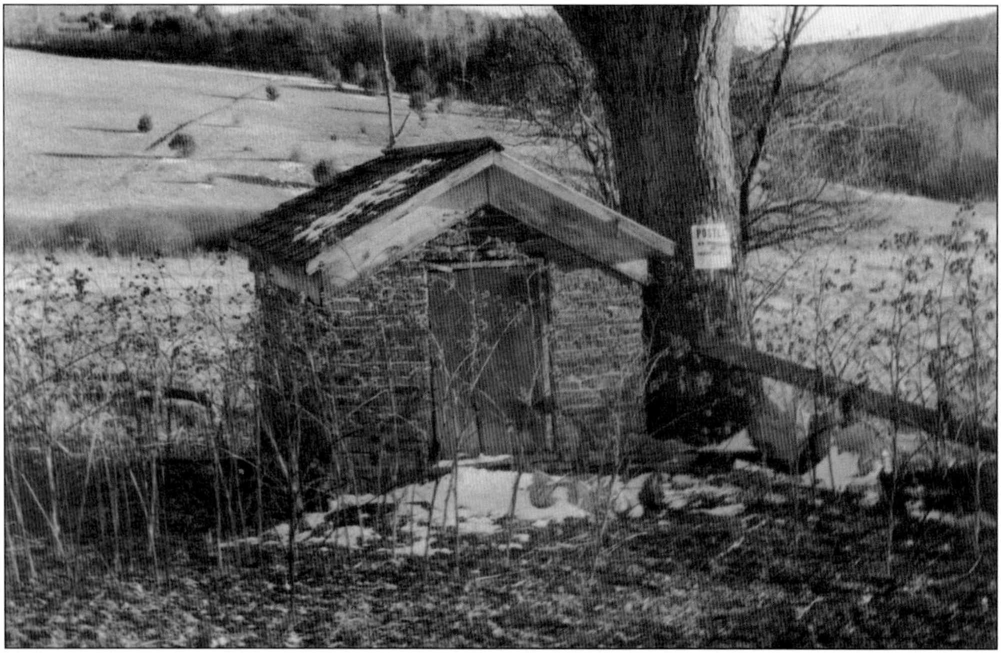

Farm families were self-sufficient, producing their own food, including everything from fruit and vegetables to milk, butter, eggs, and meat. During fall or early winter, a cow and pig or two would be butchered for the winter's meat. Some would be frozen, but more often meat would be dry-cured and preserved by smoking in a smokehouse, such as this one on the Burdick farm. (EH.)

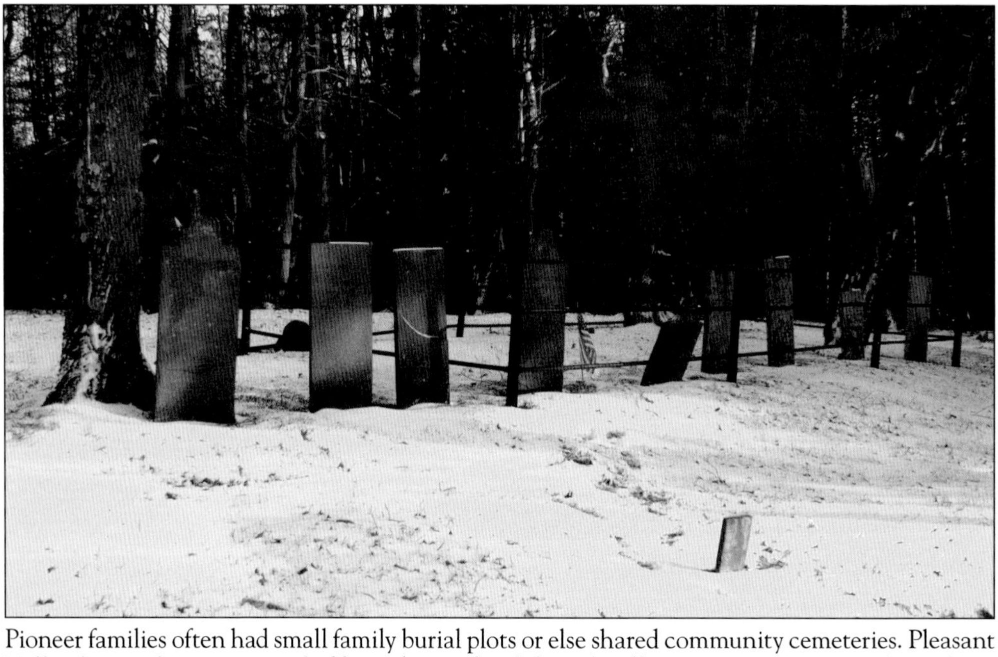

Pioneer families often had small family burial plots or else shared community cemeteries. Pleasant Valley has such a cemetery half a mile north of the schoolhouse site. Known as the Adams Cemetery, it is the resting place for Abner Adams, a Revolutionary War soldier and one of Israel Putnam's rangers. His grave site is marked here by an American flag, and immediate family, with related neighbors, are located nearby. (DC.)

Three

The Seminary Is Established

Born in 1714 in the central German province of Thuringia, John Christopher Hartwick had been in America for over half of his life when he died in 1796. He was a true pioneer, arriving in 1746 and ministering at first to five congregations in the vicinity of Rhinebeck, New York, at a time when there were only a handful of Lutheran ministers in all of the American colonies. Hartwick was eccentric and, by all accounts, cantankerous and exacting. Although not always well loved by his parishioners, he impressed his contemporaries, including prominent Lutherans such as Henry Muhlenberg. In his will, Hartwick called for the establishment of a "New Jerusalem" on land he had acquired in upstate New York, naming Jesus Christ as his heir. His executors did their best to carry out his wishes, founding in 1797 the first Lutheran seminary in America in his name. (PFCA at HC.)

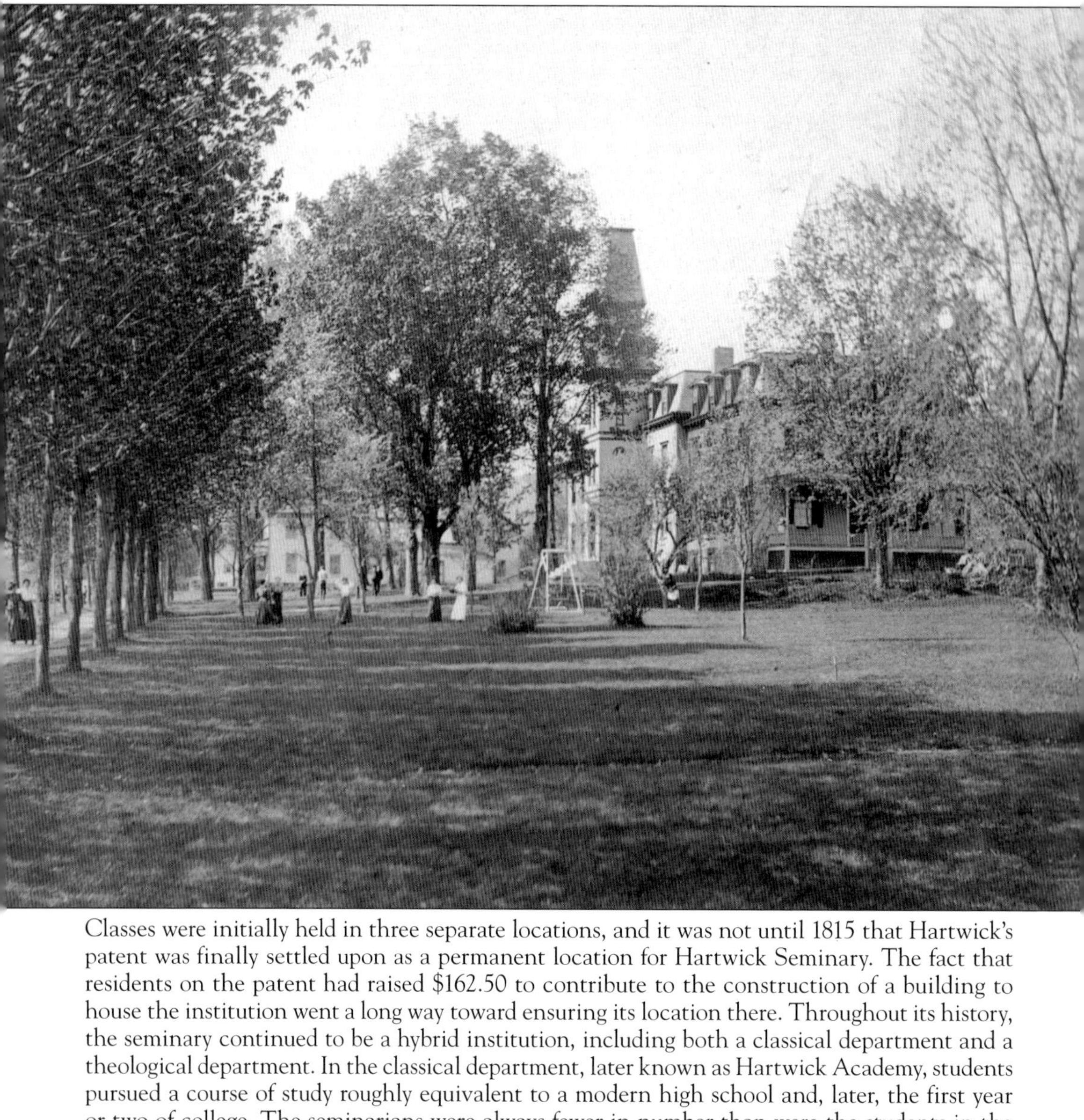

Classes were initially held in three separate locations, and it was not until 1815 that Hartwick's patent was finally settled upon as a permanent location for Hartwick Seminary. The fact that residents on the patent had raised $162.50 to contribute to the construction of a building to house the institution went a long way toward ensuring its location there. Throughout its history, the seminary continued to be a hybrid institution, including both a classical department and a theological department. In the classical department, later known as Hartwick Academy, students pursued a course of study roughly equivalent to a modern high school and, later, the first year or two of college. The seminarians were always fewer in number than were the students in the classical department. Throughout much of the 19th century, the seminary continued to require room to grow. Originally a two-story brick building, the main facility was renovated three times: in 1840, from 1867–69, and in 1915, when indoor plumbing and electricity were installed and an annex was constructed at the rear of the building. (PFCA at HC.)

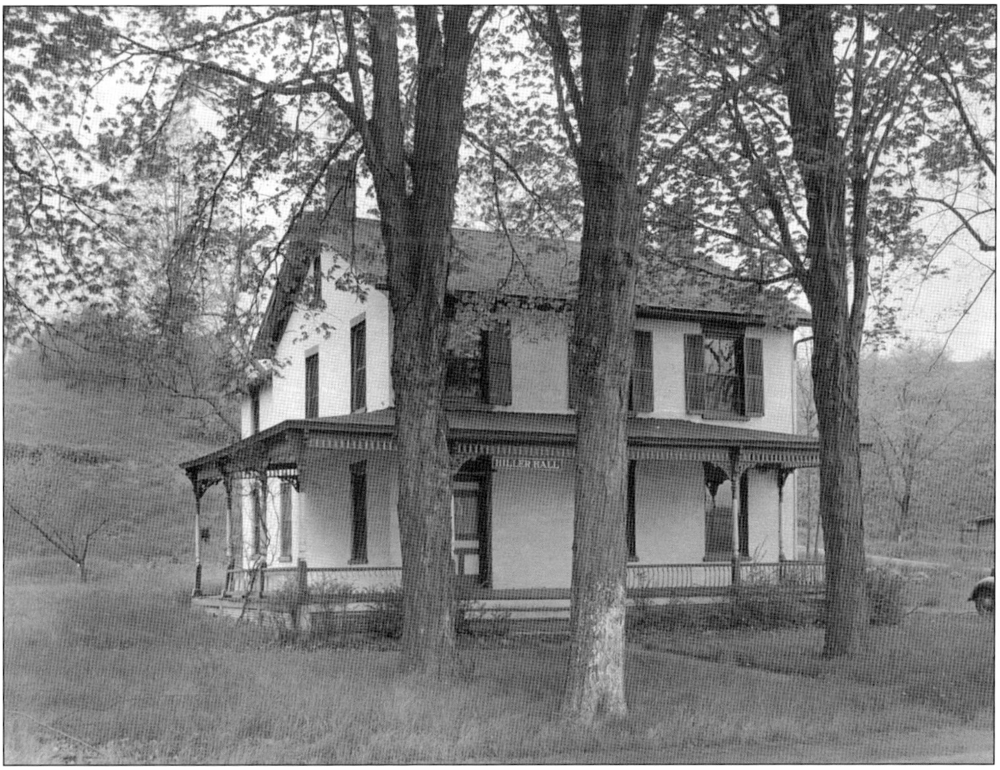

Built in 1815 for Ernst Hazelius, the first principal of the seminary, what was known as the President's House subsequently served as the home of the seminary's theology professors for decades. In 1929, the seminary and the academy formally separated, and the theological department moved to the house, which was renamed Hiller Hall in honor of Dr. Alfred Hiller, a professor of theology at the seminary for nearly 40 years. (PFCA at HC.)

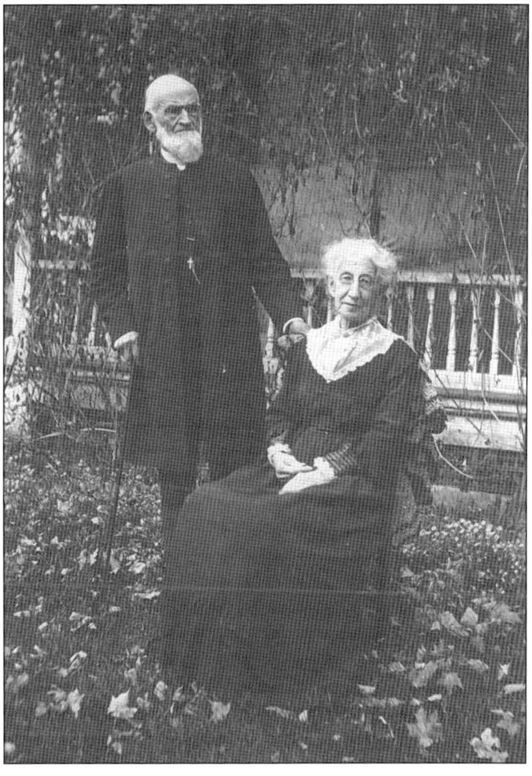

In 1881, Alfred Hiller, an 1857 graduate of the seminary, joined the faculty. His wife, Henrietta Hiller, taught French from 1882 to 1919. When the academy began to admit women in 1851, Henrietta's sister Charlotte was the first female teacher on the faculty. Both were daughters of George B. Miller, who served the seminary for over 35 years. In total, six of Miller's ten children, and three of their spouses, taught at the seminary. (PFCA at HC.)

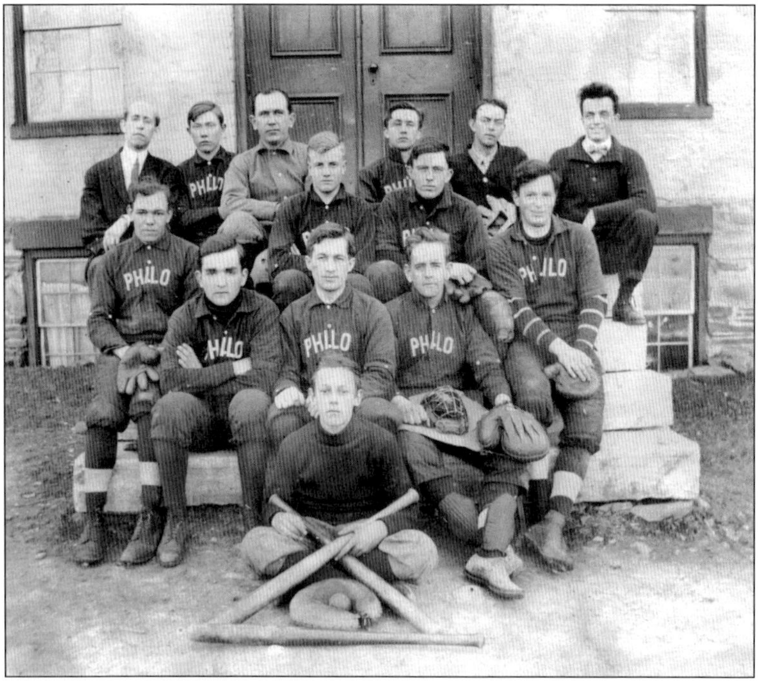

The Philophronean Debating Society was founded in 1816, and throughout its history, it played an important role in the intellectual and social life of the seminary. The Philos, as they were known, debated important issues of the day and also put on plays and concerts and sponsored lectures and sports teams. This photograph shows the Philos baseball team. (PFCA at HC.)

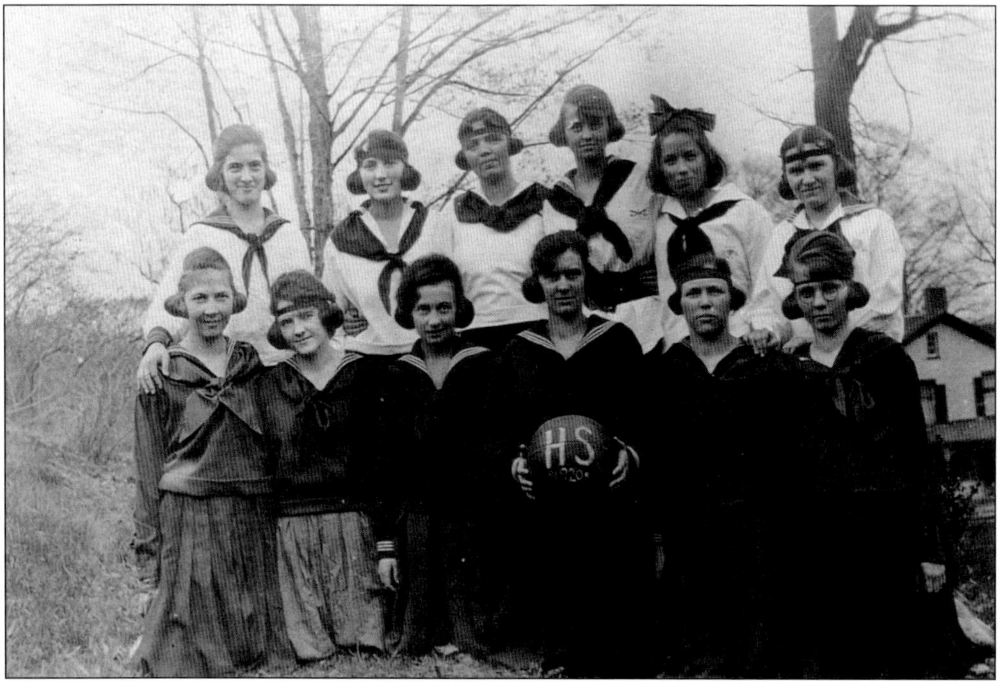

The women's basketball team in 1920 is shown here. A girls' athletic association was founded in 1912 a short time after Yetter Gymnasium was completed. The association charged members annual dues of 50¢, planned fundraisers and events, purchased equipment, and elected team captains and managers. (PFCA at HC.)

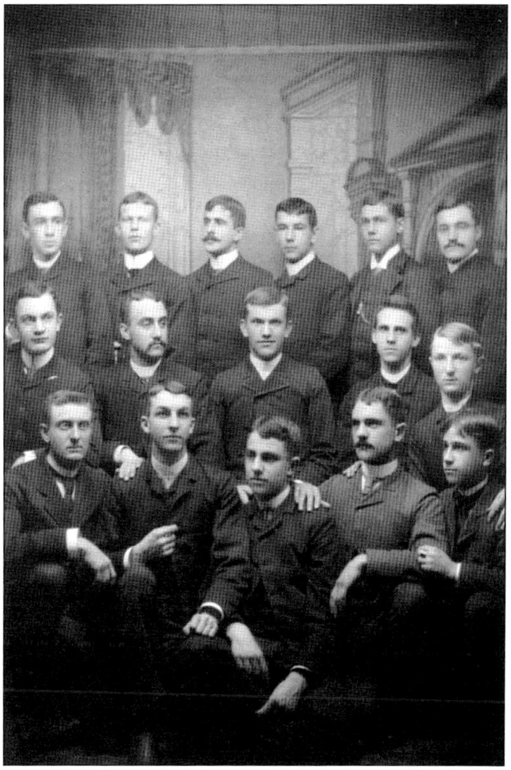

The Philos are seen here in 1887. In 1832, Isaac Newton Arnold, a Hartwick native, was a student at the seminary when the Philos debated the immediate abolition of slavery. In 1864, while serving as a Republican congressman in Illinois, Arnold introduced a resolution in the House calling for a constitutional amendment ending slavery in the United States. Arnold's resolution was the first step taken by a member of Congress toward passage of the 13th Amendment in 1865. (PFCA at HC.)

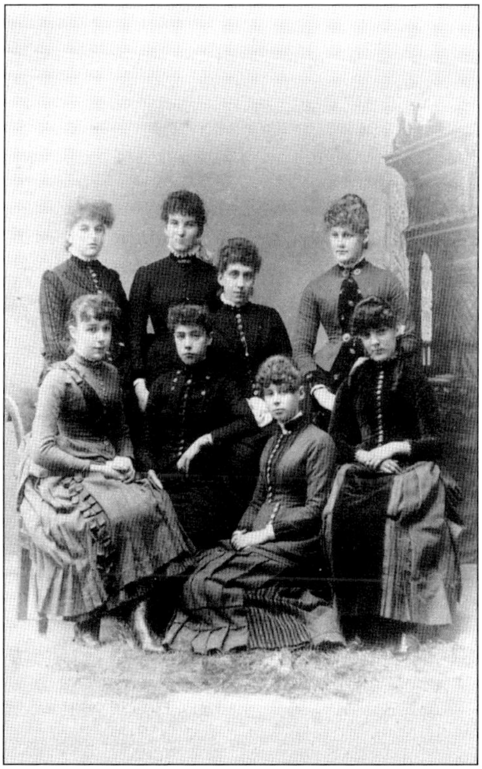

The Zetas are viewed here in 1887. Female students formed the Zetasophians, or "seekers of wisdom" in 1881. One of their first debates was whether "the mental facilities of both sexes are equal," which they decided in the affirmative. In 1885, the Philos challenged the Zetas to the first debate between the two societies, which the Zetas won. The two societies continued to debate one another in subsequent years. (PFCA at HC.)

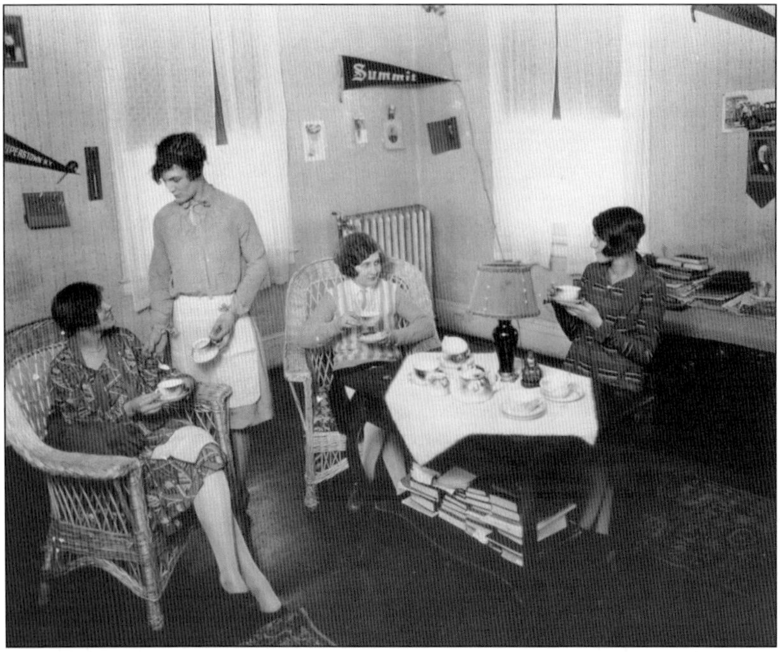

The students in this photograph by the Lockridge Studio in Oneonta are identified as Christine Meyer, Eleanor Hardy, Winifred Meyers, and Alice Cooper. It was taken in the late 1920s. (PFCA at HC.)

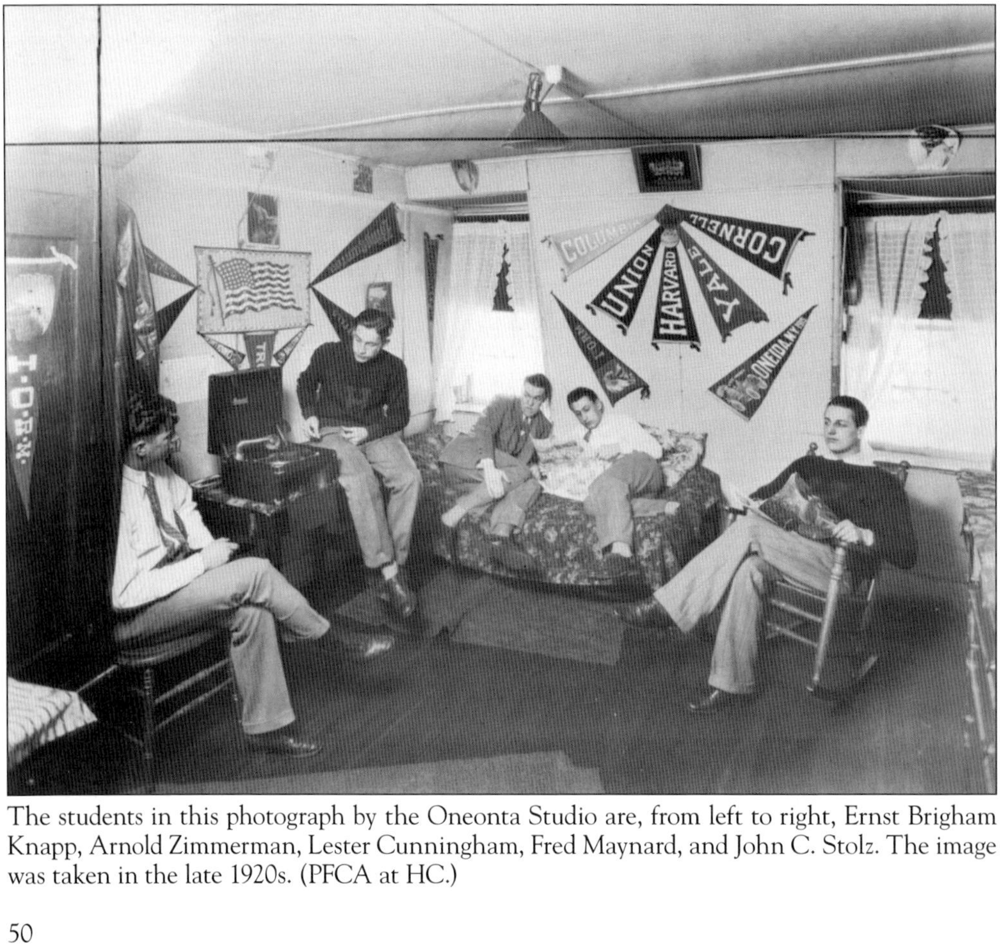

The students in this photograph by the Oneonta Studio are, from left to right, Ernst Brigham Knapp, Arnold Zimmerman, Lester Cunningham, Fred Maynard, and John C. Stolz. The image was taken in the late 1920s. (PFCA at HC.)

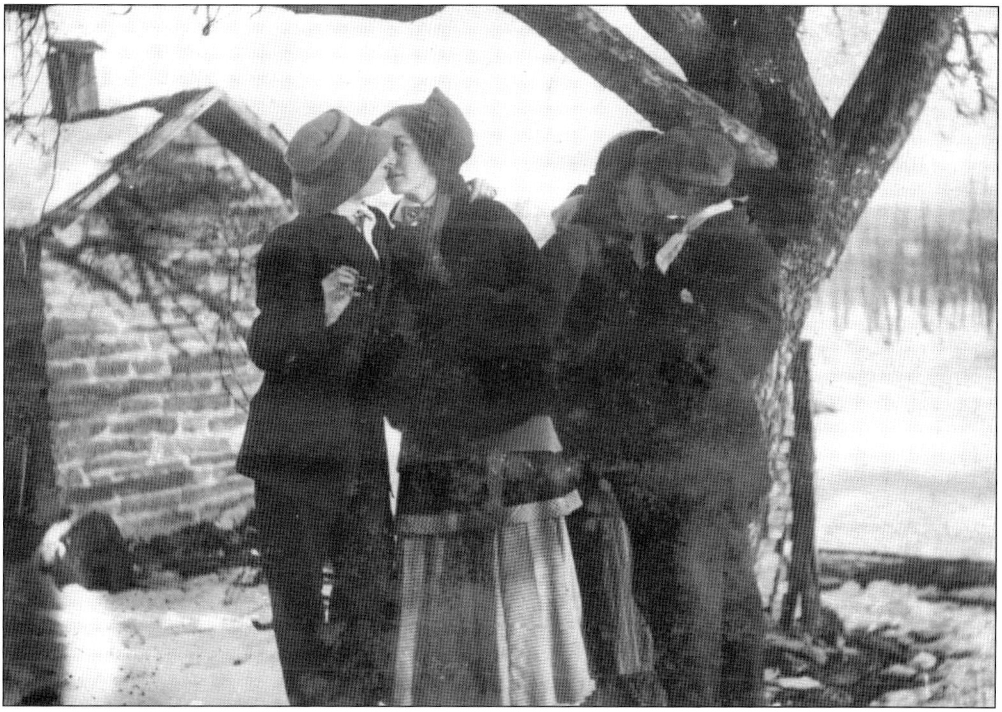

Seminary/academy student life included some extracurricular, coeducational social activities, as pictured here.

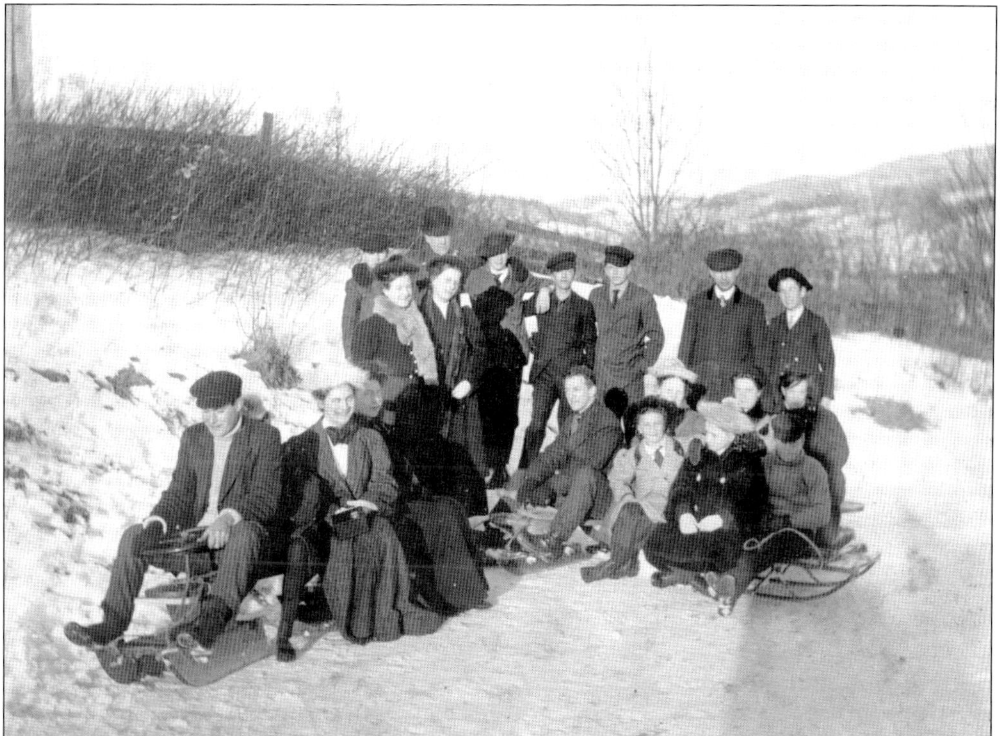

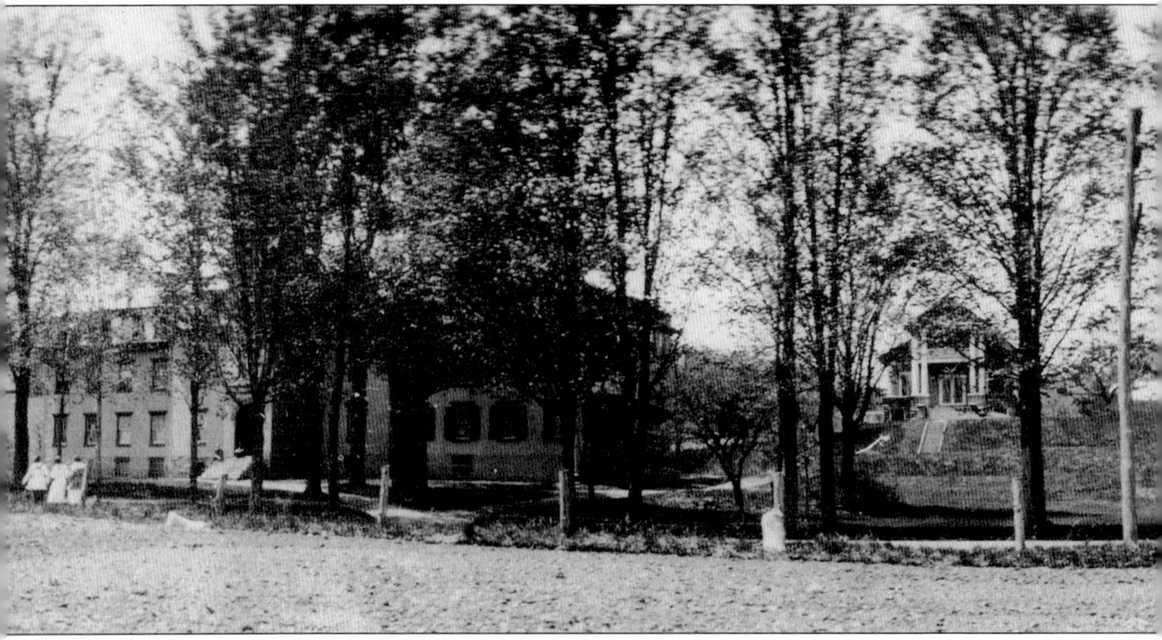

This photograph, taken sometime after 1912, shows the seminary campus, with Yetter Gymnasium in the center, the main building at left, and the president's house, or Hiller Hall, at right. According to the catalogs, the trees were older than the school, and the "spreading elms and maple lined walks" and were "beloved by every Hartwick boy and girl." The campus was quite large, encompassing

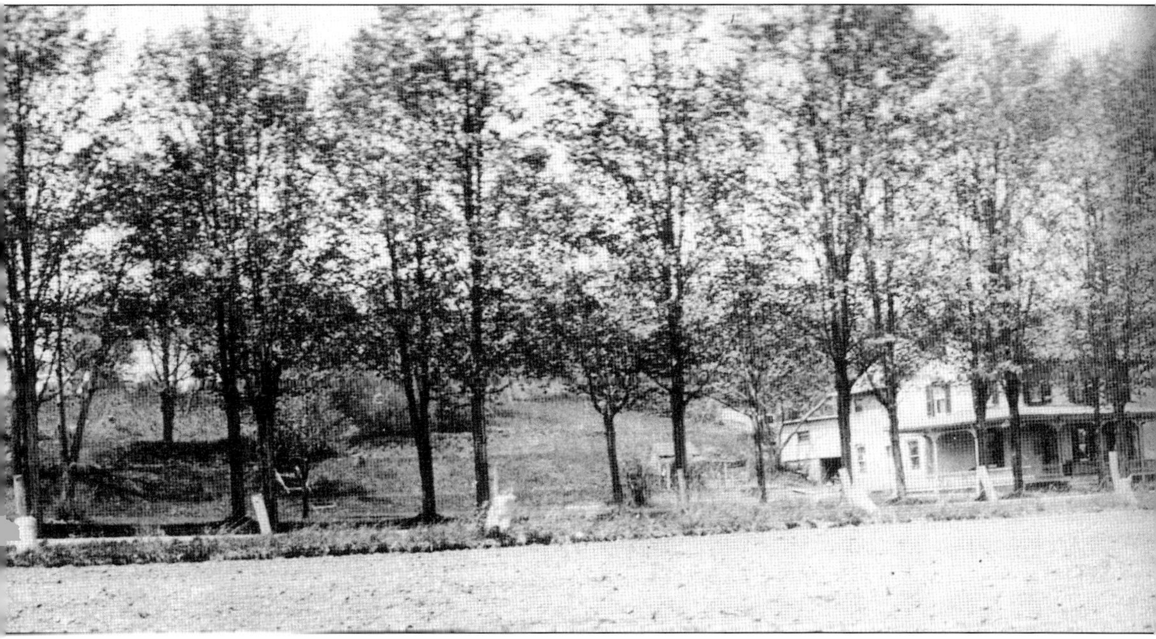

nearly 100 acres, including a farm that the school owned and operated "exclusively for the benefit of the students." According to the catalogs, "an abundant supply of rich, fresh milk is always available as well as an ample quantity of fresh eggs, poultry and pork." There were also athletic fields and a skating rink. (PFCA at HC.)

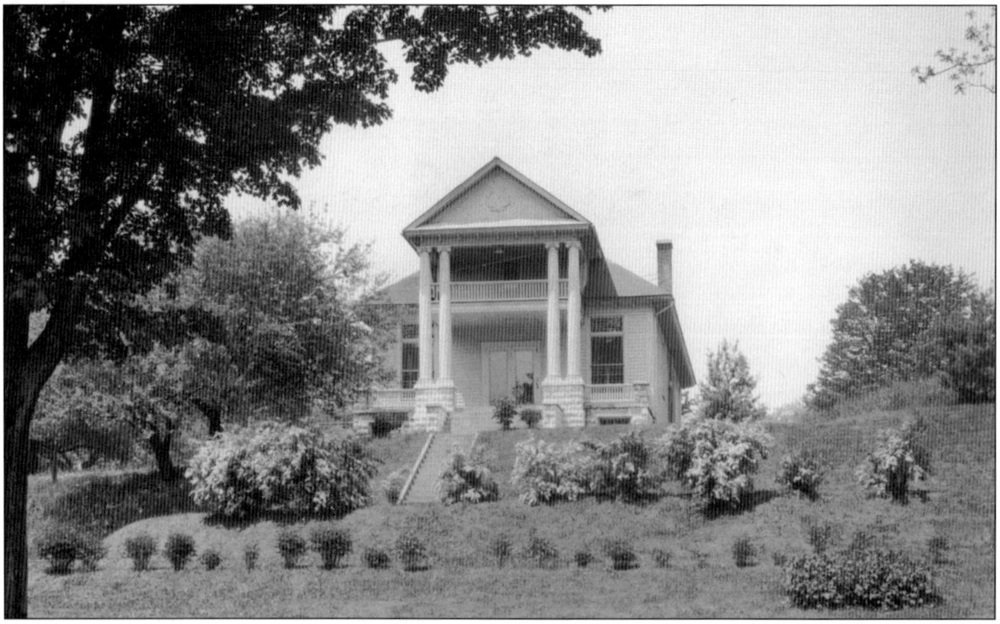

Built in 1912, the gymnasium was named for Andrew B. Yetter, an alumnus of the seminary. Neighboring residents agreed to contribute "in work or money" to excavate the foundation and to clear a site for the building. The gymnasium provided not only a much-needed athletic facility, it also served as an assembly hall for commencement ceremonies and other programs, including plays, concerts, and lectures. (PFCA at HC.)

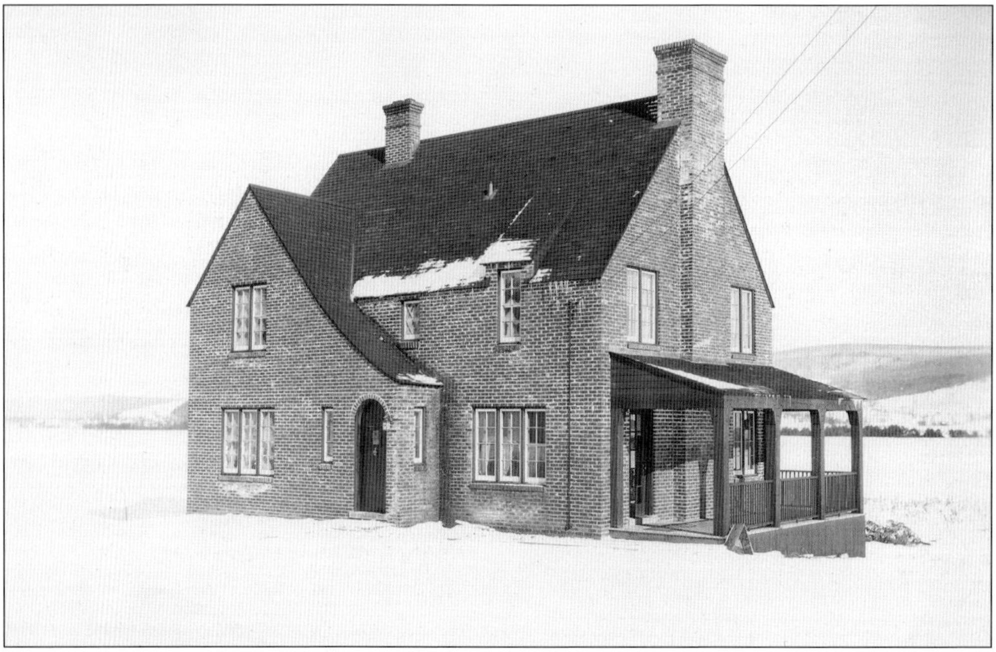

When Rev. W.H. Bruce Carney was appointed as the new George B. Miller professor in 1925, the seminary board built a new house for him and his family. In 1939, Dr. Carney became the last president of the seminary, which had relocated to New York City in 1930. It suspended operations in 1940 and legally merged with Hartwick College in 1947. (PFCA at HC.)

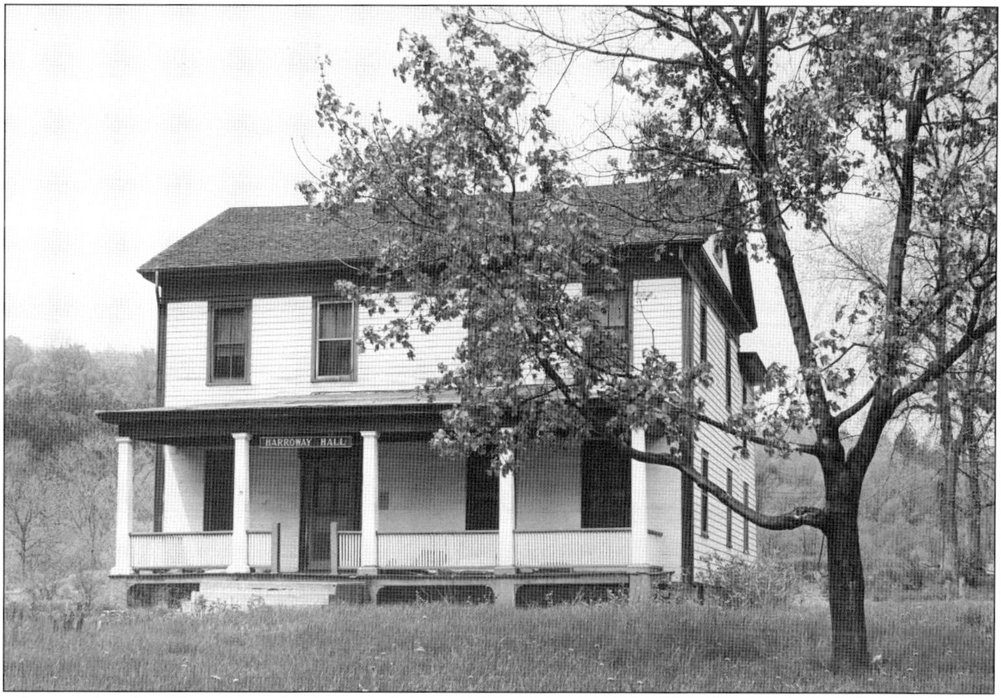

The Burditt farmhouse was purchased by the seminary in 1919 and in 1922 was named Harroway Hall in honor of Melvin W. and Etta Harroway of Richmondville. The house served as a women's dormitory for a little over a decade until the academy became an all-boy's school in 1931 (shortly before closing in 1934). (PFCA at HC.)

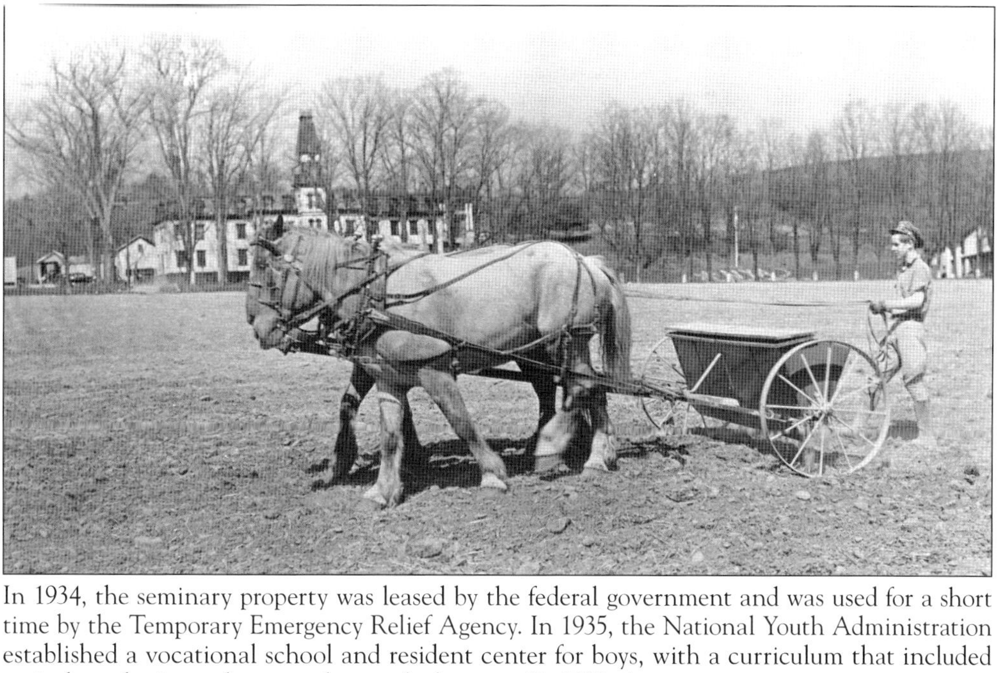
In 1934, the seminary property was leased by the federal government and was used for a short time by the Temporary Emergency Relief Agency. In 1935, the National Youth Administration established a vocational school and resident center for boys, with a curriculum that included agriculture, business classes, and general education. By 1939, the center was open to young women as well, who took courses in dressmaking, cooking, and hostessing. (PFCA at HC.)

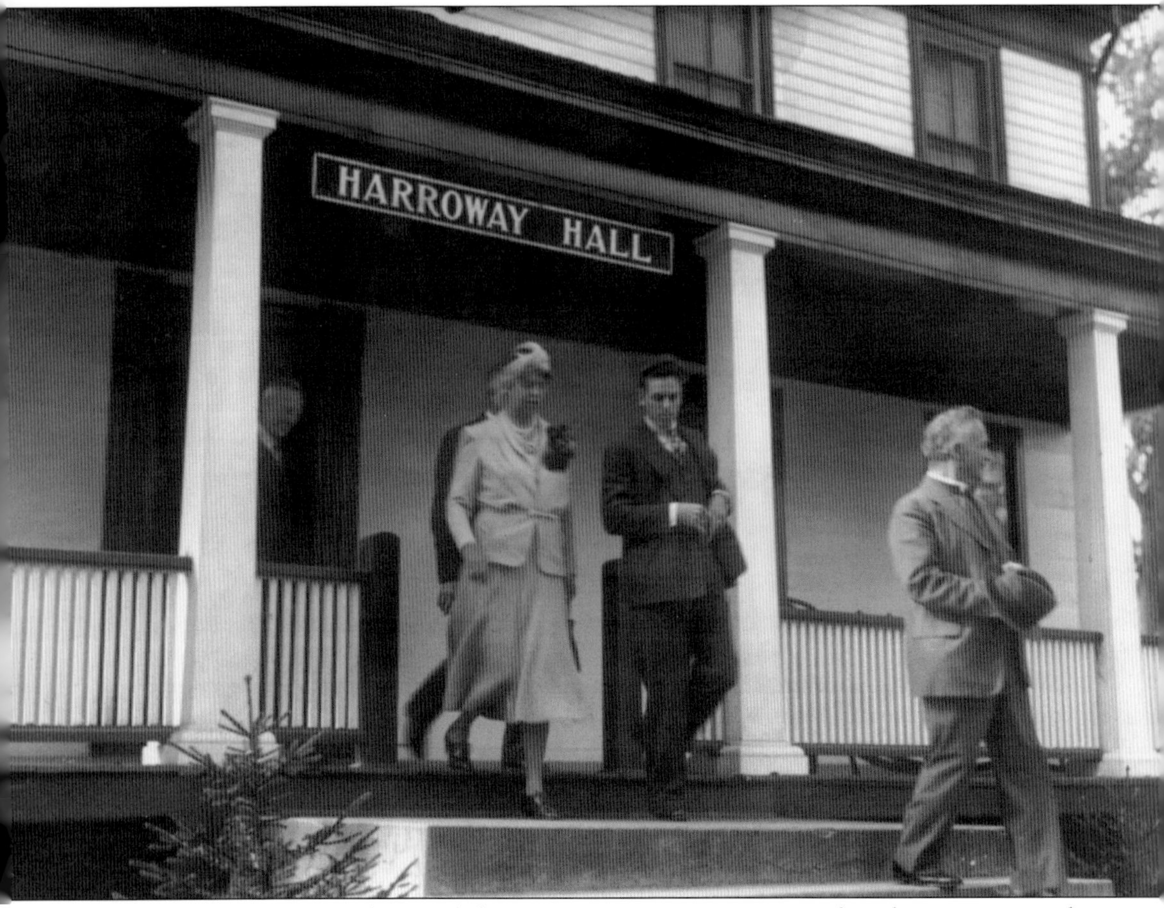

In 1940, Eleanor Roosevelt visited the seminary property on a tour of resident centers run by the National Youth Administration located at Hartwick, Utica, Solvay, and the Onondaga Reservation. According to the *Utica Daily Press*, she was presented with a cake at Hartwick Seminary in honor of her upcoming birthday. In her newspaper column, "My Day," she wrote that she was "most enthusiastic about the NYA rural center at Hartwick Seminary. I have never seen boys and girls more enthusiastic about their work . . . they are acquiring pride in what they do, and an understanding of the dignity of labor." The resident center continued to operate until as late as 1942. (PFCA at HC.)

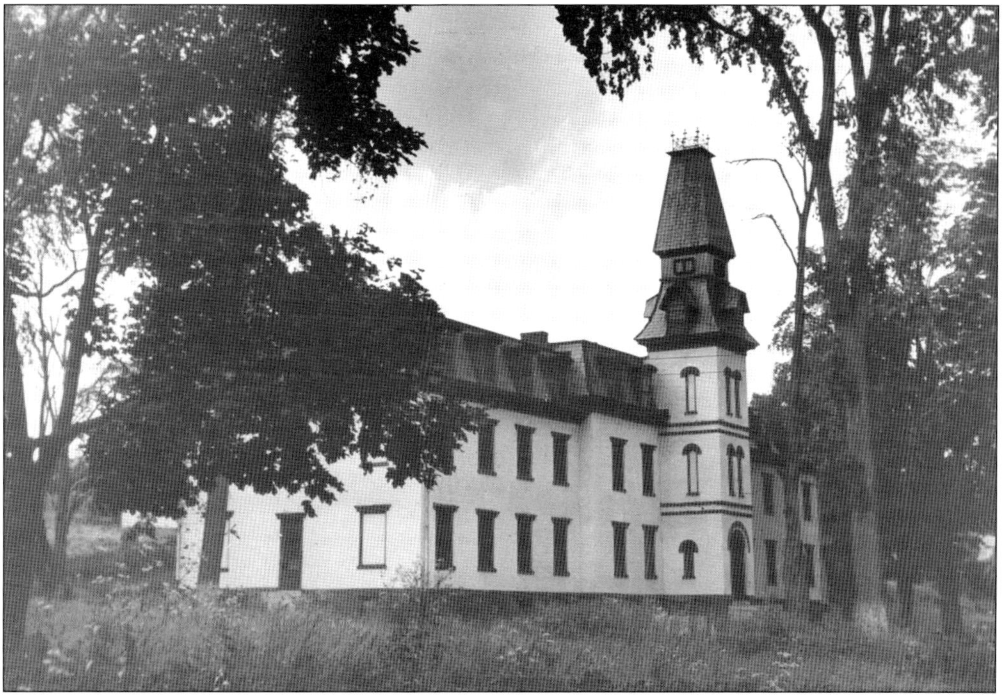

The resident center closed sometime in 1942, and the main building fell into disuse. This photograph shows the facility standing empty in July 1943, the same month that Congress voted to defund the National Youth Administration. (PFCA at HC.)

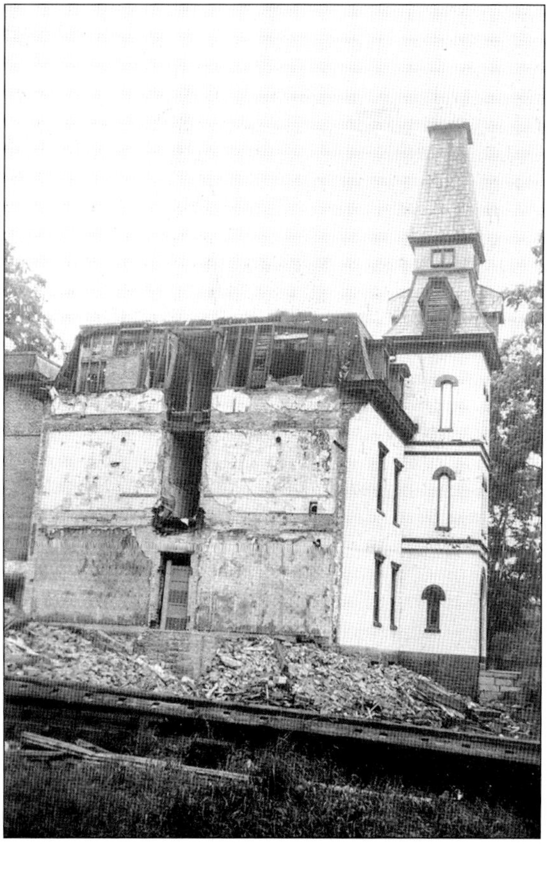

In 1944, both the academy and the seminary had closed, and the seminary property reverted to Hartwick College, which had been established in Oneonta in 1928. After failing to find another institution that could make use of the main building, the college sold it for demolition in 1946. In 1968, at the urging of seminary alumni, the college bought back the property and completed the demolition. (PFCA at HC.)

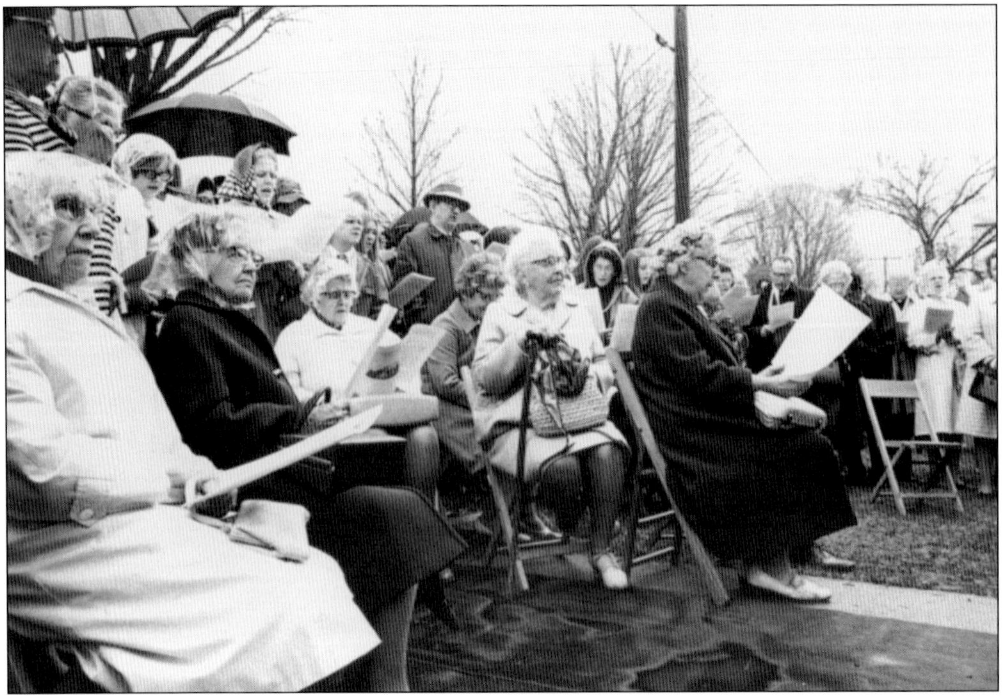

In 1972, Hartwick College held a four-day observance of the 175th anniversary of Hartwick Seminary's founding. More than 400 people, many of them seminary alumni, attended a Sunday service at the 133-year-old Lutheran church across the road from the site of the seminary, which concluded with the dedication of the Hartwick Seminary Memorial. (PFCA at HC.)

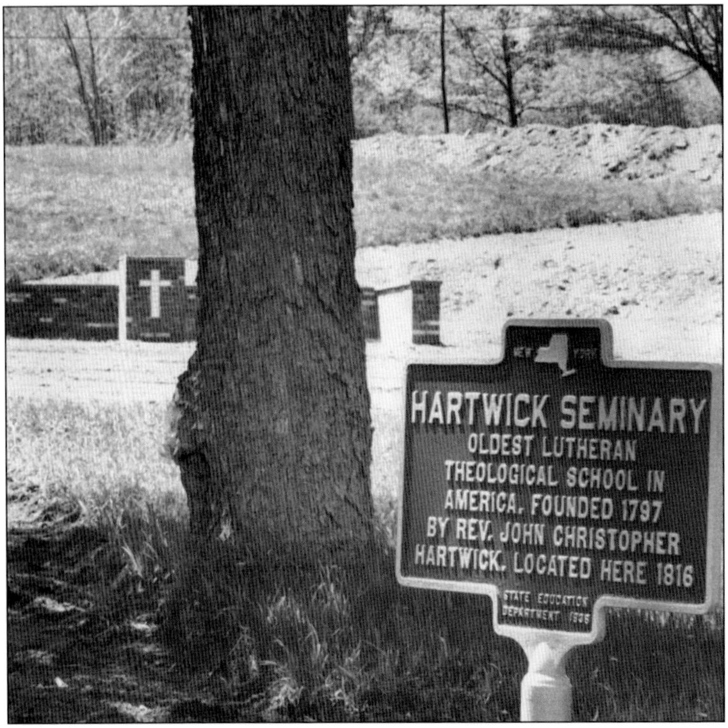

This photograph shows the Hartwick Seminary Memorial not long after its dedication. The year 1816 is actually the date the seminary was incorporated. The building was completed, and the first classes were held at the location on the Hartwick Patent in 1815. Hartwick College celebrated its bicentennial in 1997, proudly claiming the seminary's long history as its own and celebrating 1797 as its founding date. (PFCA at HC.)

Four

The Trolley Comes to Town

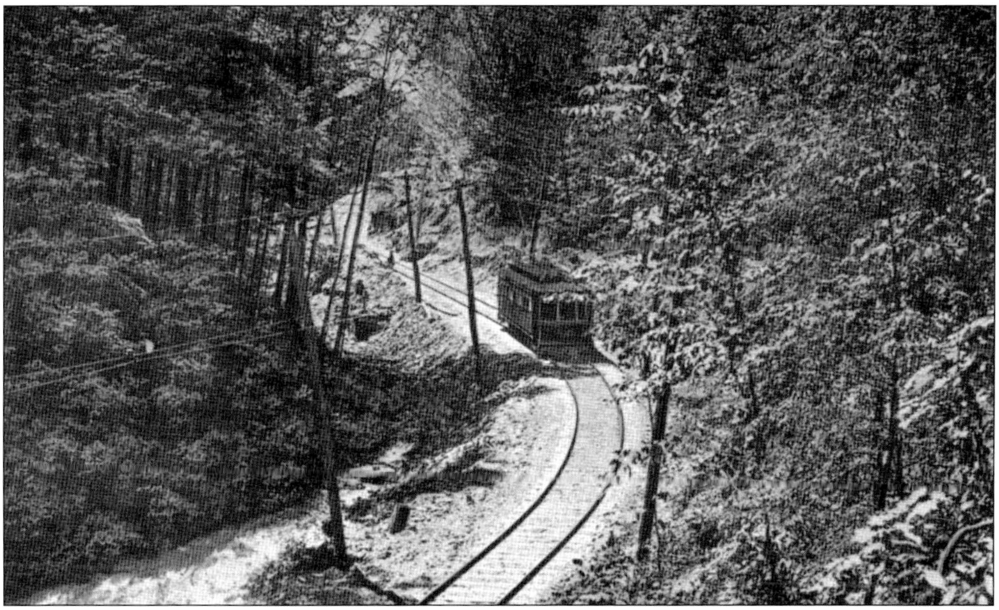

By 1897, the horse-powered Oneonta Street Railway was sold to investors interested in construction of an electric railway (trolley) line from that town north to the Mohawk Valley. When this rail line, the Oneonta & Otego Valley (O&OV), passed through Hartwick in 1901, it opened up a new era of interconnectedness and prosperity for the hamlet. In this view, a passenger trolley car winds through Chase Gorge, northeast of the hamlet, on the way to Index and points north.

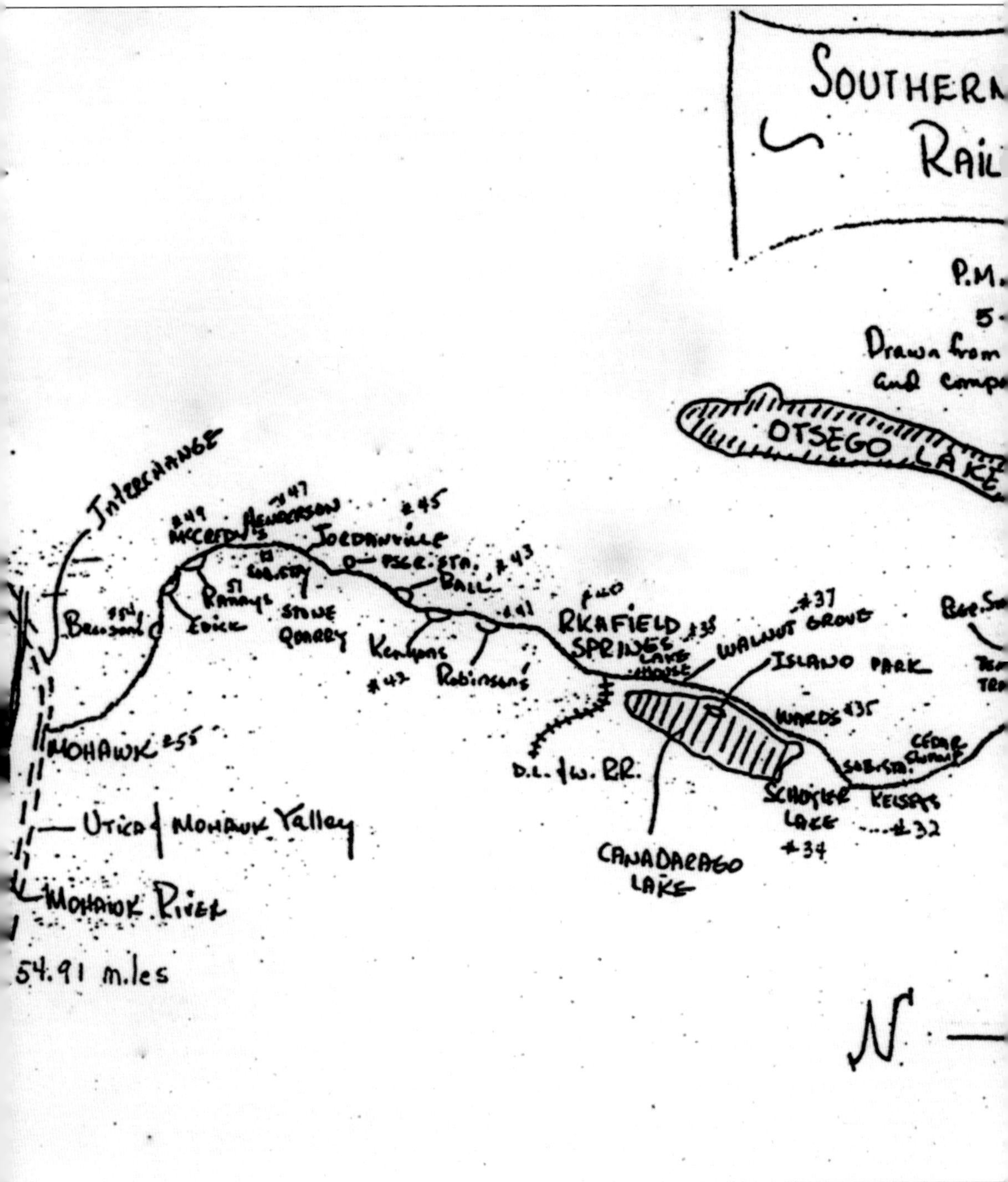

From its small beginnings in Oneonta in 1897, the electric railway/trolley moved steadily north through the Otego Valley to reach Mohawk and Herkimer by 1904. As it advanced northward along Otego Creek, the line connected some of the early neighborhood settlements in the Hartwick Township, opening up vital passenger and freight links to Hartwick and beyond. Through the years, the name of railway changed many times as the current destination of the route altered or financial difficulties led to new ownership. As this completed route map from about 1924 shows,

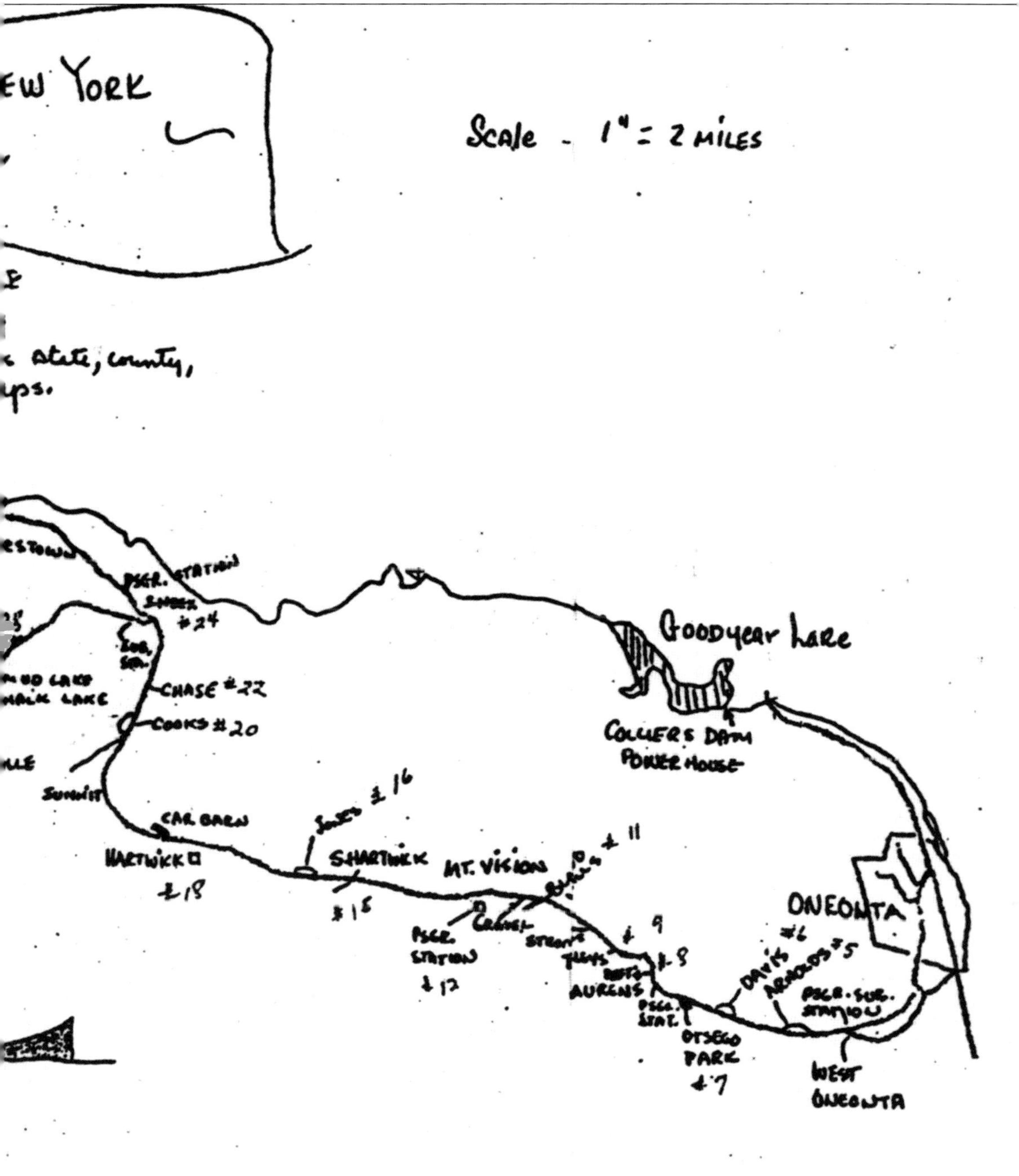

the final company name was the Southern New York Railway, and the mainland route covered 55 miles with 55 station stops. As seen, Hartwick hamlet was the midpoint on the route and as such had become the location for company headquarters, a large carbarn, and the primary electrical power source for the entire line. The hamlet had developed into a town commercial center, meeting housing, business, and service needs for outlying settlements, passengers, and employees of the trolley company.

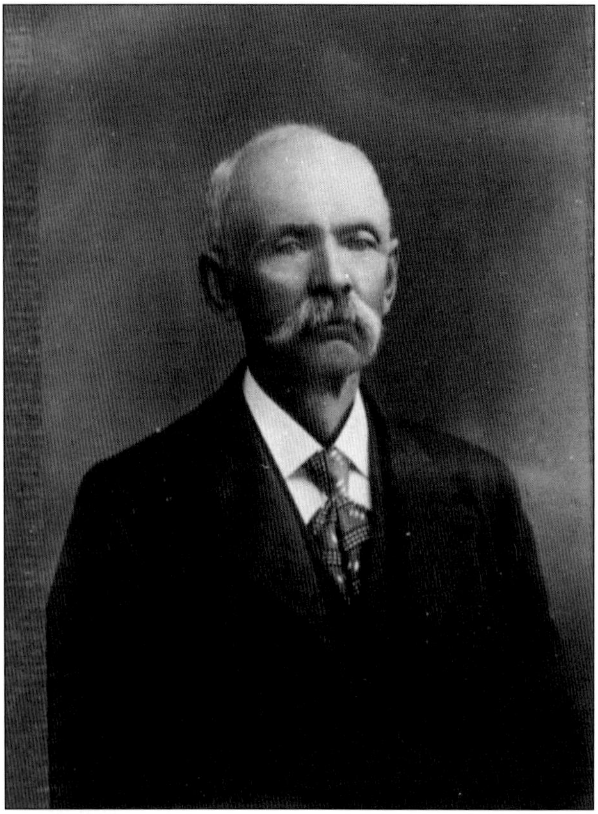

The first portion of the northbound electric trolley line was a short extension from Oneonta to West Oneonta. Soon after, a plan developed to extend the route north to Richfield Springs along the right-of-way of the existing highways. Owen Phillips, seen here, was selected as the original surveyor of the Oneonta, Cooperstown & Richfield Springs Railway (OC&RS.)

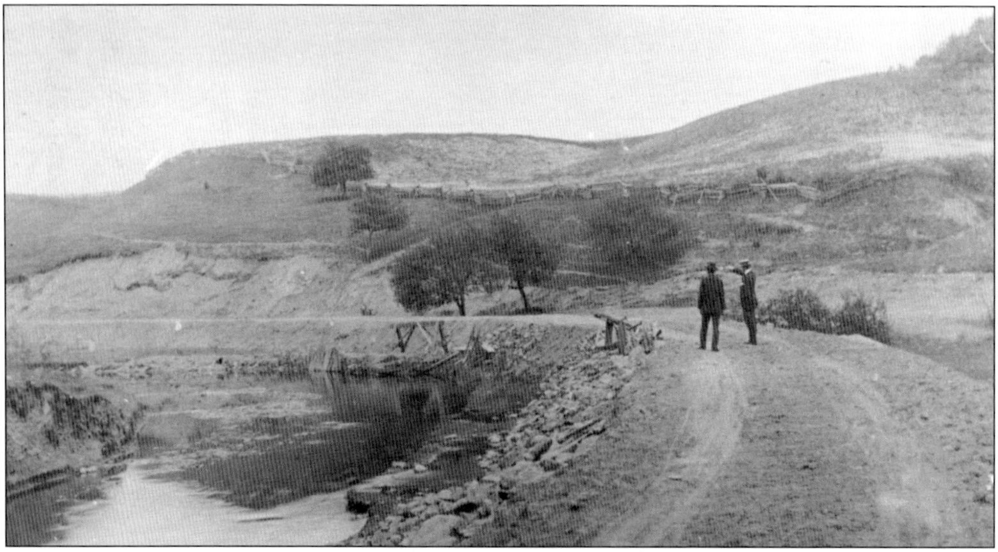

Plans to follow the existing highways proved unworkable for the trolley because of the steep grades of the roads. The decision was made to build the trolley with the easiest possible grade by following a "creek to creek route." This image shows early construction of the rail bed along a stream, possibly Otego Creek, as the line inched north through the Otego Valley toward Hartwick. From there, the route turned east over Cooks Summit to Chase Creek and on to Index, then north along Oaks Creek (the border of the Hartwick Township) and on toward the Mohawk Valley.

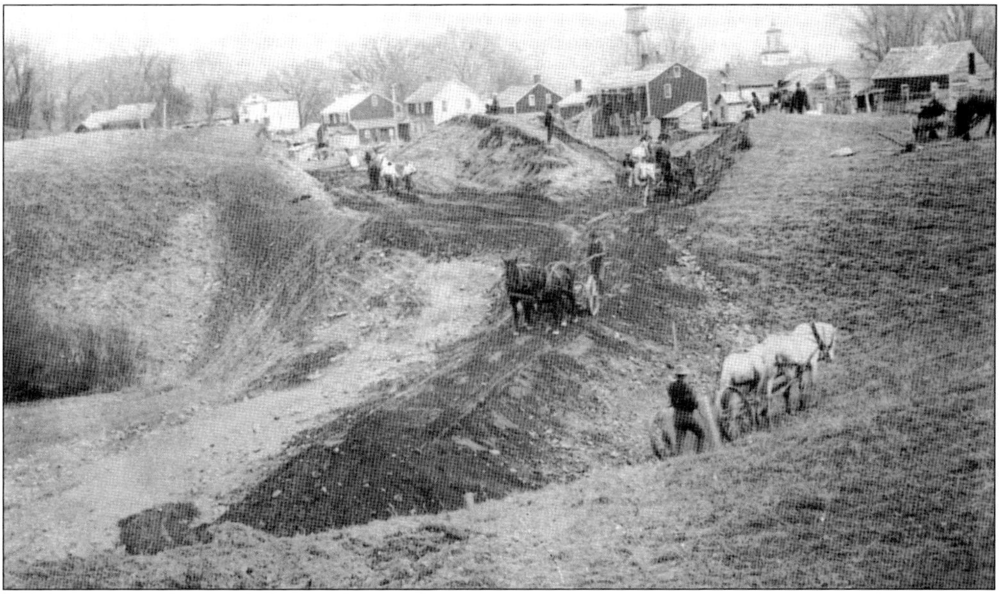

Without modern machinery, construction work was strenuous, backbreaking labor done by hand with pick and shovel. After blasting and shoveling, rock and dirt were removed from the roadbed cuts and hauled away by horse-drawn carts. Large work crews then lifted and laid ties and rails, preparing the way for steam locomotive–powered work trains to move construction materials forward. These photographs show a typical work crew and work in progress along a section of roadbed.

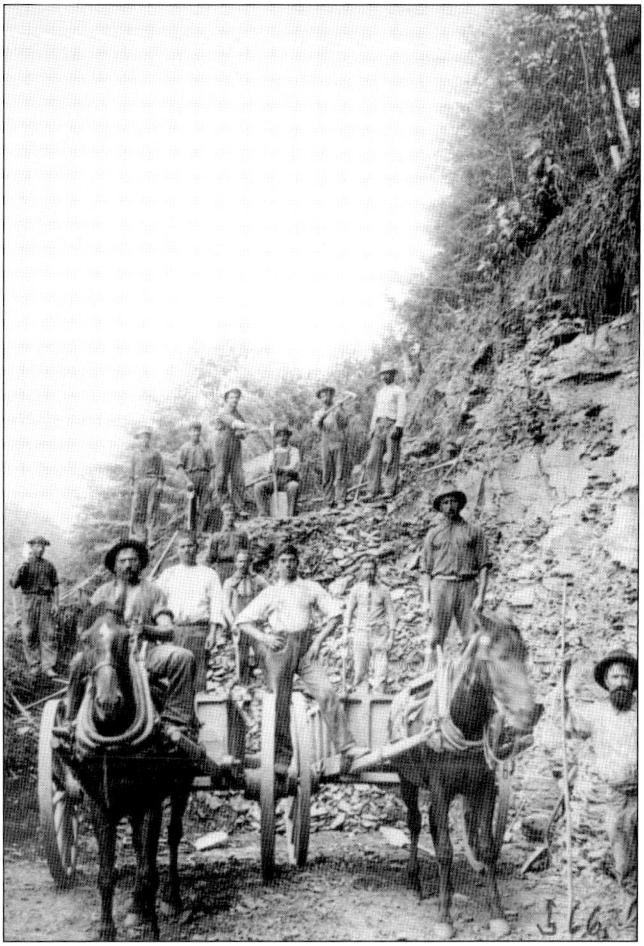

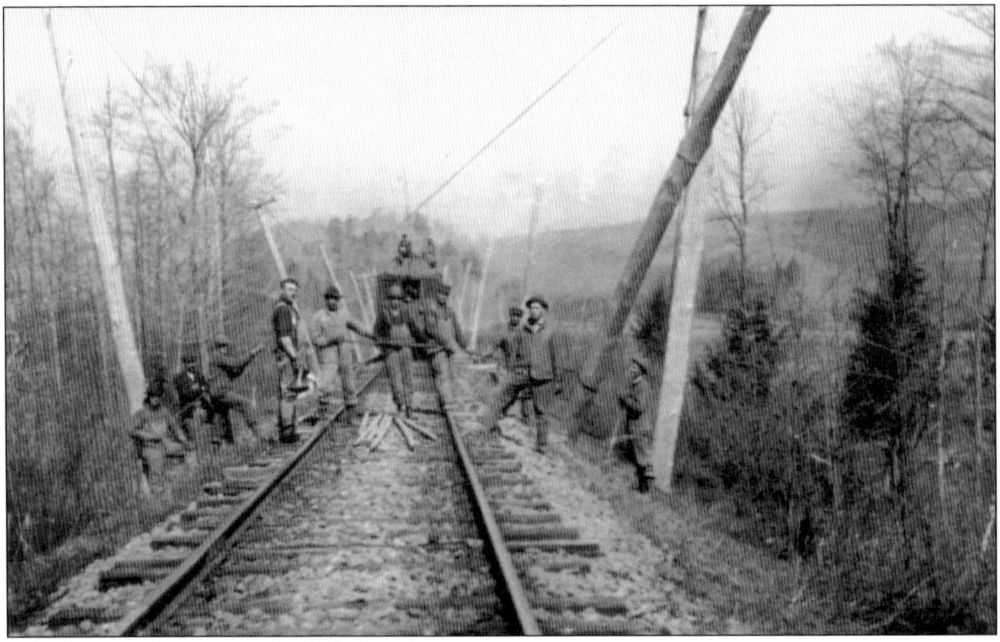

After poles were set along the trolley bed, line crews, such as the one seen here, would begin the task of stringing electric power wires.

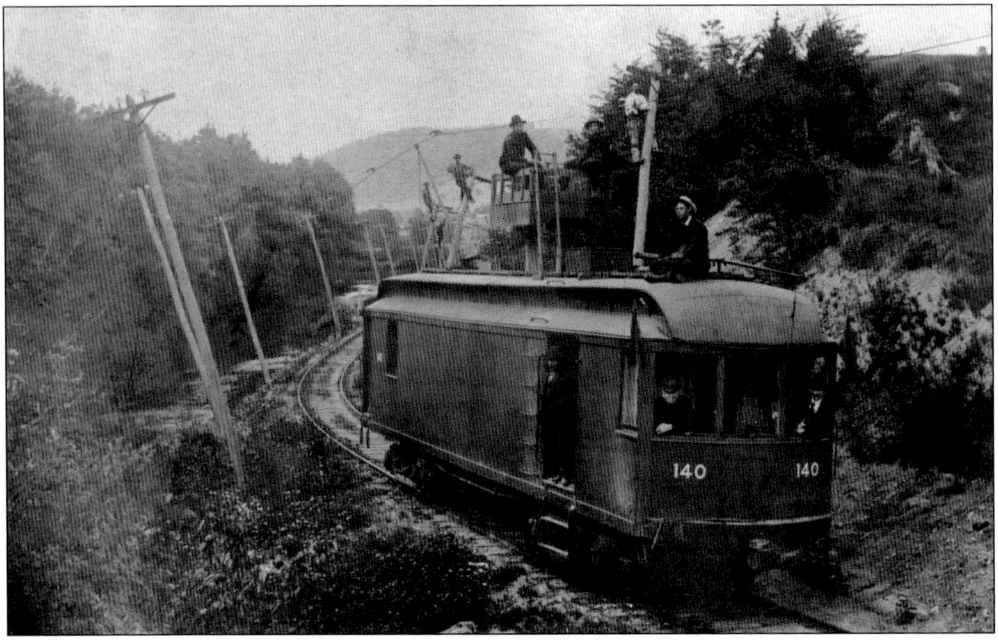

A line crew makes use of a tower mounted here on top of car No. 140 to string electric wires. After the wire was energized by the power plant, electric locomotives were used to power construction trains along the route (RF.)

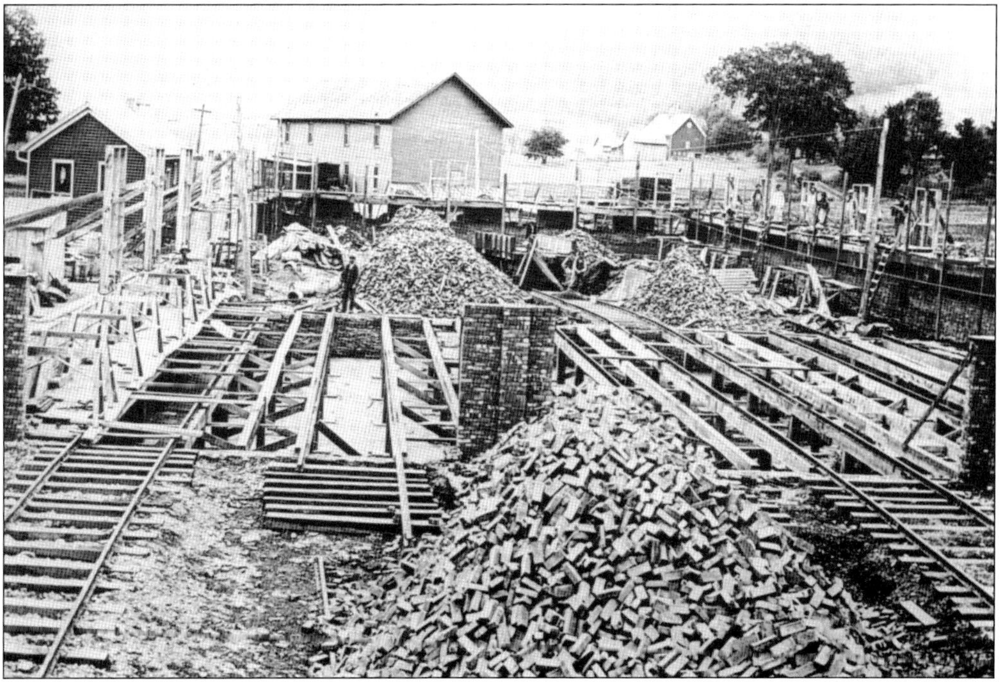

The carbarn for the OC&RS was built in 1905 in Hartwick. As the image shows, it was a large building (260 feet by 75 feet) constructed of wood and brick and used to house the majority of rolling stock for this trolley line. The man in the center of this construction image gives some perspective on the enormous size of the building.

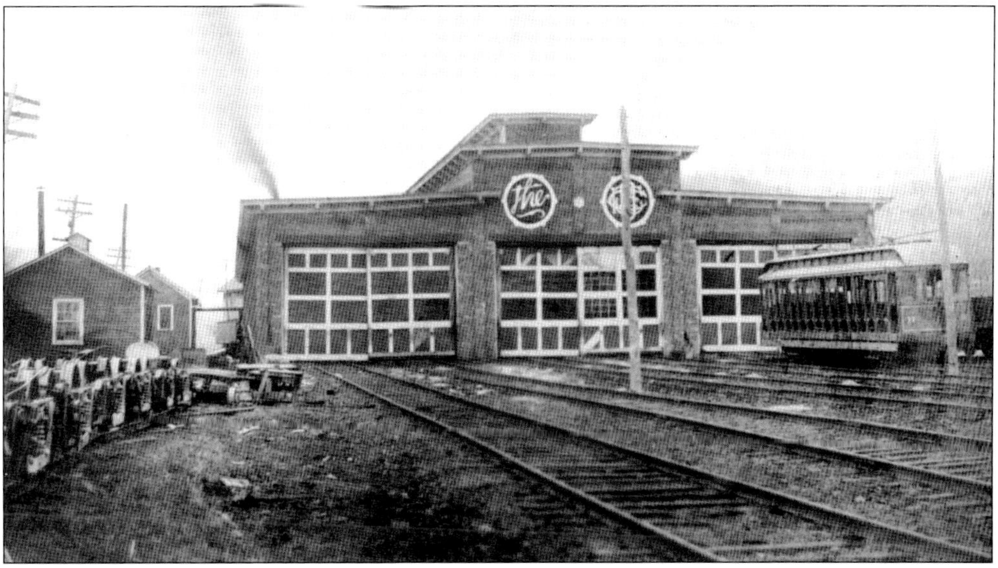

By 1907, the Oneonta & Mohawk Valley (O&MV) was completing 14 round-trips a day between Oneonta and Mohawk, with 109 trains operating over the line (not counting Oneonta City cars). These trains all passed through Hartwick, and much of the rolling car stock was housed there. When a December 1910 fire destroyed the freight house and car shed in Oneonta, the only surviving trolley cars were those in Hartwick. (RF.)

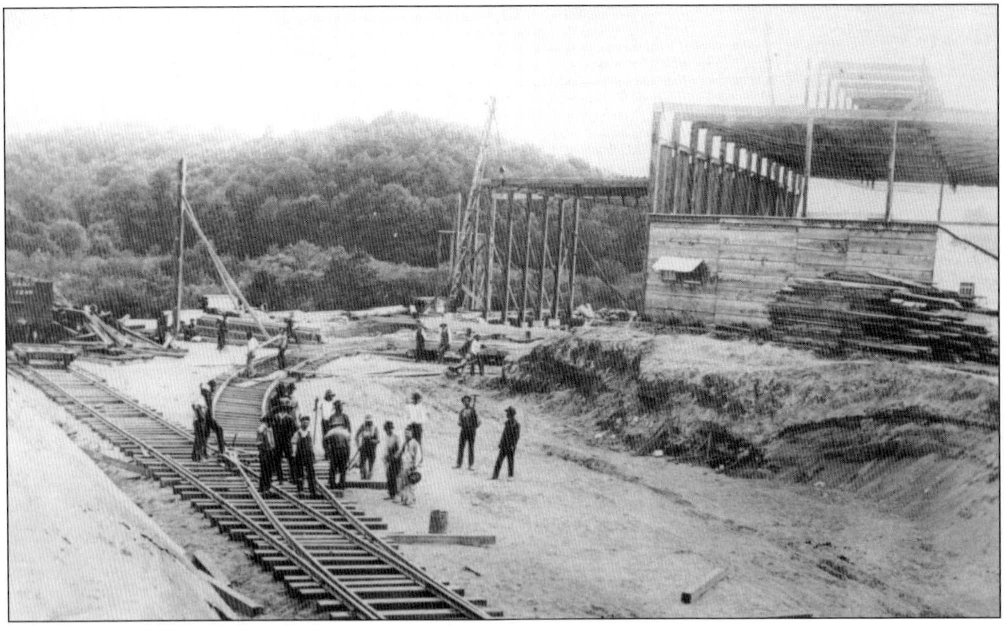

The original O&OV powerhouse in Oneonta was replaced in 1900 by the power plant in Hartwick. The first powerhouse, seen here, constructed from locally milled lumber, burned in 1904 and was replaced by a second building of brick, which remained for the duration of the trolley line. The powerhouse under construction in these photographs was 100 feet by 125 feet and produced electric power for the entire trolley line and many private homes. When demand for electricity exceeded what the powerhouse could supply in 1907, a hydroelectric dam was constructed 15 miles to the east on the Susquehanna River to transmit additional power to the trolley lines.

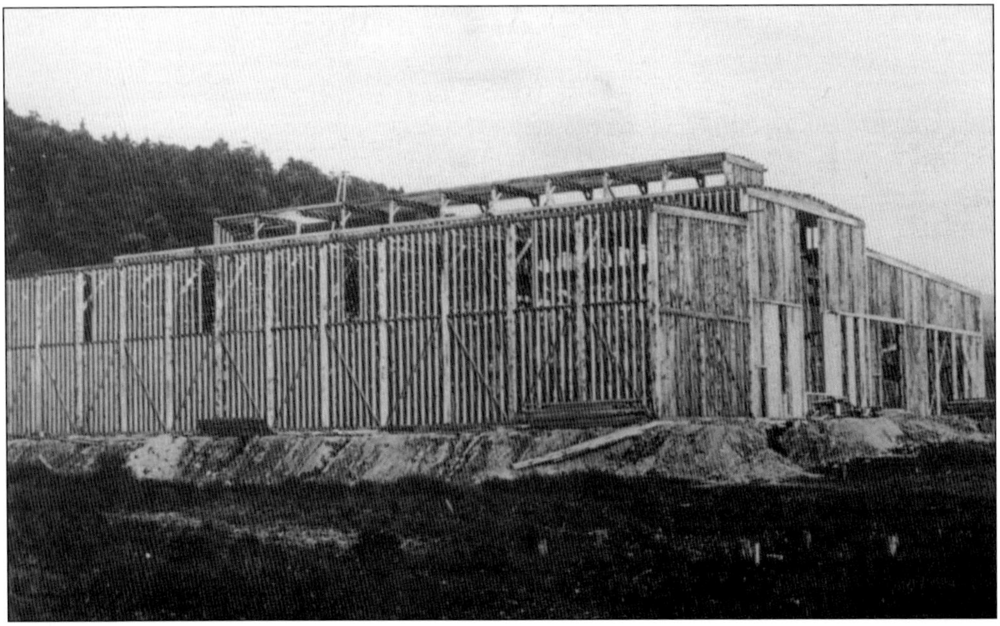

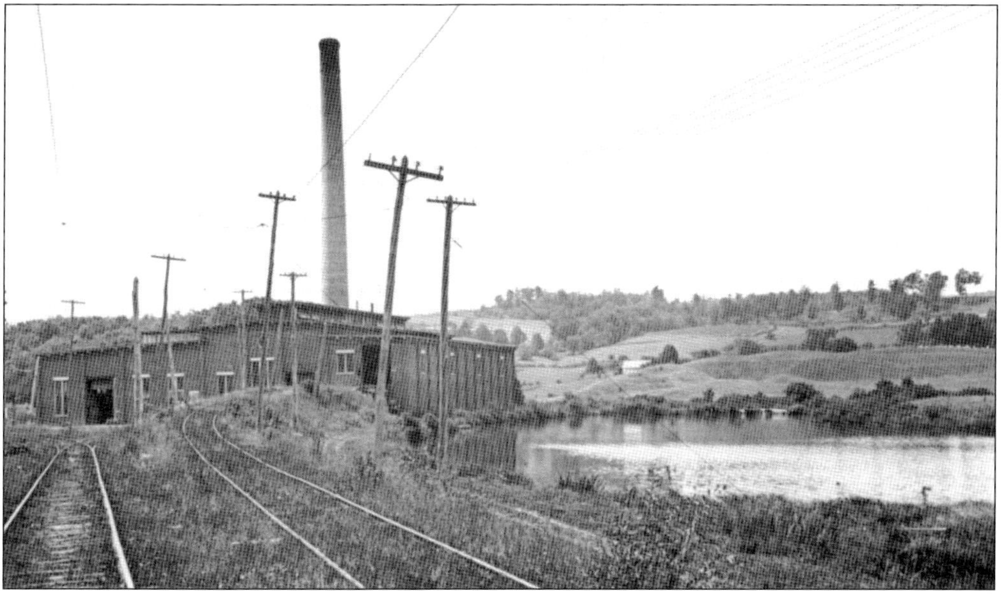

The powerhouse in Hartwick, as viewed here, was a large brick structure located beside a pond, not far from Otego Creek, south of the hamlet. Two 1,000-horsepower steam-powered engines produced electrical power for the railway. When the trolley ended all service by 1941, the powerhouse was closed and later torn down. The last remaining structure, the 185-foot-high smokestack, was dynamited in May 1953, and the bricks were used for an Oneonta building on Chestnut Street. The Hartwick Rod and Gun Club now stands on the powerhouse site.

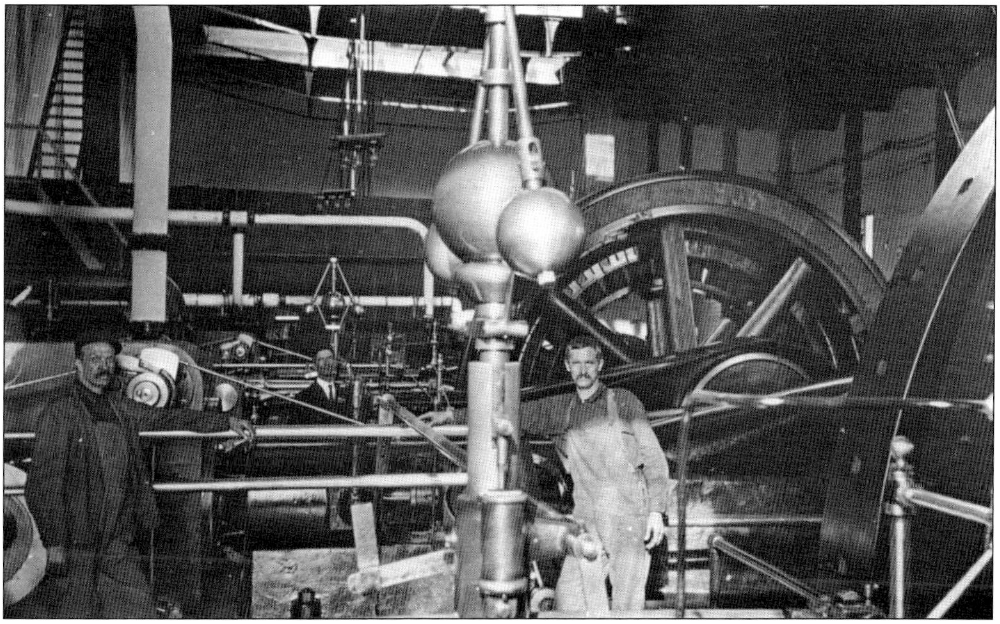

This photograph shows a section of the interior of the Hartwick Power Plant. Three 300-horsepower fire-tube boilers were installed in 1900 to provide the steam needed to generate electricity. Steam engines drove the alternators (one is seen in the right background) to generate the electricity, which was then transmitted through power lines to substations near the trolley power lines.

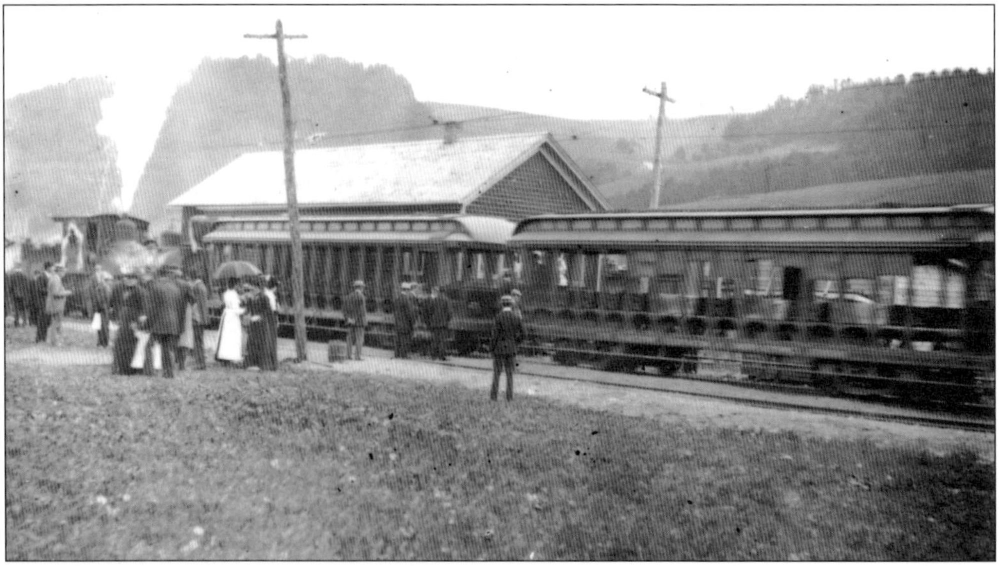

The trolley reached Hartwick in the summer of 1905. The opening day, viewed here, must have been very exciting for those embarking on travel aboard the new service through Hartwick.

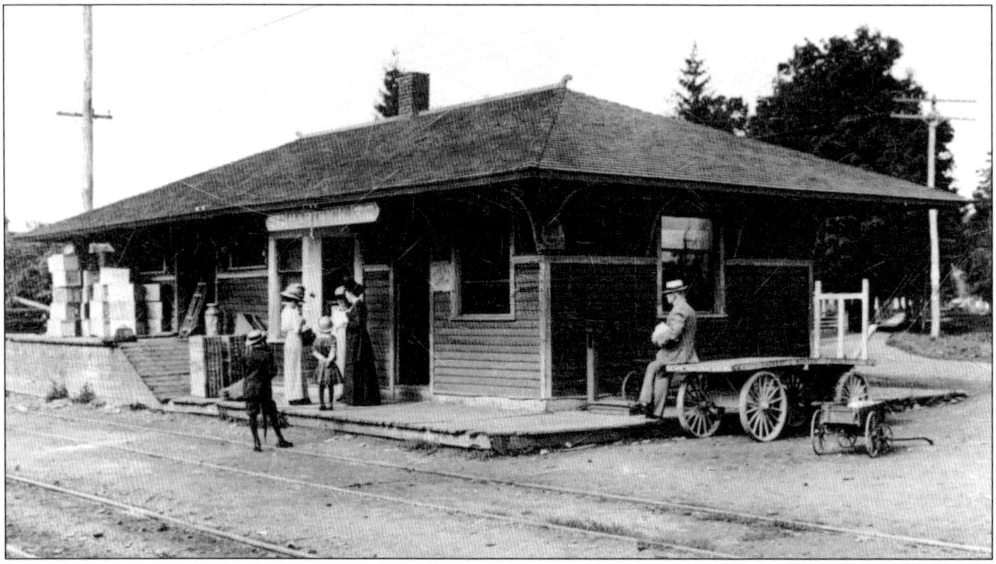

This wooden depot in Hartwick was built by J.W. Packer of Laurens and served as a local hub for passengers and freight service (including a variety of express, mail, milk, and agricultural products) for nearly 40 years. By 1905, the railroad operated eight daily round-trips from Oneonta through Hartwick to Mohawk and 14 through Index and Cooperstown, with 45 trains in all. Theatergoers enjoyed evening runs between Cooperstown and Hartwick. When trolley services ceased, the depot was used by three feed stores. Today, it is the manufacturing location for the Cooperstown Bat Company.

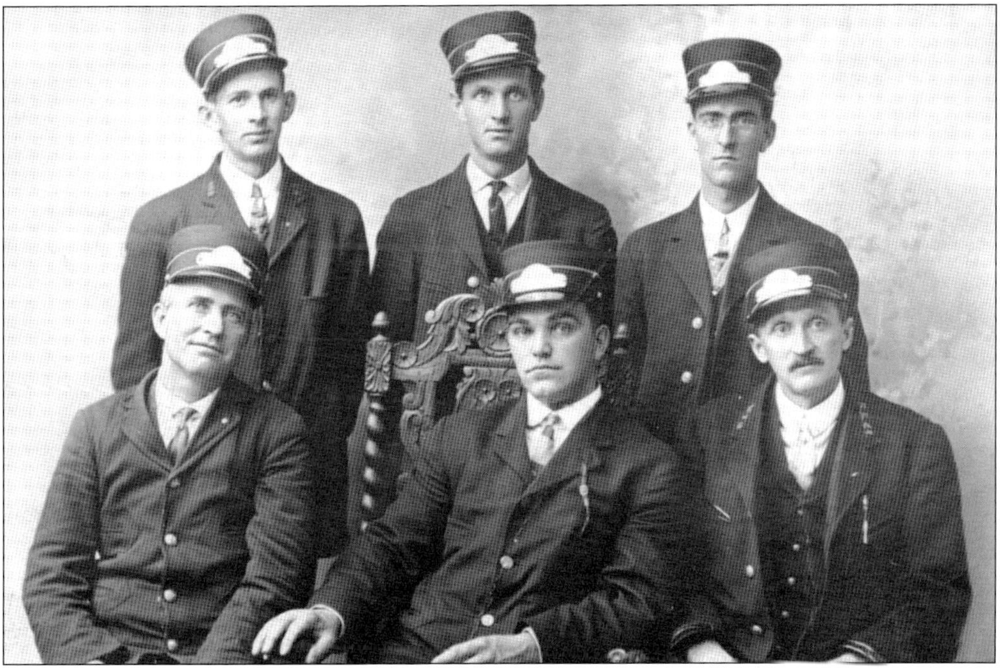

The trolley company was the major employer for Hartwick in the early 1900s. Employees filled positions at all levels needed for maintenance and operation of the system. This image identifies a few of the local conductors who made daily trips aboard the trolley cars. From left to right are (first row) Henry Bergman, Earl Ellsworth, and George Hyer; (second row) Henry Aplin, unidentified, and Howard Bush.

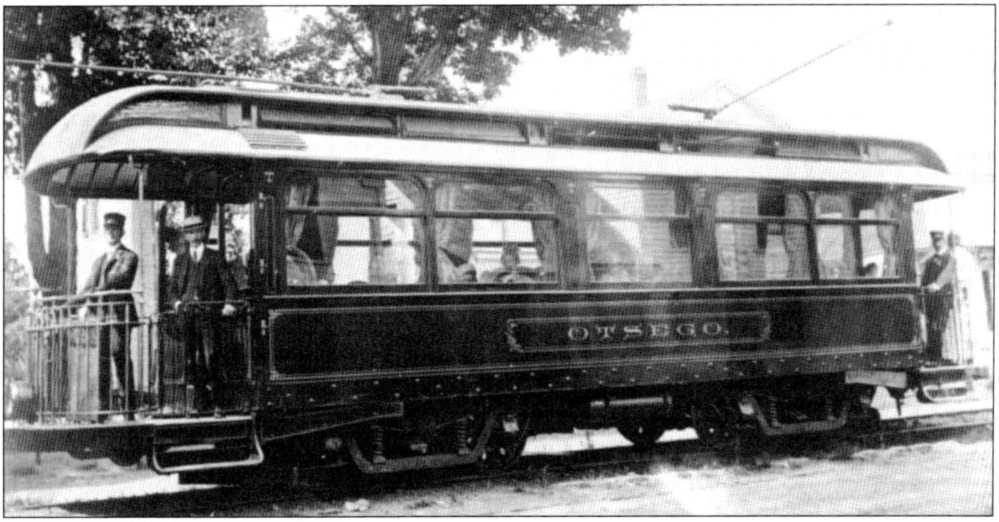

Various types of enclosed or open-air cars were used on the trolley lines for passenger service or for the popular summertime excursion trips. One of the more famous enclosed cars is pictured here, the elegant parlor car *Otsego*. Named after the famous lake in Cooperstown and for the county in which the OC&RS operated, it was purchased in 1901. The car was finished in figured African mahogany and had fine wicker chairs, carpeting, curtains, a brass-railed observation deck, a toilet, an icebox, and a bar on board. Notables such as Theodore Roosevelt and the Anheuser-Busch family enjoyed its accommodations.

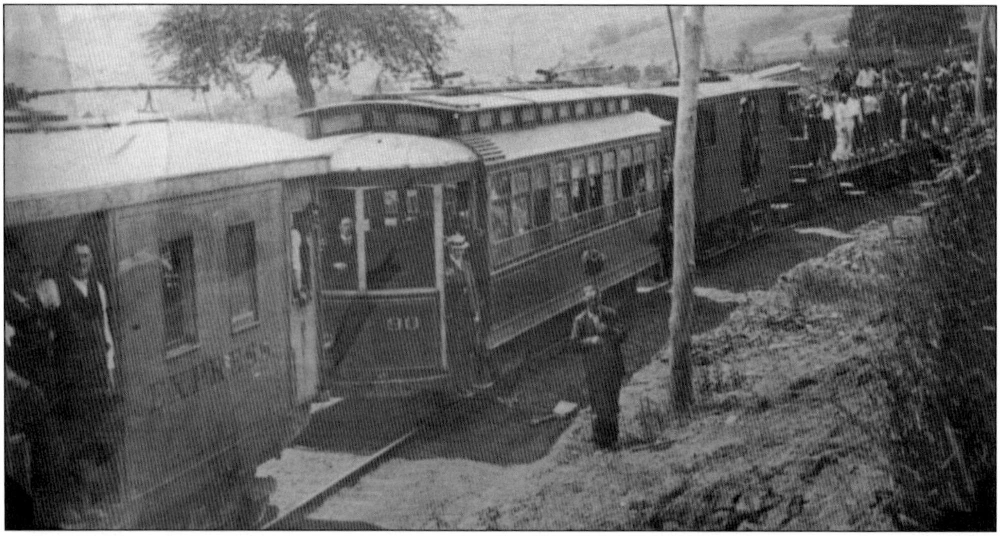

In early days, excursion trains were popular and ran through Hartwick, either en route north to Canadarago Lake near Richfield Springs or to beautiful Otsego Park located south of Laurens along Otego Creek. Otsego Park, opened in 1902, featured rustic buildings and benches for outdoor relaxation and a pavilion for special entertainment. At night, the park was lit by 200 electric lights.

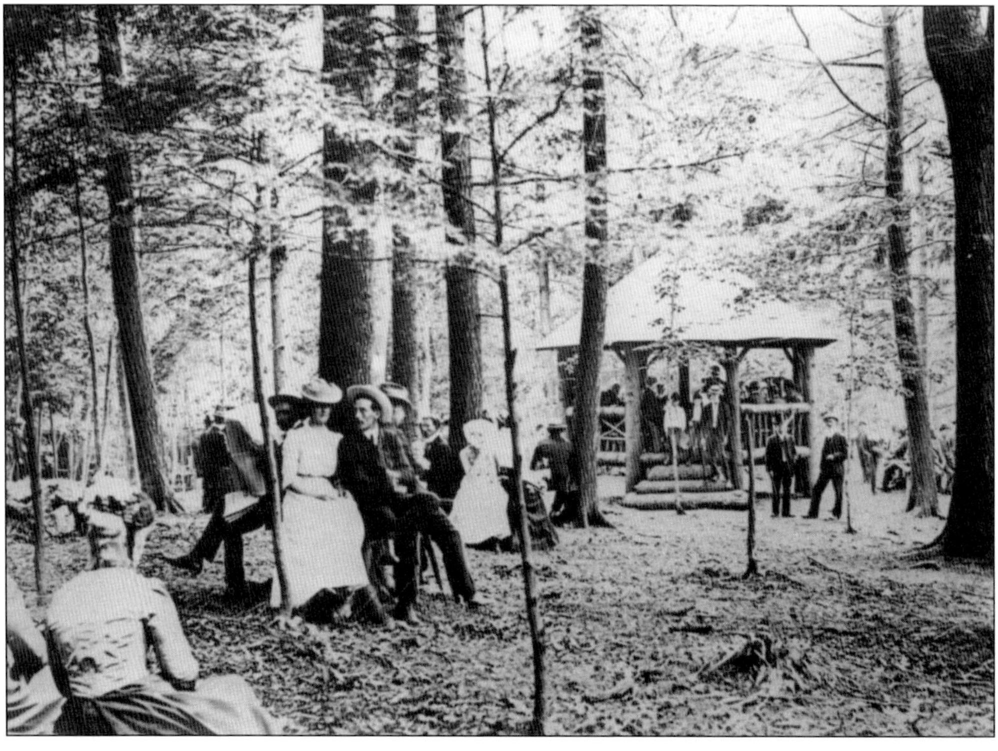

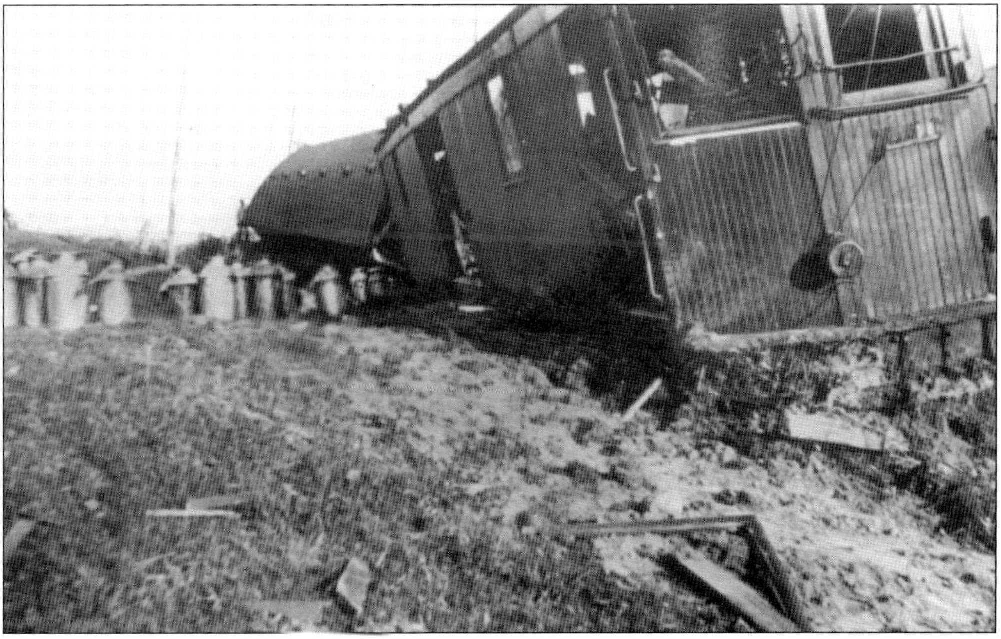

The local railway system had its share of accidents and injuries through its approximately 30-year history. The year 1902 was an especially troubling one, with at least seven reported accidents, including some serious injuries and one fatality. Two of these collisions occurred near the Hartwick powerhouse. This photograph shows an undated milk-car train wreck along the line.

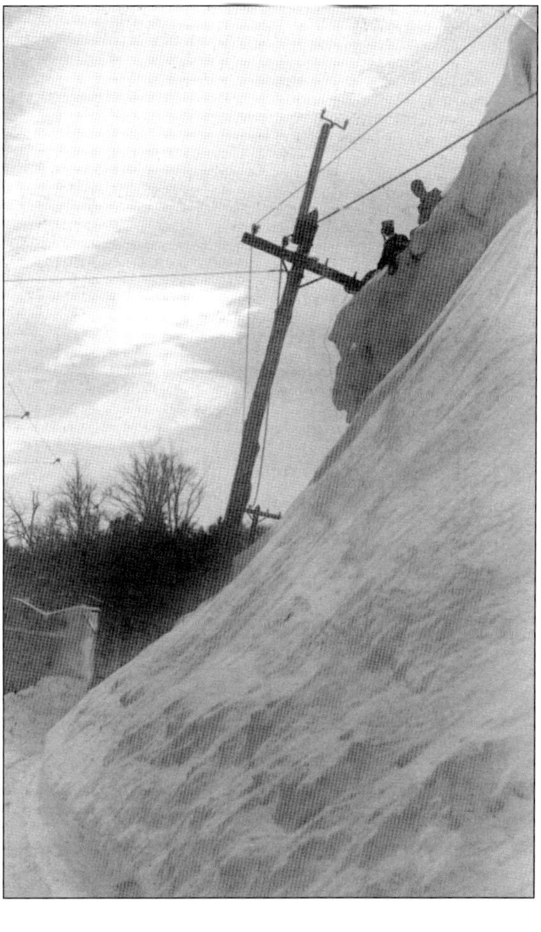

The railway ran year-round in all weather conditions, but the winter of 1920 brought an extreme challenge to the operation as blizzard conditions of snow, ice, and wind brought the trolley to a standstill. Snowdrifts, created by strong winds and the struggling rotary plow, reached the top of the poles along the roadbed. (RF.)

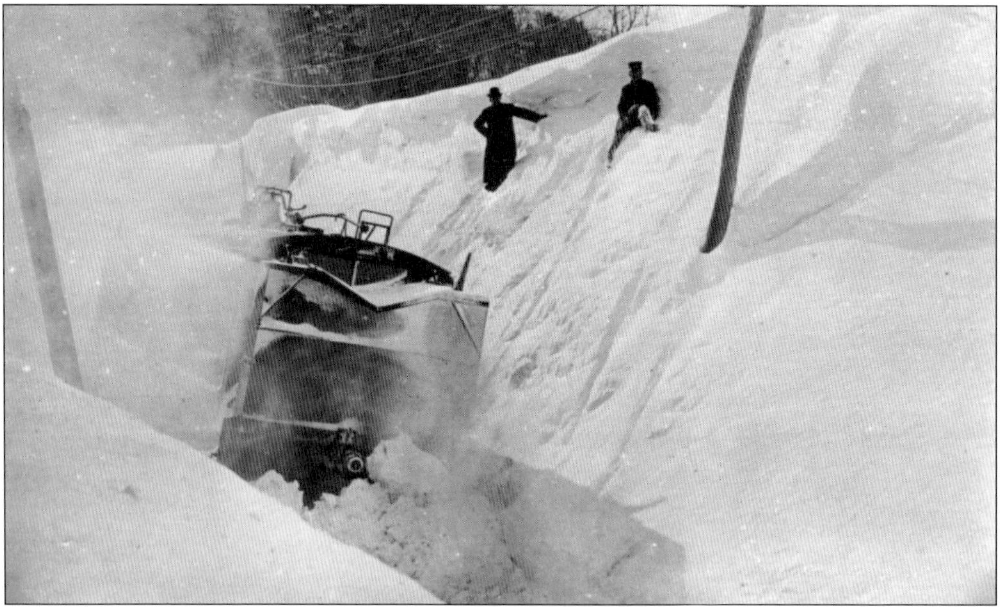

During February 1920, Hartwick and surrounding areas were paralyzed by major snowstorms that forced the trolley to suspend service while huge rotary plows labored to break through the snow and ice to clear the tracks. According to the *Oneonta Herald*, "General Manager Stone received but six hours rest out of 87 consecutive hours on the job." After two and a half days, the line was finally cleared through to Herkimer, and the trolley resumed its schedule. The image above shows one of the large rotary plows in action, operating much as a modern-day snowblower. Below, a trolley car is moving along a cleared rail track while overshadowed by a massive snowbank.

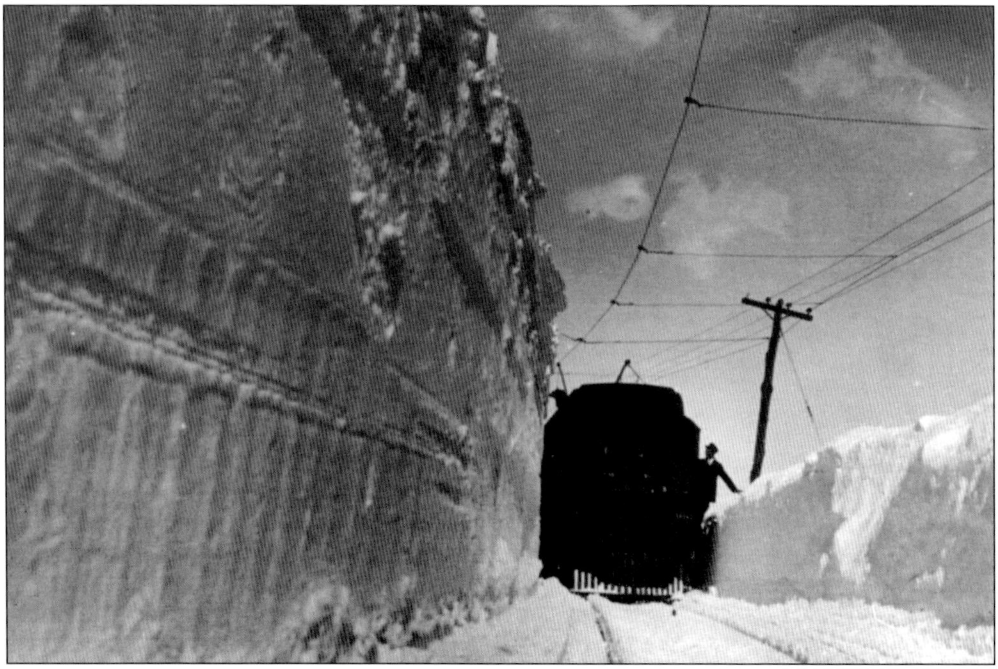

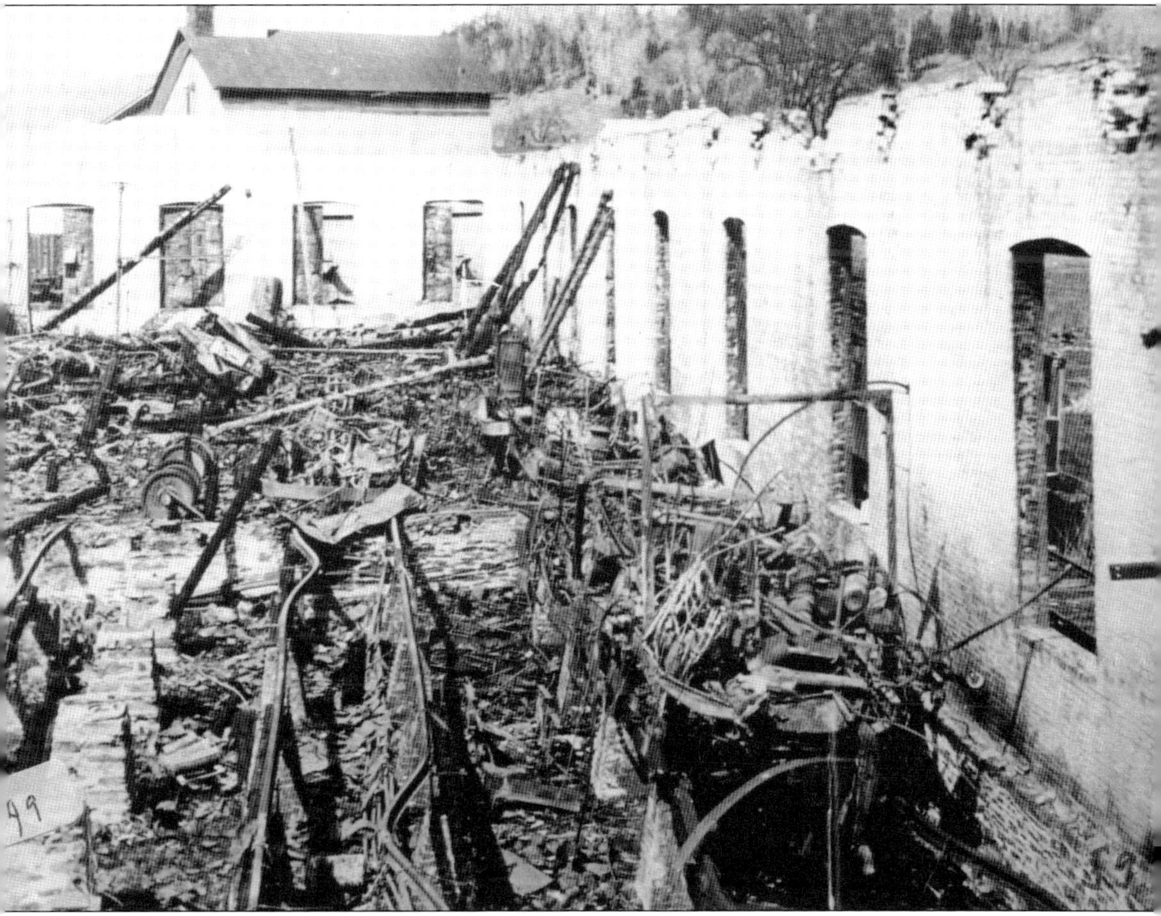

Disaster struck on March 27, 1925, when fire consumed the carbarn at Hartwick. Eight cars were destroyed, and passenger service was severely curtailed. Loss of the building and rolling stock was estimated at $200,000. The trolley company never fully recovered from this loss, and train service, along with Hartwick's economy, slowly declined. A new carbarn was never rebuilt, although passenger service continued on a limited basis until 1932. Mail and express had been carried on the daily passenger train until then, and the trolley continued to operate only as a freight line through the end of the 1930s. The line could no longer compete for profit with modern motor vehicles, and by 1941 all but one and a half miles of track near West Oneonta was abandoned.

Little Old Hartwick

n a little place called Hartwick, a town that's known so well.
That has three good churches, and four places they call hotels;
s a little dinkie railroad, with its car shops and its barns,
That carries the farmers' produce, as they bring it off the farm

There's a little Kill O'Watt factory, about a mile below the town
That furnishes the power, for miles and miles around.
t keeps a gang of men that labor, night and day,
To make the towns along the line, look like the Great White Way

t keeps the cars a-running, almost every day,
f we do not have a snowstorm, and the cows keep out the way.
And if they drop a motor, or a car goes in the creek,
They put a brand new tie in, and it always does the trick.

For the man that does the head work, is a man that is well known
nd the boys on this ere pike, all call him Daddy Stone.
But he has to have a helper, each department has a head,
And the man, that is the super, to the boys is known as Fred.

Then we have our freights and tariffs, and other things going on
So we have a man from Richfield, and the boys, they call him John
But Charlie tends the Kill O'Watt factory, as it grinds from hou
to hour
For to run the New York Southern, we have to have the power.

And when we have a snow storm, or the cars get acting mean,
We start right off for Hartwick, to see friend George Killeen;
So among all the fellows, you never hear a kick,
For the cars always get there, but it sometimes takes a week.

The era of the trolley had come to an end. This poem, written by H.O. Hintermister, appeared in the *Freeman's Journal* on January 2, 1918, and describes that time when Hartwick was still booming because the trolley had come to town.

Five

Hartwick Hamlet

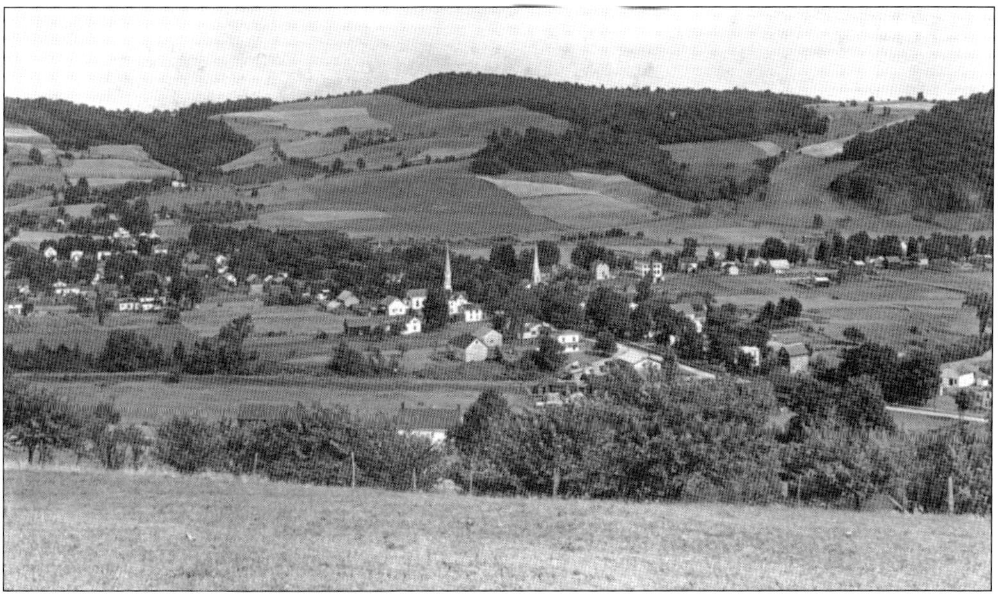

As this mid-1800s view from the west shows, the hamlet of Hartwick had grown in size from the first small settlement along Otego Creek. The raceway along Otego Creek, which powered Samuel Mudge's early gristmill and sawmills in 1802, can be seen across the lower middle of the photograph. Spires of two of the three churches of this time are visible in the distance. (RF.)

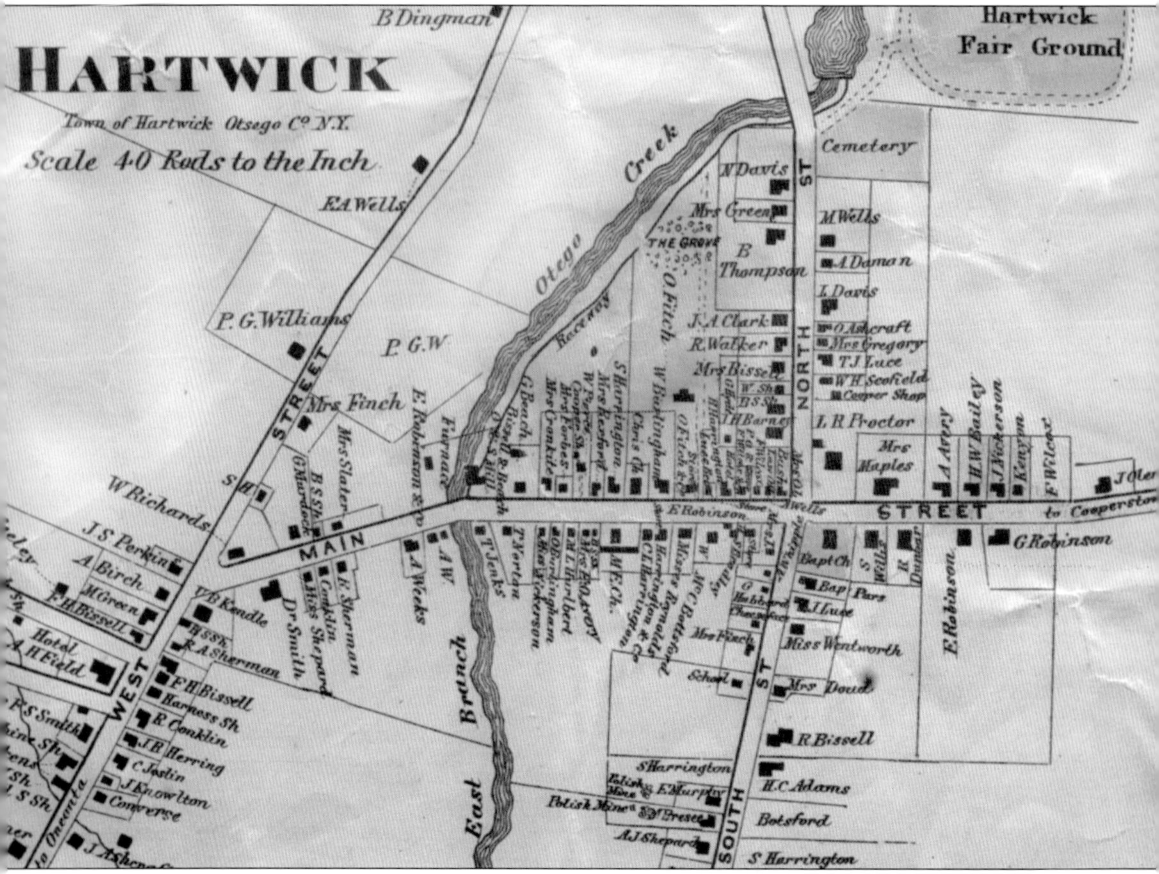

As this 1868 map shows, the hamlet had spread out in all four directions from the initial settlement along Otego Creek. At this time, a business directory listed 15 businesses, including a blacksmith, two coopers, a physician-surgeon, an attorney, three hotel proprietors, a wagon/carriage maker, a miller, and several dealers in flour, feed, lumber, agricultural implements, groceries, dry goods, and general merchandise. There was also one dealer of the famous Peter's Polish, a silver-polishing grit from the mines on South Street. The population was about 500 people in 1872. Other township settlements, notably the mill towns of Toddsville, Clintonville, and South Hartwick, had grown in manufacturing importance as well. Only after 1901, with the extension of the trolley line through Hartwick, did the population grow, and the hamlet expand greatly to become the largest center of commerce within the township.

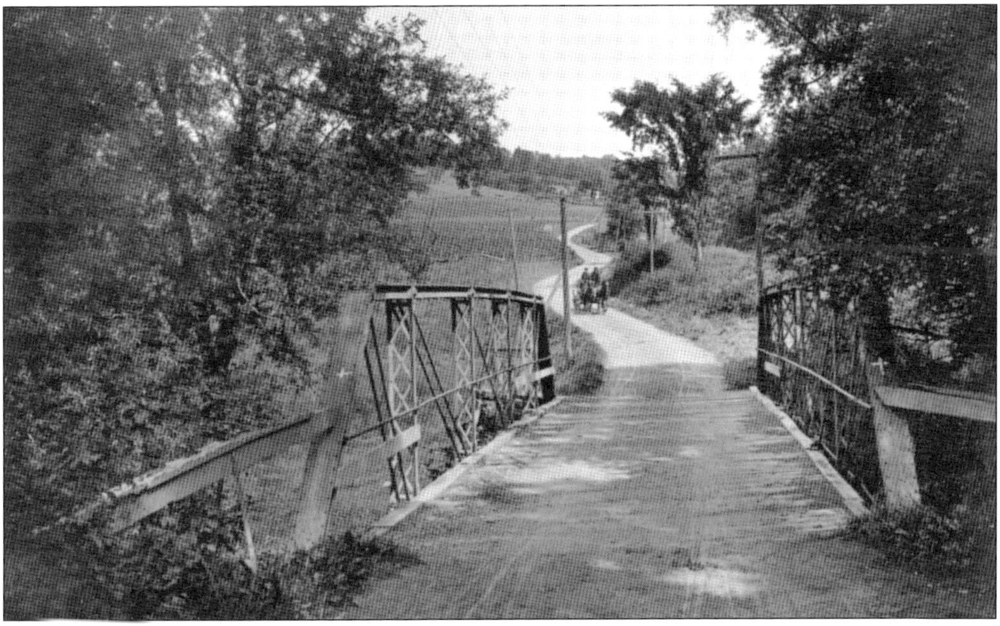

One approach into the hamlet is over Otego Creek on the North Street Bridge. Here, an unidentified farmer heads into town (known early on as Peth) from the farm country of White House or Scotch Hill. Near the bridge, on the right out of this view, was a path leading to a pleasant wooded and floral area known as "the Fly," and to the left, the raceway followed the stream southwest to the grist/sawmill. (OB.)

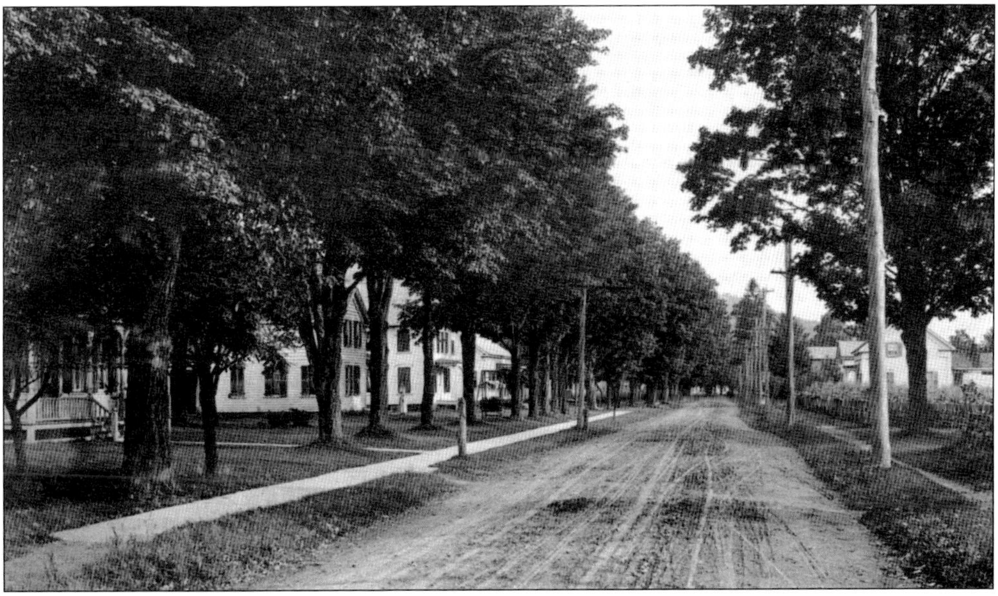

This early view of North Street looks south toward the four corners street intersection. The first house on the left is the home of Marcus Wells, the famous hymn writer of "Holy Spirit, Faithful Guide." It is now the parsonage for Hartwick Christian Church. (RF.)

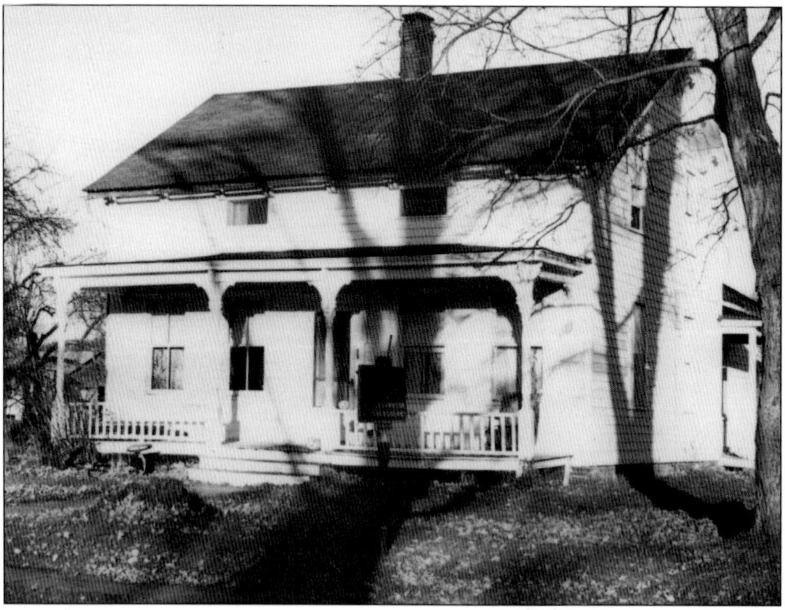

This image shows the one-time home of Marcus Wells, a well-known hymn writer, inventor, and businessman. He held a patent for a wood barley fork and produced them, using steam-powered machinery, in a fork factory located between this home and cemetery to the north.

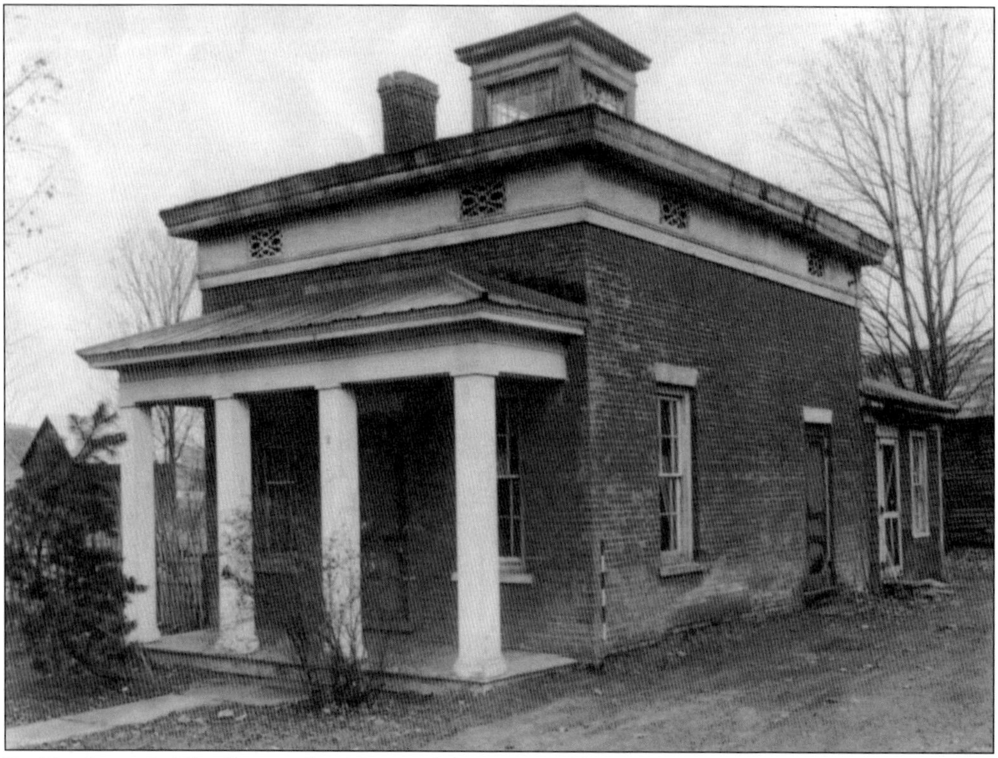

Dr. Freeborn G. Thrall moved to Hartwick by 1833 and bought the medical practice of Dr. Paris Pray and the large stone house at Hartwick's four corners. Across the driveway, along North Street, was a small brick building used as a doctor's office and "an anatomical theater lighted by a skylight" used for anatomy lectures and dissections. That redbrick building, shown here, was sold after Dr. Thrall moved away, and in 1951 it was moved to the Farmers' Museum, where it now serves as Thralls Pharmacy.

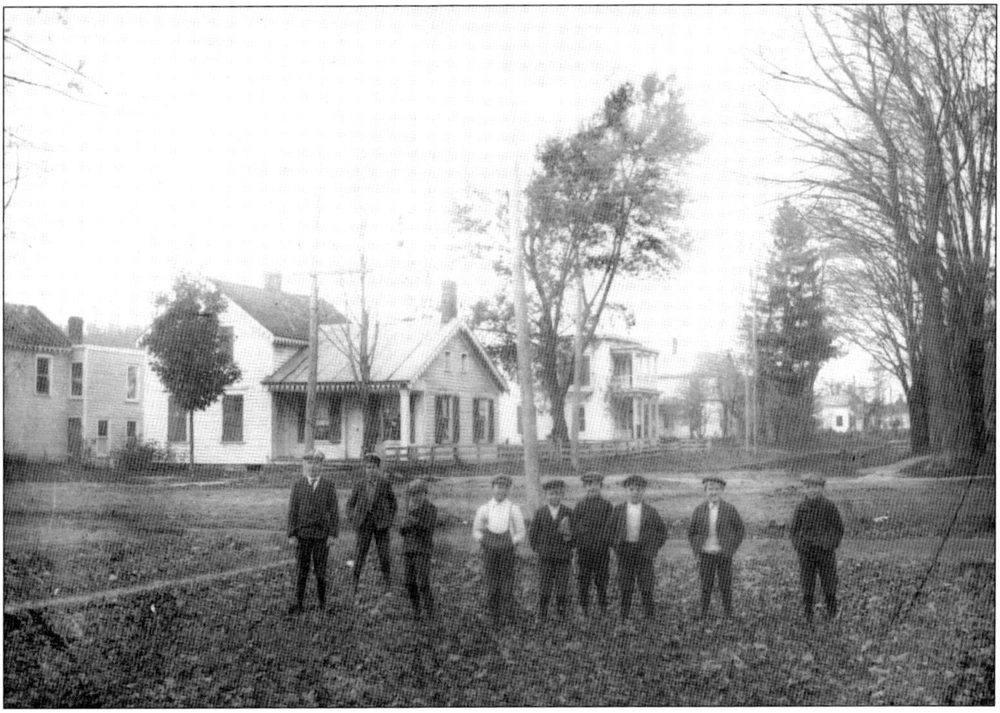

This group of young boys is standing in the yard of First Baptist Church near the four corners. In this image looking north across the corners, the home and office of Dr. George Schoolcraft can be seen first. Next to it, on the right, is the home and possible early photographic studio of Arthur "Putt" Telfer, a well-known area photographer. (ST at FAM.)

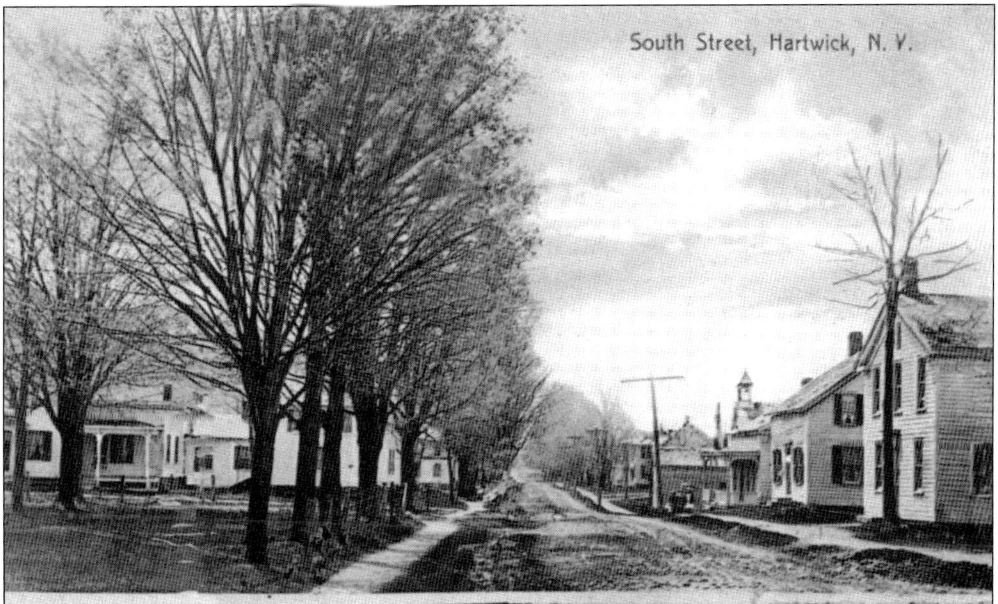

This early view shows the unpaved dirt road of South Street across the four corners intersection. The first house on the left became an early parsonage for First Baptist Church (out of sight to the left). The cupola of School No. 4 can be seen on the right side, midway down the street. (RF.)

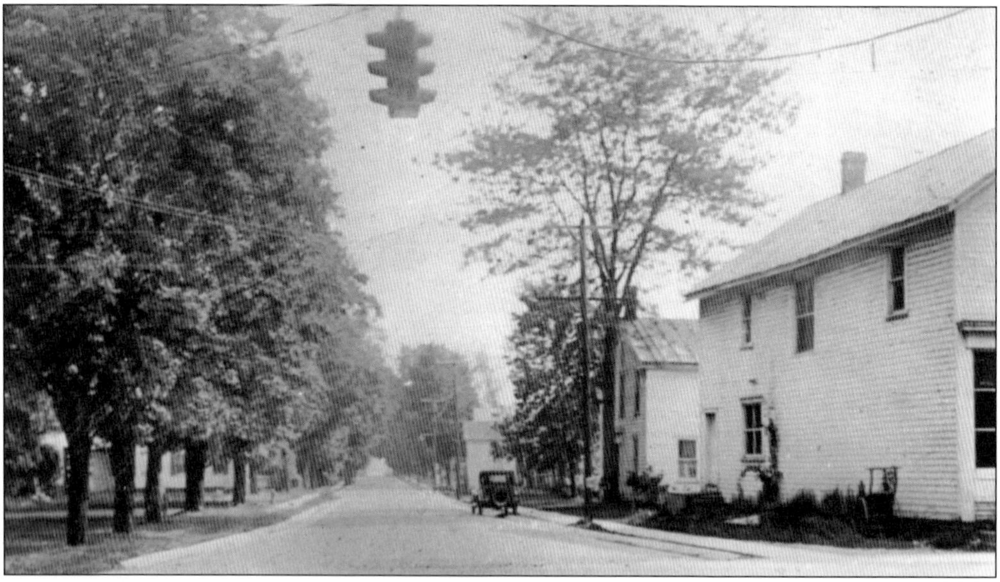

Construction was begun in May 1931 to change the narrow dirt road heading south from Hartwick into a wider state highway. Seven miles of newly paved road were completed in November 1931. A petition signed by 112 people requested a stop-and-go light at the Hartwick four corners, but state officials would only authorize a yellow blinker light. That traffic light, seen here, was installed but only used for a short time before being replaced by legal stop signs at each side of Route 205. (RF.)

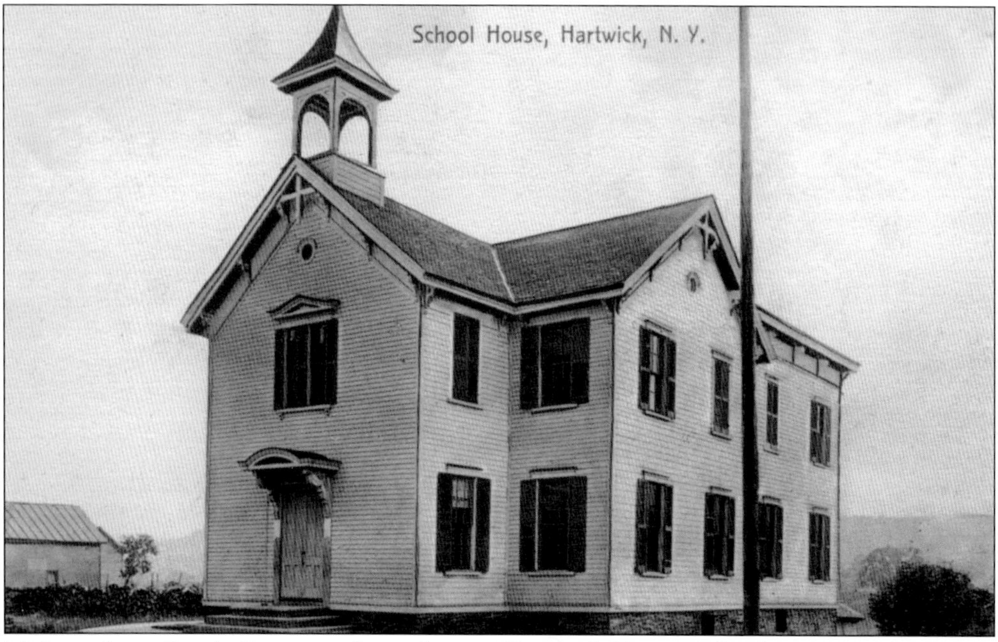

Midway down South Street on the right was Hartwick Union School No. 4. Built in 1878 amid local controversy about size and location, the new school united smaller districts No. 17 and No. 4. This new building provided much-needed space and greater variety of courses for a growing population of students. In later years, the building was used as a car dealership and service station. (RF.)

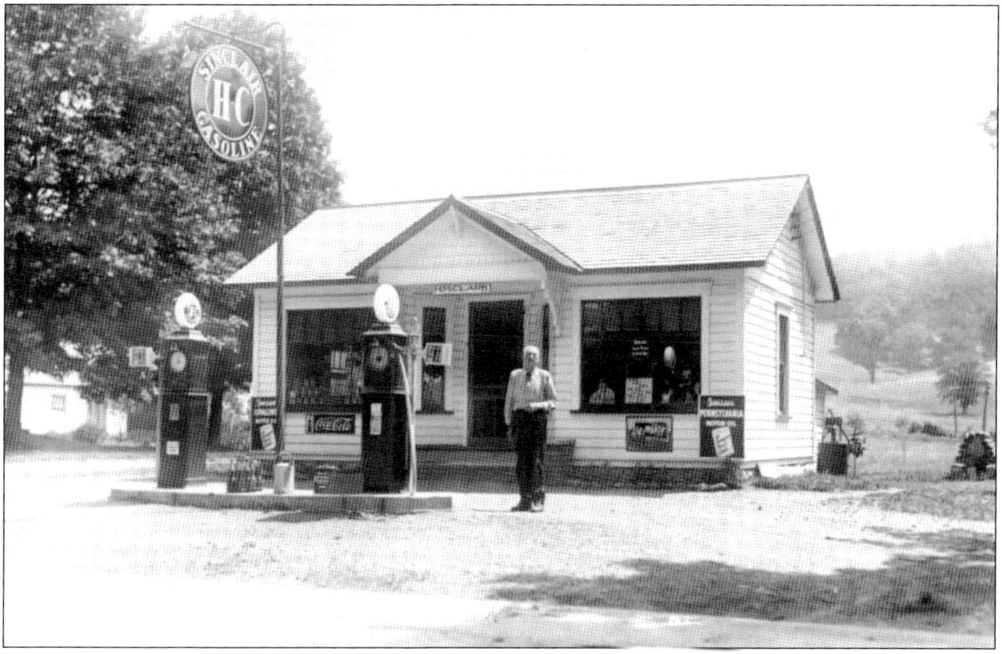

With the transition from horsepower to mechanical transportation, a number of garages and gasoline stations came to the hamlet. In this photograph from the 1930s, John Parr stands in front of his gas service station at the southern end of South Street. Today, a Quickway convenience store and fuel station occupies the same site. (ST at FAM.)

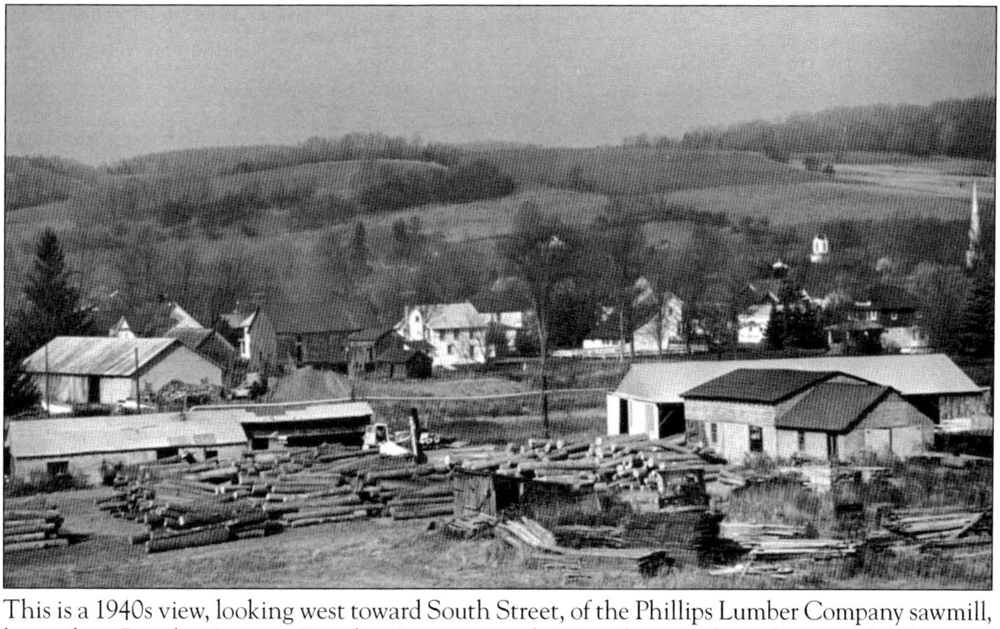

This is a 1940s view, looking west toward South Street, of the Phillips Lumber Company sawmill, located on Popular Avenue. Popular Avenue was the site of an employee housing development when the trolley came to town in the early 1900s. The sawmill later occupied the site of the trolley office headquarters and warehouse building, which had been moved closer to the depot and carbarns on Main Street. To the upper left of the lumberyard is the Town Highway Equipment Barn, constructed there in the 1930s.

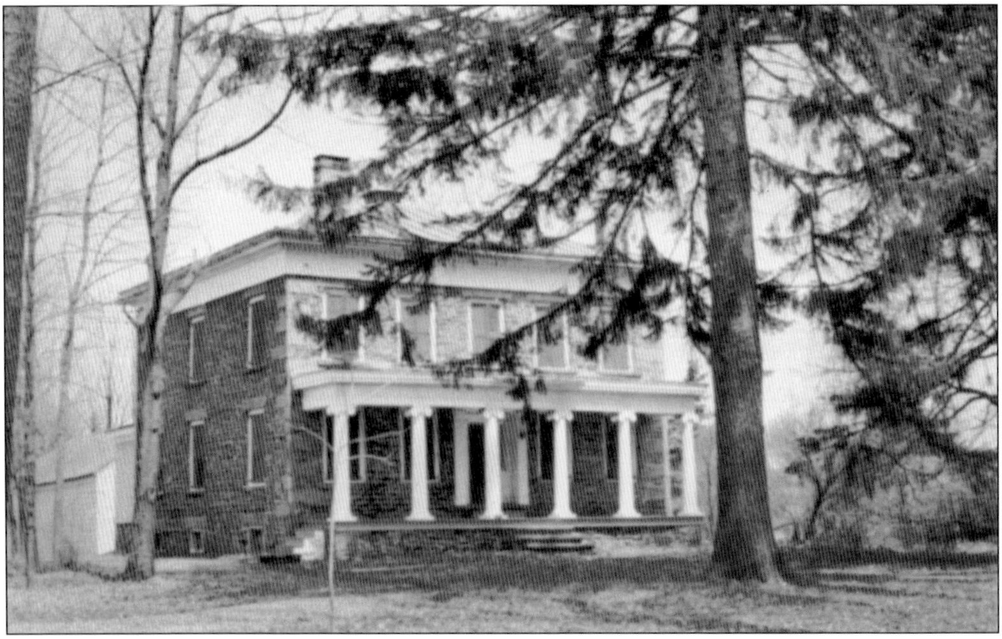

The stately old stone house known as the Proctor House stands on a large lot near the four corners of the hamlet. The early home of Dr. Freeborn Thrall, it was purchased in 1850 by Leonard Proctor and remained in that family for many years. The landmark home, at the center of Hartwick hamlet, is owned today by Orrin Higgins (RF.).

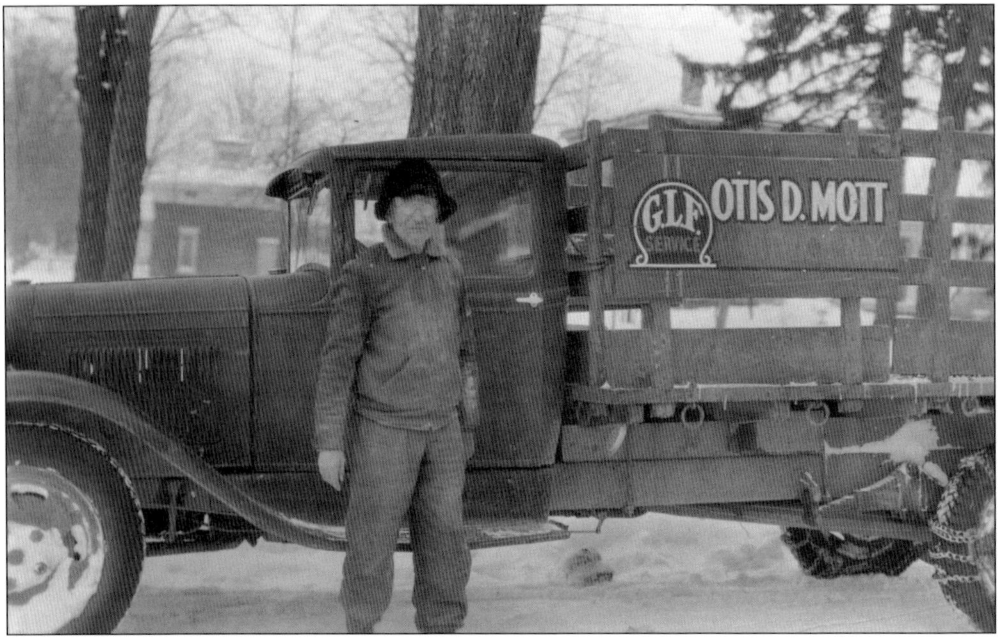

Otis D. Mott owned and operated the Grange League Federation (GLF) Feed Store on East Main Street. Feed was both sold directly to farmers off of the freight car and also delivered to some farms from the store. In this late-1930s image, Mott and the feed delivery truck have stopped near the four corners in front of the Proctor stone house. Behind him, the roof of the brick doctor's office/pharmacy can be seen. (CG.)

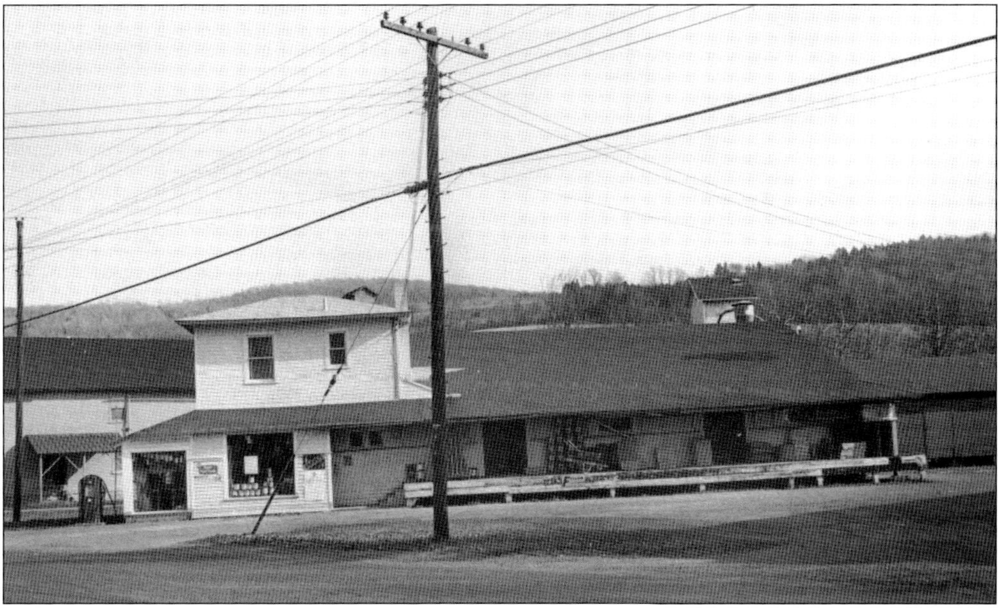

The depot and freight station was an essential part of the local trolley/railway system during the 30 years of operation in and through Hartwick. During that time, a second story was added to the building for dispatch of trains along the single line. With the demise of the railway, the building was converted, as shown, to serve as the GLF Feed Store and later as the Agway store. The Harrison Feed Store is seen in the background.

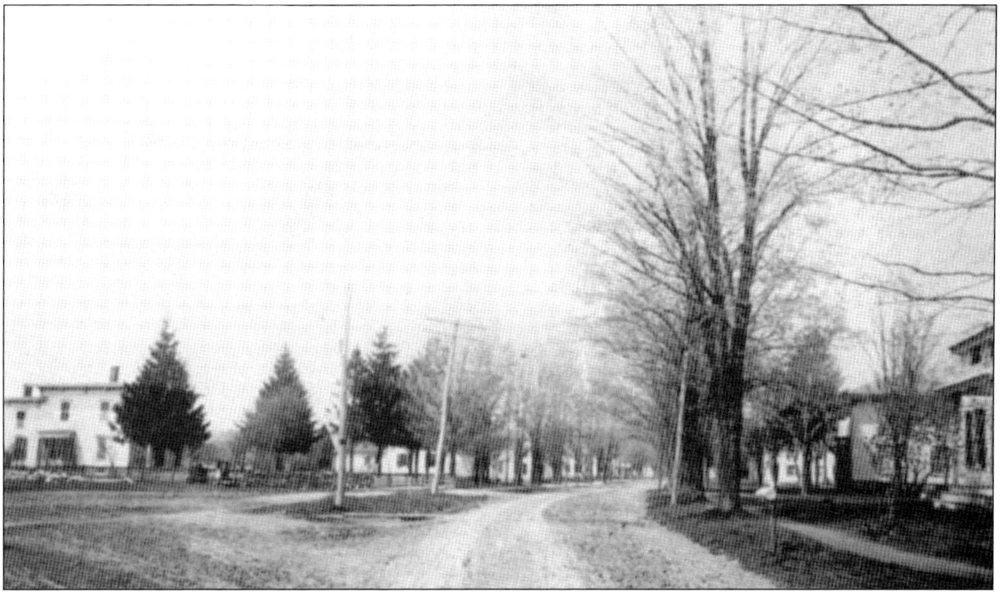

This is an early view west from the trolley station toward the four corners at the center of town. The open land at left would soon become the site of the EMBA (Employees Mutual Benefit Association) Hall.

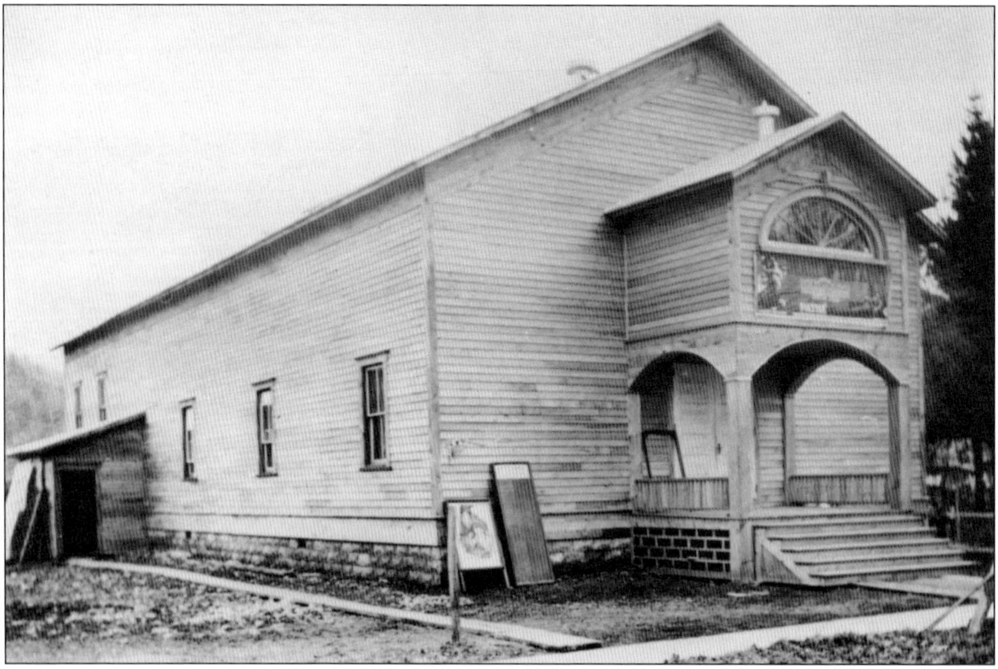

Sometime after 1912, when railway offices were transferred to Cooperstown, the former office building was donated by the company and moved to a site near to the depot on East Main Street. The building, known as Tammany Hall, became the social hall for the Employees Mutual Benefit Association. The 40-foot-by-90-foot EMBA Hall, seen here, was later used as a gymnasium for Hartwick High School and today is the Hartwick Community Center.

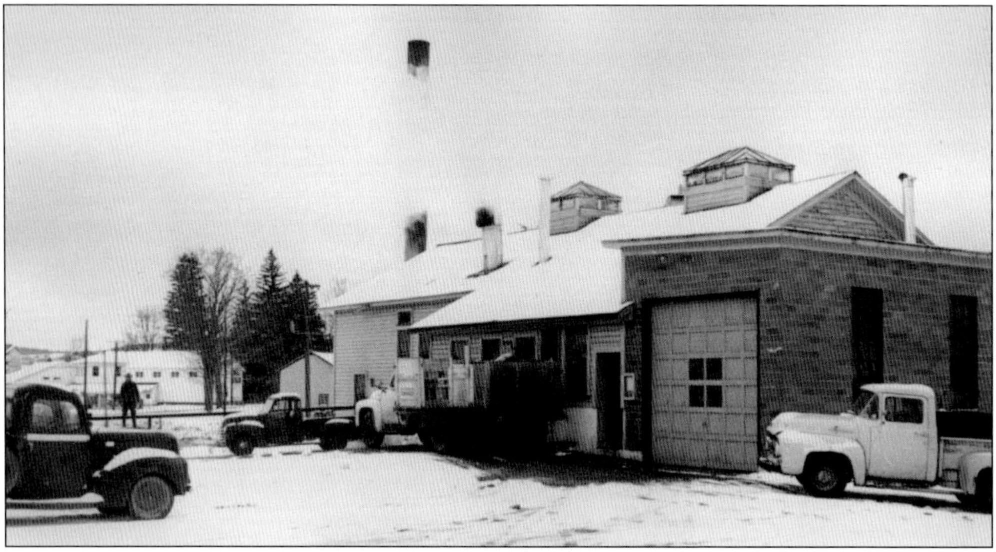

Dairy farming with milk production provided the livelihood for many local families. In early days, milk met the needs of family farms and community cheese factories. Later, milk was transported either by horse and wagon or by trolley to milk plants in neighboring towns. After formation of the Dairymen's League Cooperative and the 1919 milk strike, local milk-processing plants were built. As shown in this 1940s view, milk was delivered in cans to the Hartwick plant for bulk collection and shipment by tanker trucks to a downstate urban market.

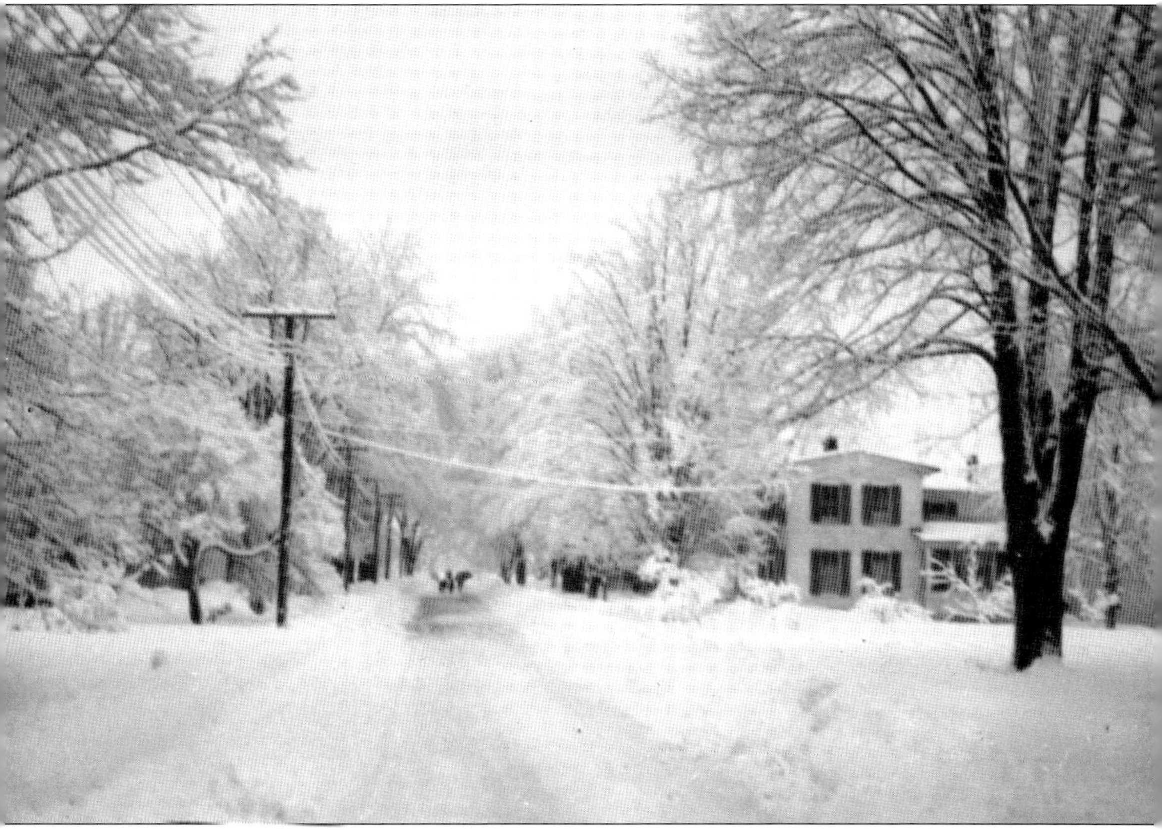

This side street near the EMBA Hall runs toward the north and was called both Wells Avenue and Mill Street in the early 1900s. It was later renamed School Street when the high school was built there in 1921. Howard Murdock and Russ Bresee owned the sawmill next to the future school building. That mill burned in 1904. Chan Naylor also had a mill and a small door and window-sash shop along the street before the school was constructed. (RF.)

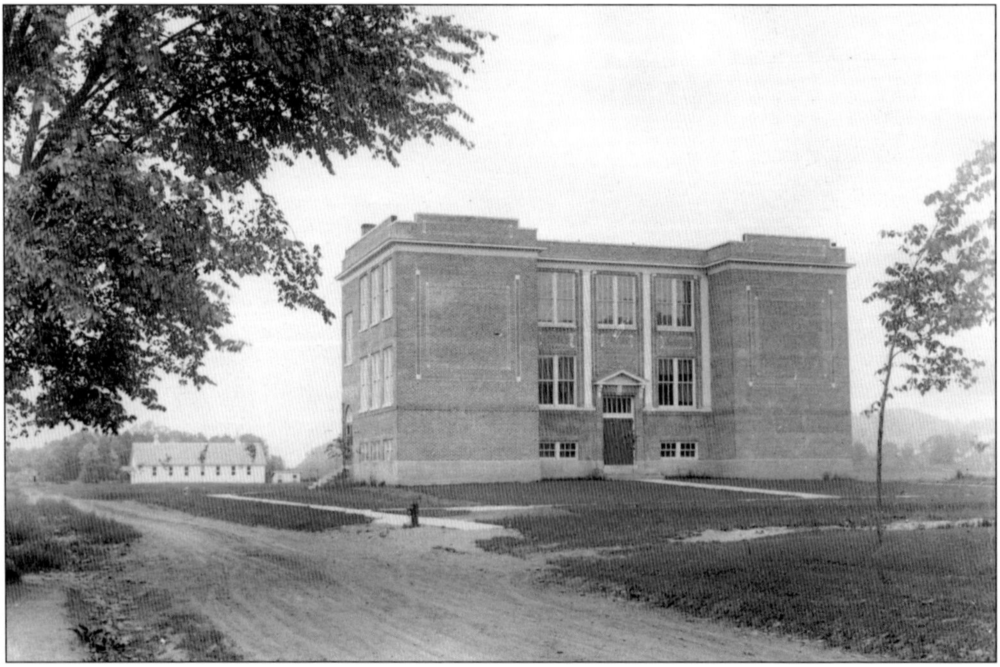

This new brick Hartwick School building was completed in the fall of 1921 at a cost of $60,000. By 1934, there was an enrollment of 100 pupils, with classes for all ages through high school. Hartwick High School consolidated with Cooperstown Central School in 1957, and the final senior class here graduated that year, followed by the last eighth-grade class in 1958. The school continued in operation as the Hartwick Grade Center until its closure in 1977. Seen beyond the school in this image is the Hartwick Hatchery.

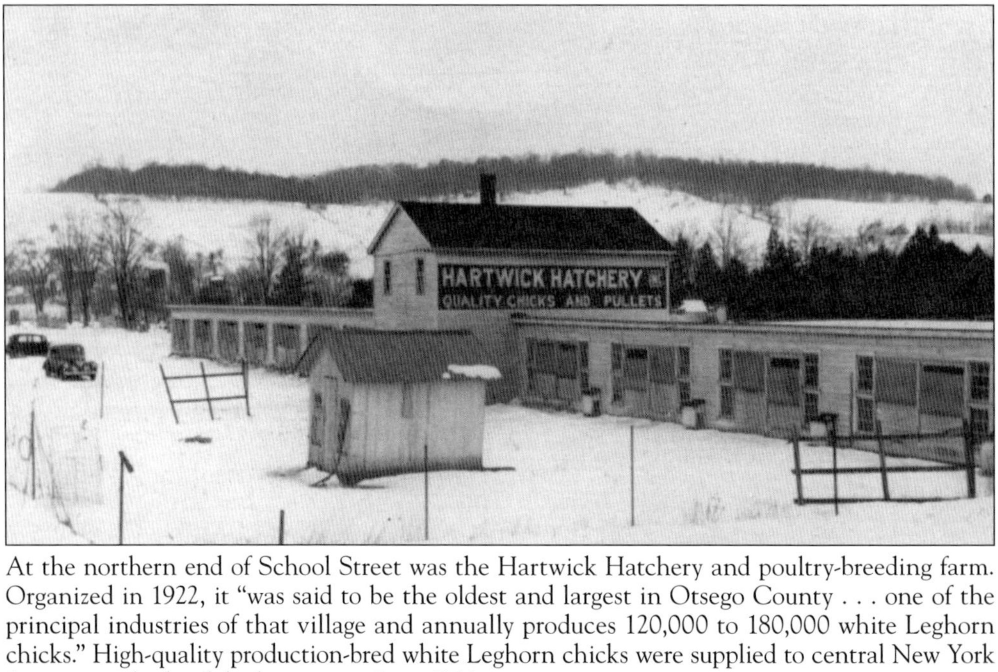

At the northern end of School Street was the Hartwick Hatchery and poultry-breeding farm. Organized in 1922, it "was said to be the oldest and largest in Otsego County . . . one of the principal industries of that village and annually produces 120,000 to 180,000 white Leghorn chicks." High-quality production-bred white Leghorn chicks were supplied to central New York farmers until sale of the business in June 1956.

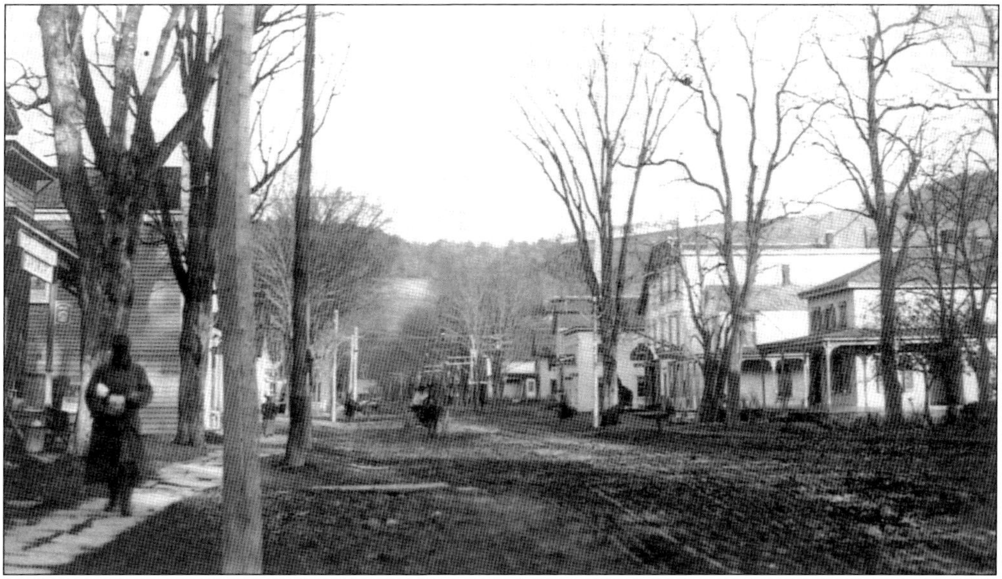

The commercial center of the hamlet lay west of the four corners along Main Street and included a variety of shops and businesses through the years. In this 1905 photograph, the trolley depot is visible in the distance to the east. At center right are the Sergent Block, Augur Hardware, and Cottage Hotel. In the far-left foreground is the Porter Block, later operated as the W.L. Risley Store. (GW and R.)

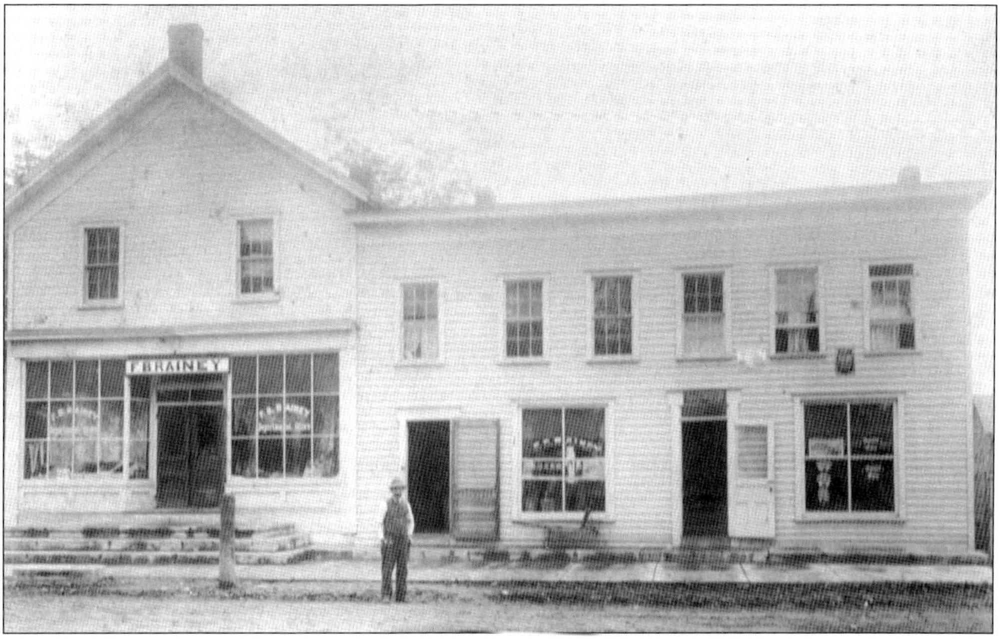

Sometime after 1868, Leroy Sergent erected a large white building for a store at the corner of South and Main Streets. A two-story addition in May 1878 soon filled with a shoe shop, jewelry store, and law office. Second-floor rooms were later used as lodge rooms for the Maccabees and Eastern Star, as a telephone office, and for community banquets. The store had many proprietors, including Frank Bresee, founder of the famous Oneonta Department Store, and in this c. 1916 image (about 1916), the building housed the F.B. Rainey Department and Grocery Store.

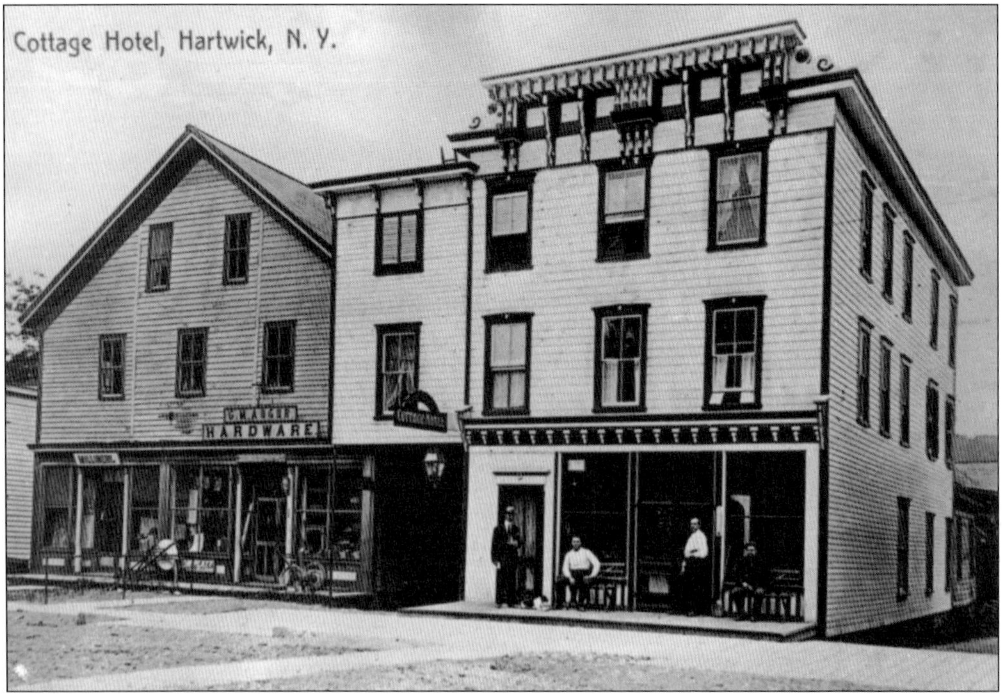

Peleg Gardner operated the Cottage Hotel along the south side of Main Street as early as 1893. The building, with a 24-foot-wide frontage and a depth of 238 feet, was attached to the Augur Hardware at the second floor, with a narrow alley between that gave access to the hotel's livery stable. On the left of the hardware store, a millinery shop can be seen.

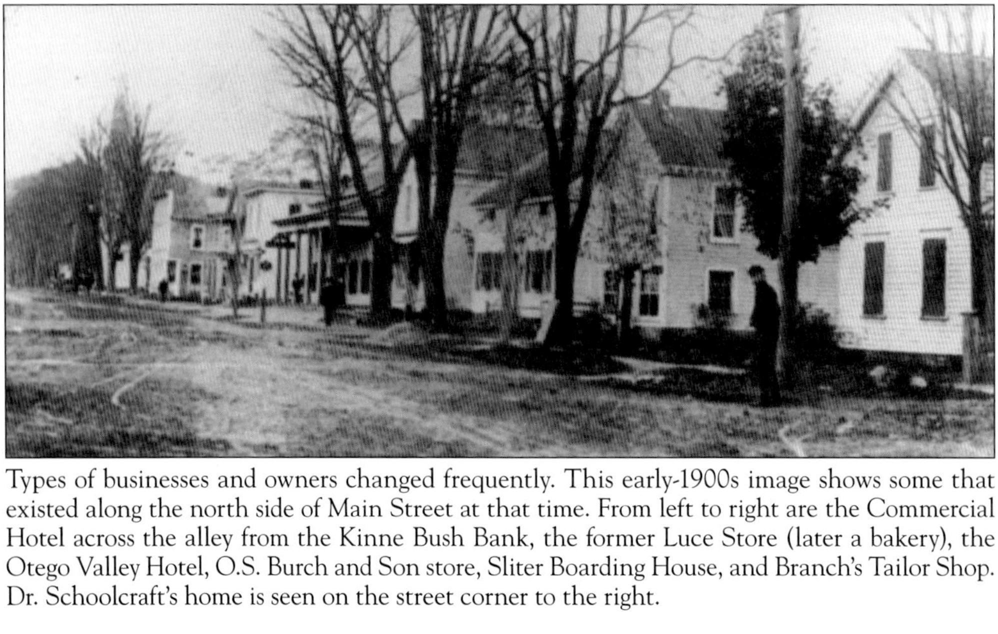

Types of businesses and owners changed frequently. This early-1900s image shows some that existed along the north side of Main Street at that time. From left to right are the Commercial Hotel across the alley from the Kinne Bush Bank, the former Luce Store (later a bakery), the Otego Valley Hotel, O.S. Burch and Son store, Sliter Boarding House, and Branch's Tailor Shop. Dr. Schoolcraft's home is seen on the street corner to the right.

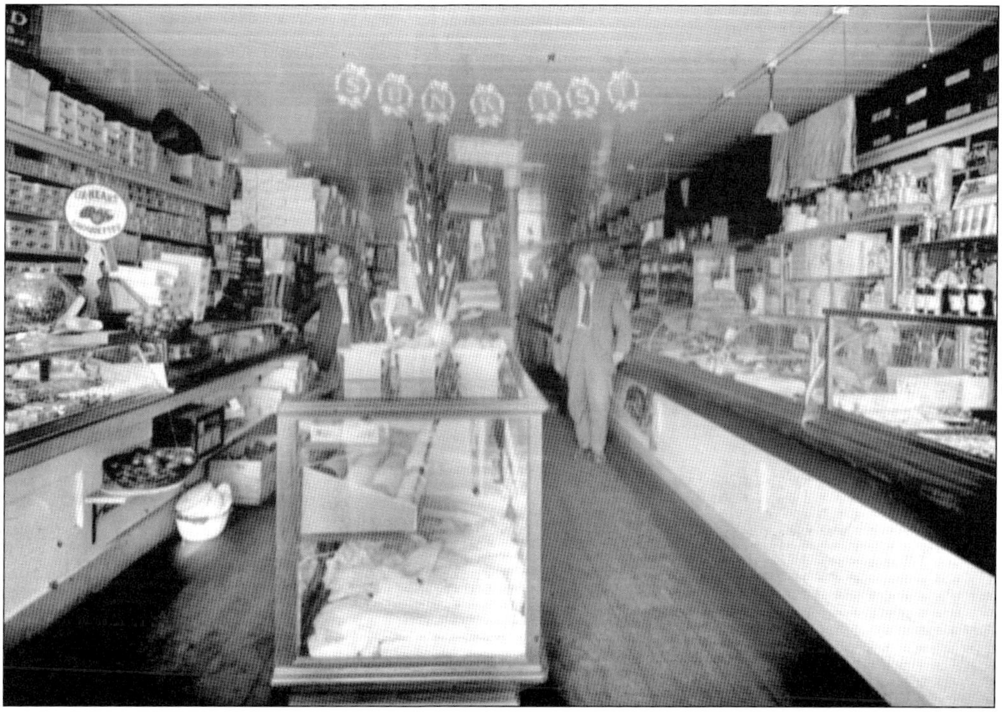

The O.S. Burch and Son store was established in 1870 selling general merchandise in a building across the street from the bank on Main Street. The business later relocated a few buildings east, next to today's American Legion building. This photograph was taken around 1915 and shows the interior of the building with A. Monroe Burch on the left and Orlo S. Burch, or "O.S.," as he was known to most people, on the right. O.S. started his business at the age of 21 in partnership with Frank H. Robinson selling dry goods, groceries, boots, shoes, drugs, and medicine and accepting produce in exchange for goods. This building is currently being restored by Martha and Paul Clarvoe. (OB.)

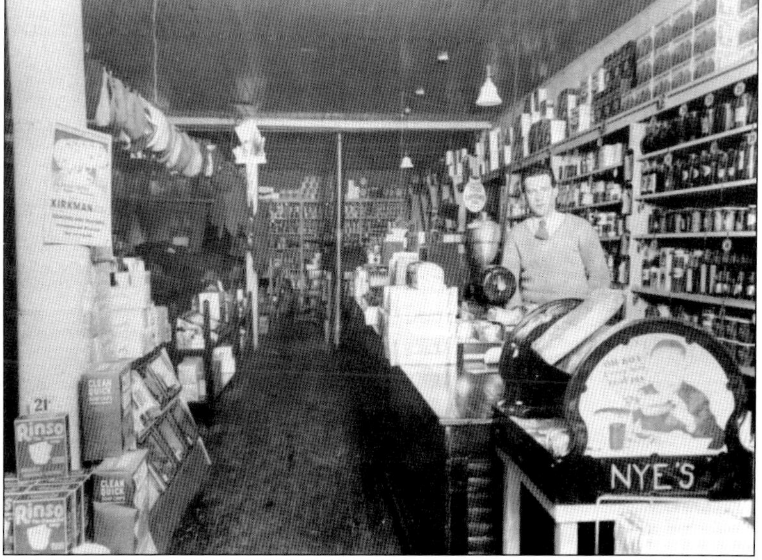

Ford Risley, pictured around 1930, is tending the counter in Risley's store on West Main Street (the second building east of Christian Church). The Risley family operated the store over two generations. (GW and R.)

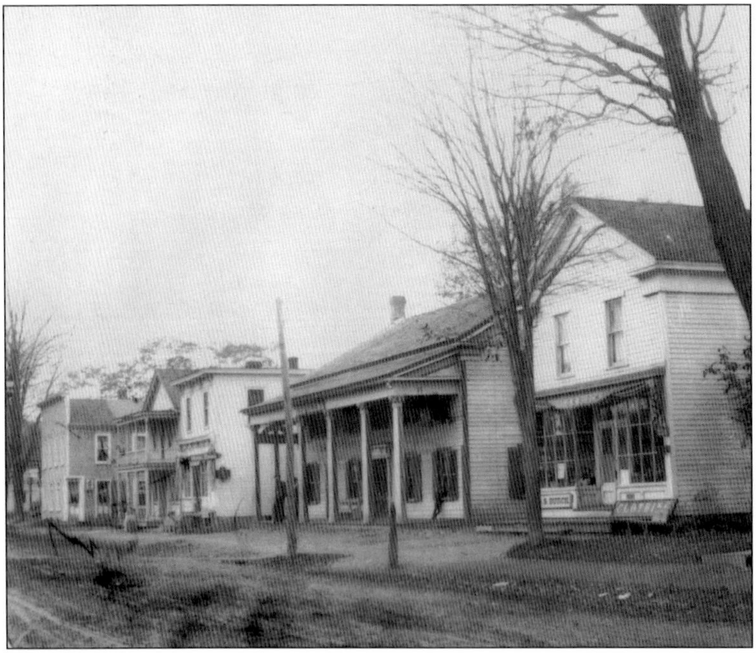

The Otego Valley Hotel at the center of Hartwick's Main Street is said to have been built as early as 1805 by Andrew Elbridge. The large, pillared hotel seen here to the left of the Burch store was a busy stagecoach stop and gathering place. The landmark hotel, with a large ballroom, was the site of church suppers, plays, and concerts. Today, the building is home to the Hartwick Post Office. (ST at FAM.)

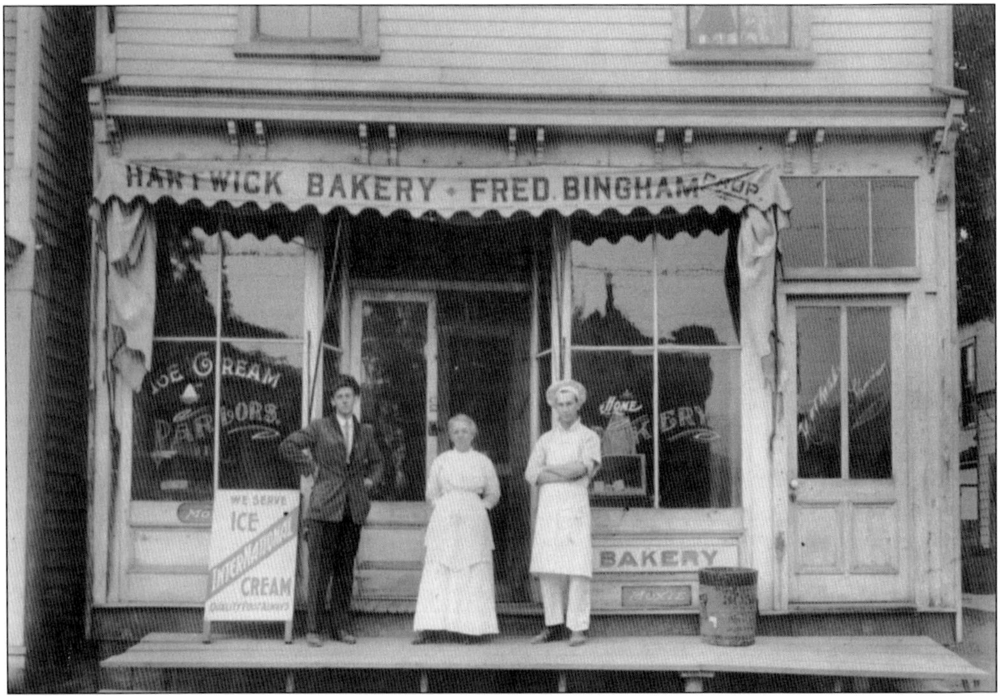

The Hartwick Bakery seen here was located to the near west of the Otego Valley Hotel. In the 1850s, the building was the site of Torry Luce's store. It later housed the ice cream parlor/bakery, and then a basement butcher shop with a harness shop above. In the 1930s, the Victory chain grocery store operated here.

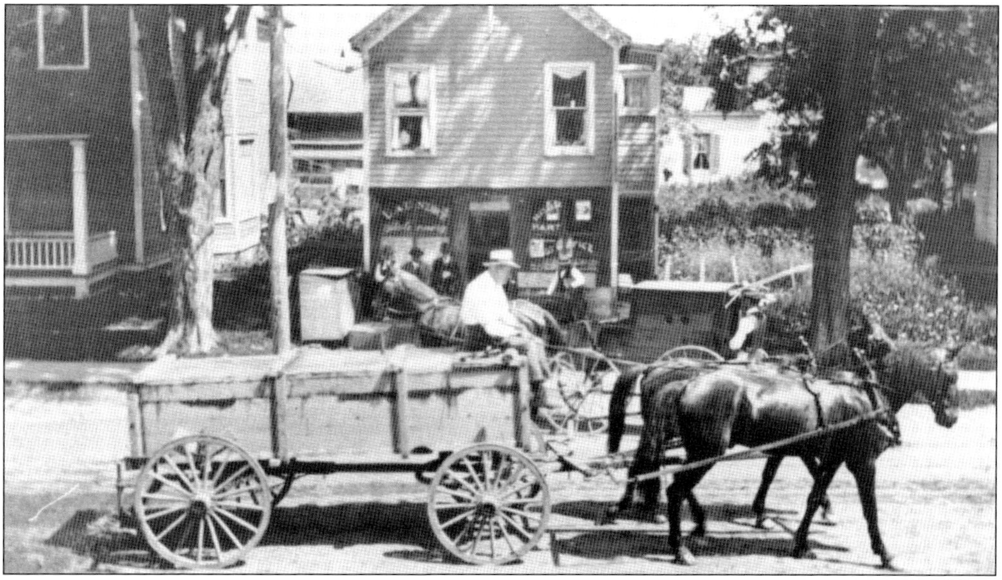

Dirt roads in town could be ankle deep with dust or mud and riddled with ice- or snow-filled ruts in wintertime. This horse-drawn water wagon dampened Main Street dust in 1915. The small building behind the wagon once held a lawyer's office and a variety of businesses, including a tailor shop, a harness and repair shop, a telephone office, and a post office.

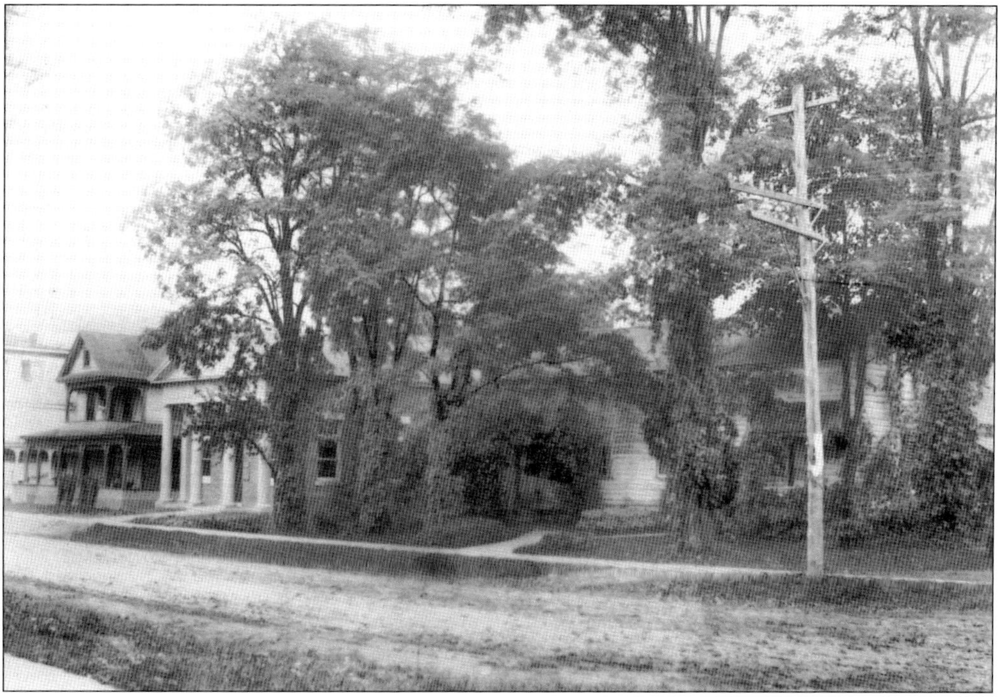

A view of the south side of Main Street depicts the columned brick building of Kinne, Bush & Company Bankers of Hartwick. The private bank organized in June 1908 at the time of great trolley-related growth in the hamlet. Today, the building is occupied by a branch of the Citizens Bank. The vine-covered Snodgrass home seen to the right of the bank was a millinery shop in 1868 and is a private home today.

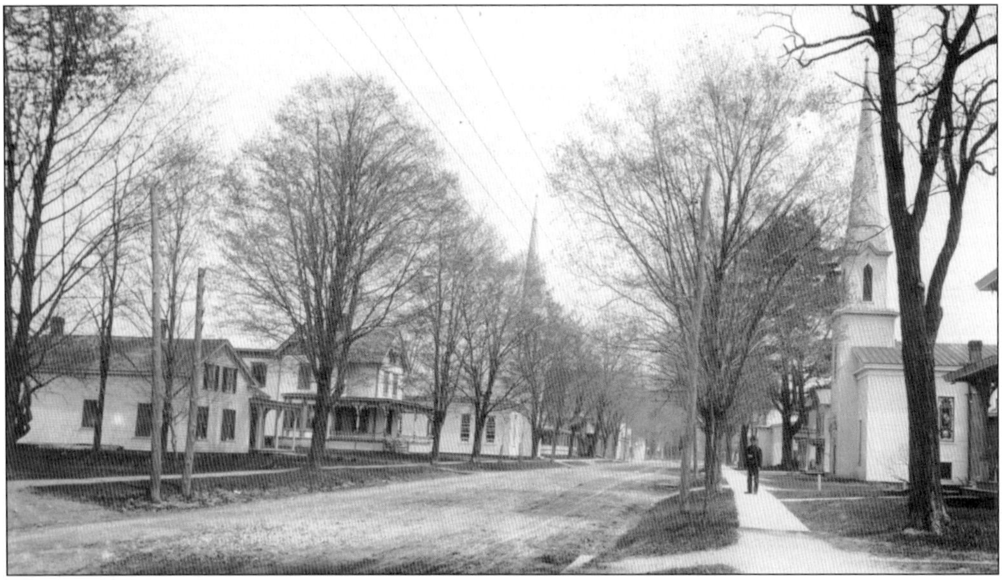

This photograph of West Main Street looking east shows Christian Church at the left center and the Methodist church on the right. The Methodist steeple seen here was removed in 1924 at a cost of $150. (RF.)

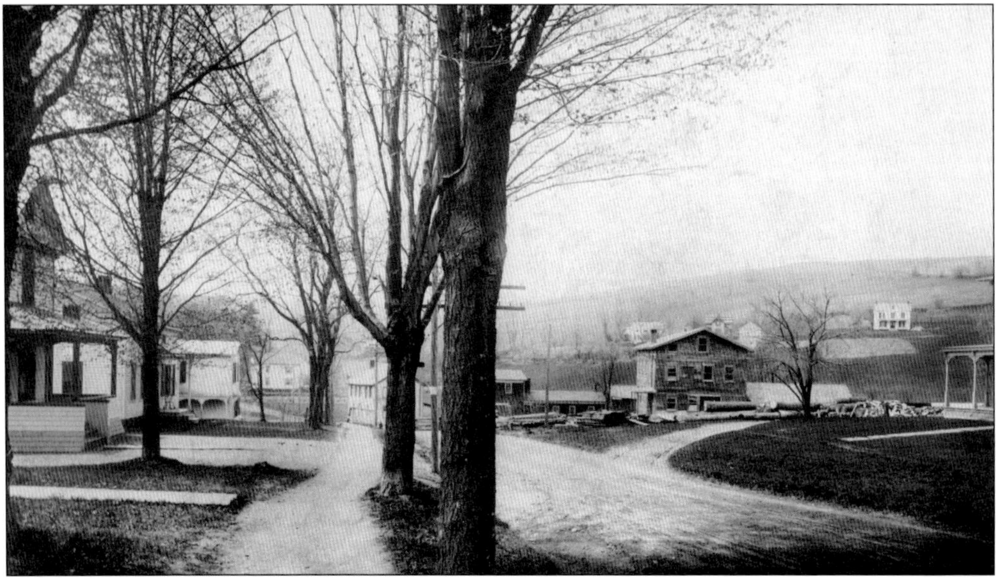

Another view of West Main Street, in 1912, looks toward Otego Creek with the cheese box factory partially hidden at the center. The grist and sawmill seen clearly on the right and built by Samuel Mudge in 1802 was owned by Marvin Duly in 1860. Louis Lake operated this mill business in 1912. (RF.)

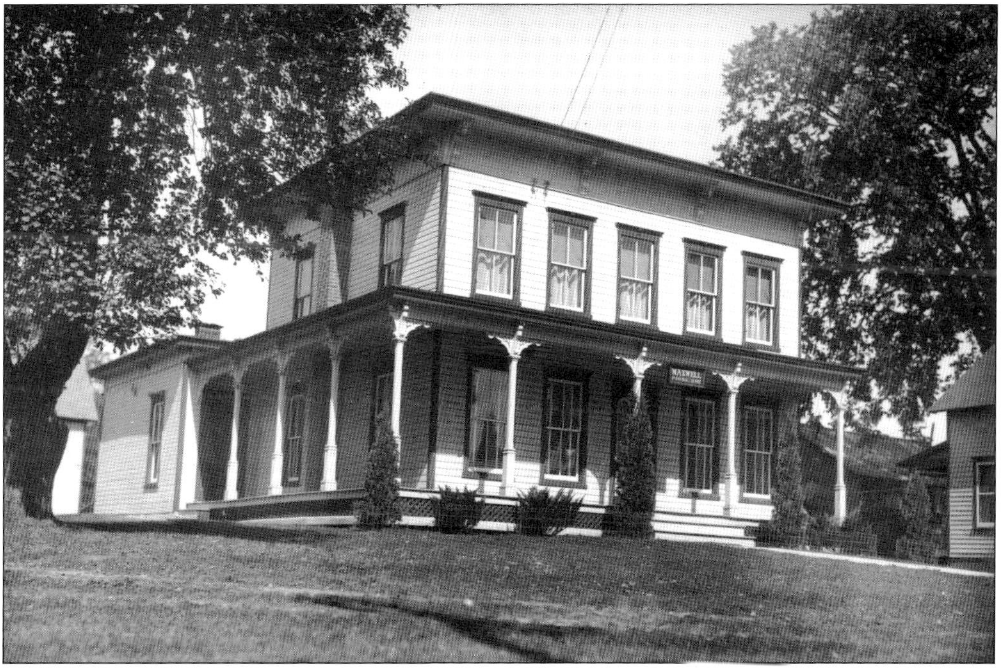

Research shows a number of funeral directors and homes in the late 1880s and 1900s in Hartwick. This image shows just one of these, the Maxwell Funeral Home operated by J.A. Maxwell between 1932 and his untimely death in 1951. The home was located just east of Ainslies sawmill along West Main Street.

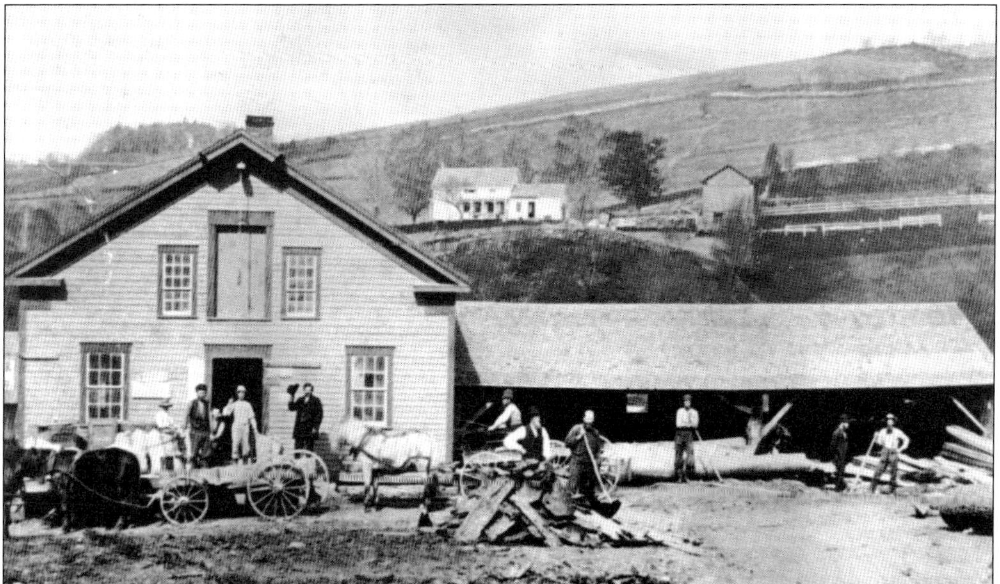

Among the earliest settlers of Peth (Hartwick hamlet) was Samuel Mudge, who built this grist and sawmill along Otego Creek in 1802. It was powered by a raceway along the creek from a small dam near the North Street Bridge. Operated through the years by various owners, such as Marvin Duly (around 1860) and Lewis and George Beach (1862–1867), it continued into the 1950s. The last owners were John and James Ainslie.

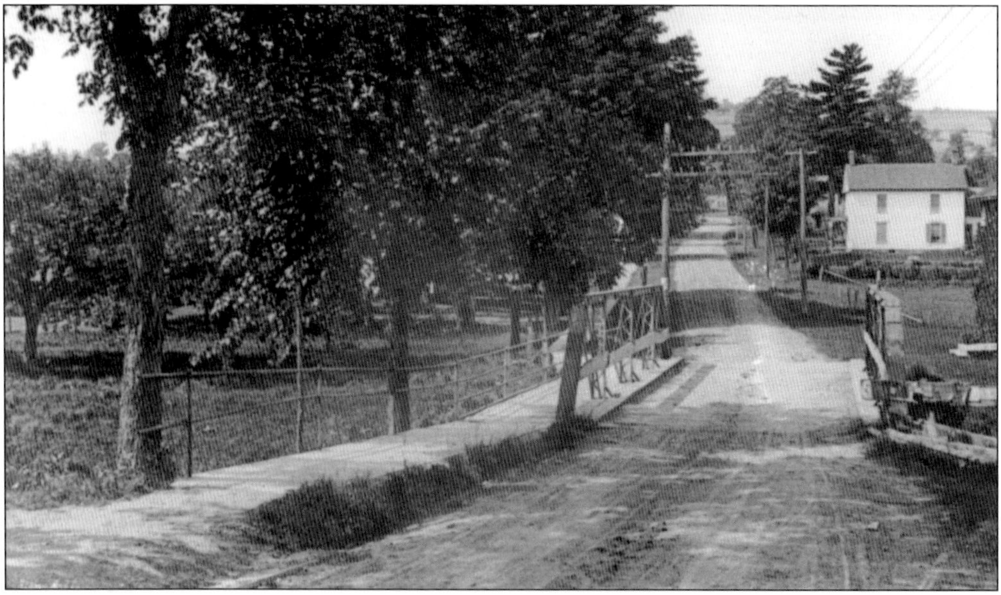

The early Hartwick settlement flourished along and to the west of Otego Creek. This view shows the road leading west from the bridge into the Brooklyn end of town. Parmer Williams operated an iron foundry, which cast cook stoves, patent ploughs, and other farm equipment. The foundry furnace was located just beyond the creek to the right. Closer to the road was a cheese box factory.

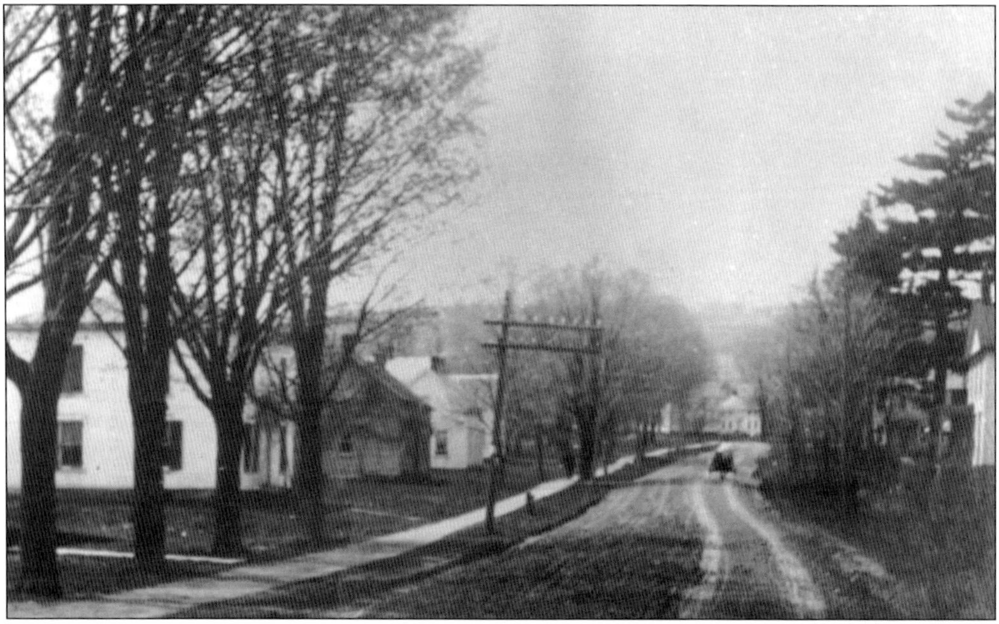

Another view shows West Main Street winding down to the west. Among businesses located here in 1860 were the Converse butcher shop, Sherman blacksmith, Cushman and Vincent wagon shop, Ashcraft's cabinet shop, and Delos Merrill's sulfur match factory. Hartwick's first John Deere tractor dealership was started in 1921 by William Ainslie and operated in the 1930s and 1940s in this West Main Street area. Some original hamlet homes still exist along the south side of the street.

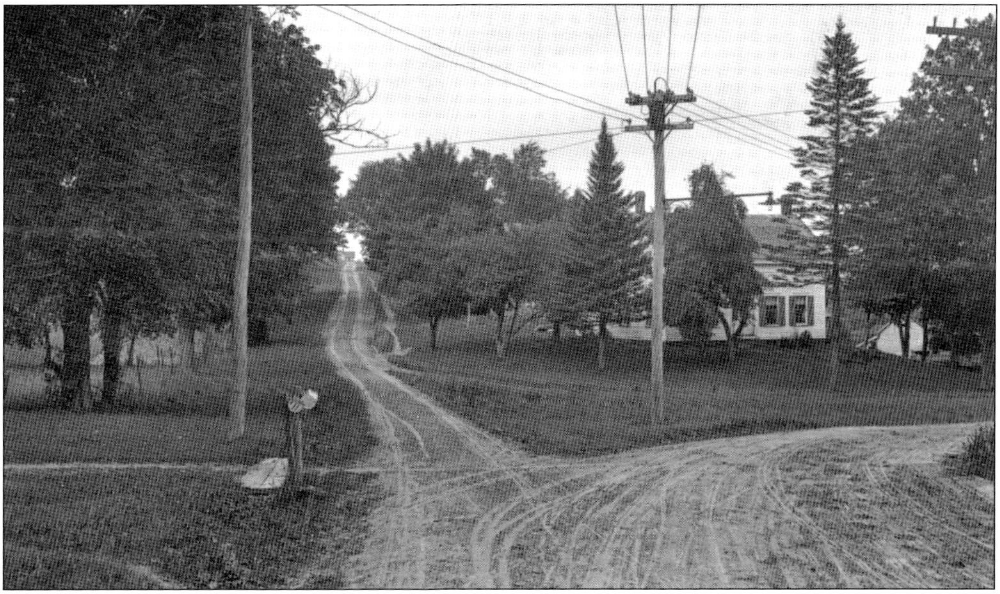

The street curves south at a point known as Whooping. The old West Street, now called Weeks Road, came into the west end settlement from the north. Because it was a straight downhill stretch, a good team of horses would come down into town "a whooping," giving the area this name. At this crossroads, to the right, was the first church in Hartwick (Presbyterian), and north of it were both the old Grand Army of the Republic (GAR) headquarters and District School No. 17. (SC.)

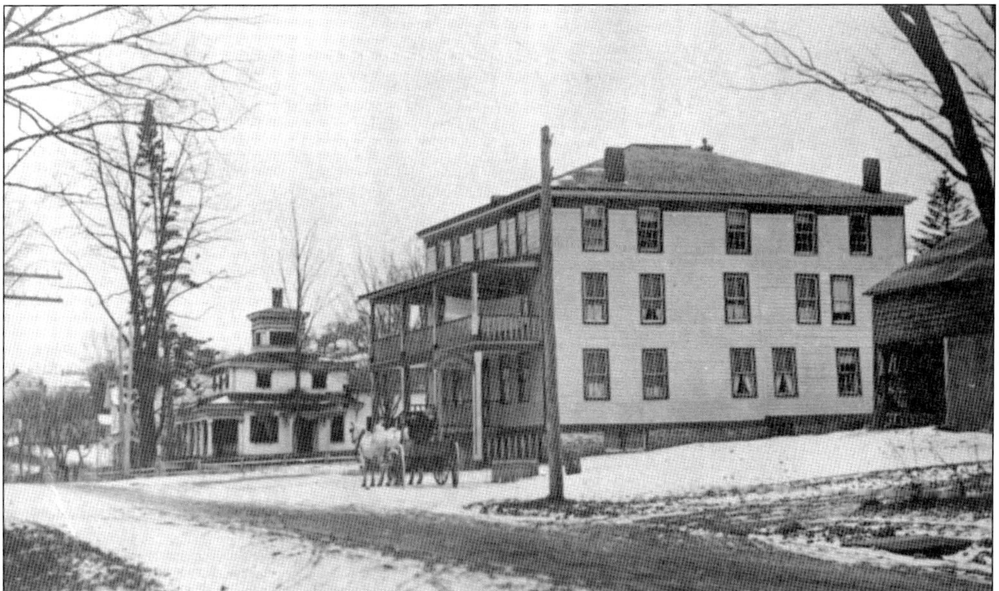

A short distance south along the street was the imposing Brooklyn House Hotel, shown here in 1905. The largest building in Hartwick with three stories and a basement, it was the center of business in this section of town. The basement of the hotel featured a saloon with swinging doors. Beyond the hotel was the home of Harlan Murdock.

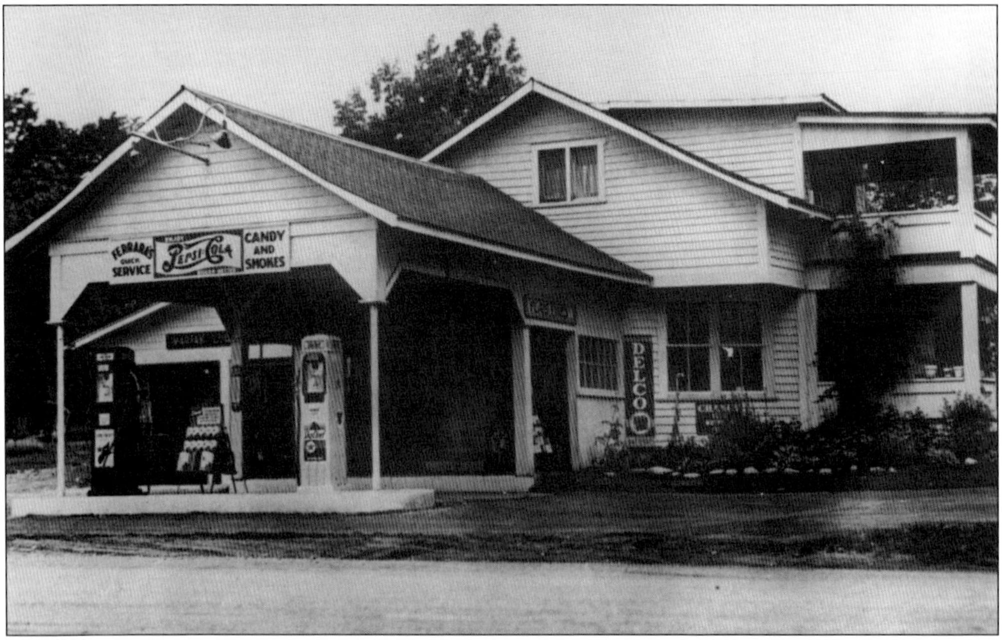

With the advent of motor transportation came gasoline and service stations. One of these was Ferrara's, located on the site of the old Brooklyn House in west end Hartwick. Operated by the Ferrara family during the 1940s and 1950s, it was later owned by Floyd Bresee and Wrights Farm Supply. It is now a private home.

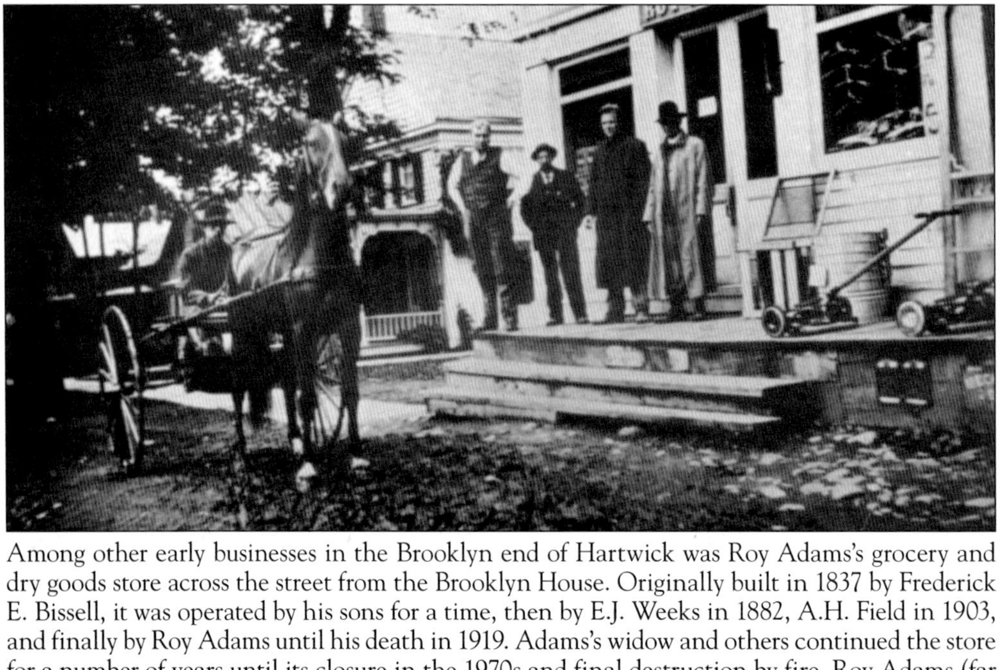

Among other early businesses in the Brooklyn end of Hartwick was Roy Adams's grocery and dry goods store across the street from the Brooklyn House. Originally built in 1837 by Frederick E. Bissell, it was operated by his sons for a time, then by E.J. Weeks in 1882, A.H. Field in 1903, and finally by Roy Adams until his death in 1919. Adams's widow and others continued the store for a number of years until its closure in the 1970s and final destruction by fire. Roy Adams (far left, in the vest) is seen in this early-1900s photograph on the steps of the store.

Six

Churches, Organizations, and Community Life

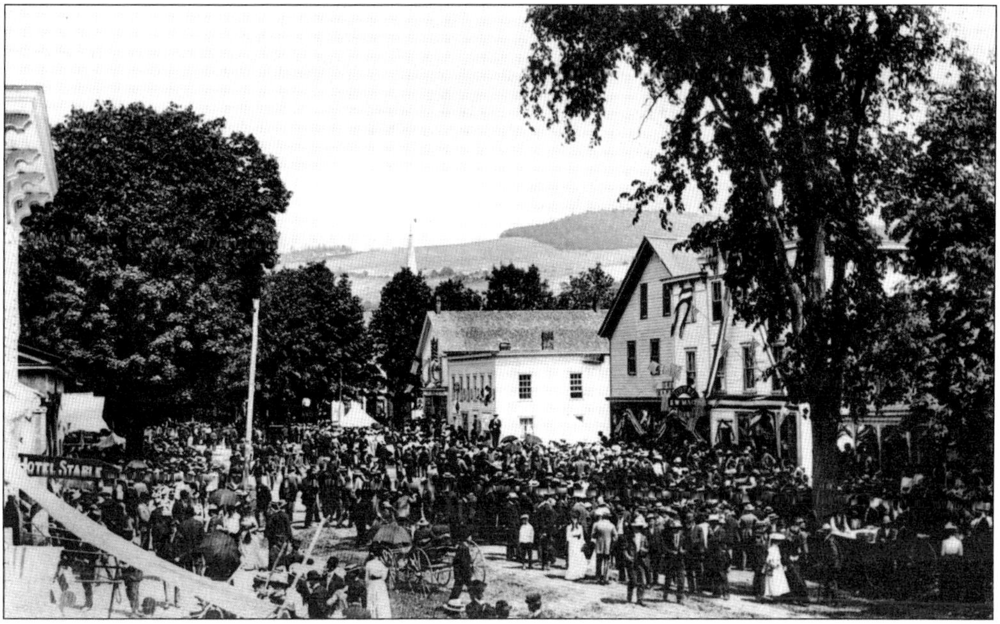

Apart from daily work on farms and in business, Hartwick families enjoyed active social lives, both in their neighborhoods and the larger township community. The number and variety of organizations to join meant many shared cultural events, dinners, dances, and frequent celebrations with parades. The Fourth of July Hartwick centennial celebration of 1902, seen here, was one of the largest community gatherings on Main Street in the hamlet. (ST at FAM.)

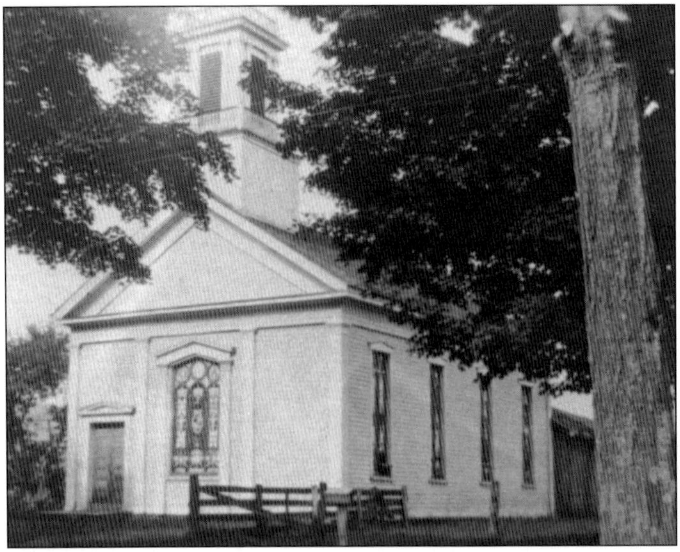

Early neighborhood social life centered around family homes or the community church or school. Pictured here is Union Church in Toddsville. Dedicated in 1876, the church was built for shared services of five different denominations: Presbyterian, Methodist, Christian, Baptist, and Universalist. After closing in the late 1940s, the community church reopened in 1960 as Toddsville Baptist Church and is now known as Community Bible Chapel.

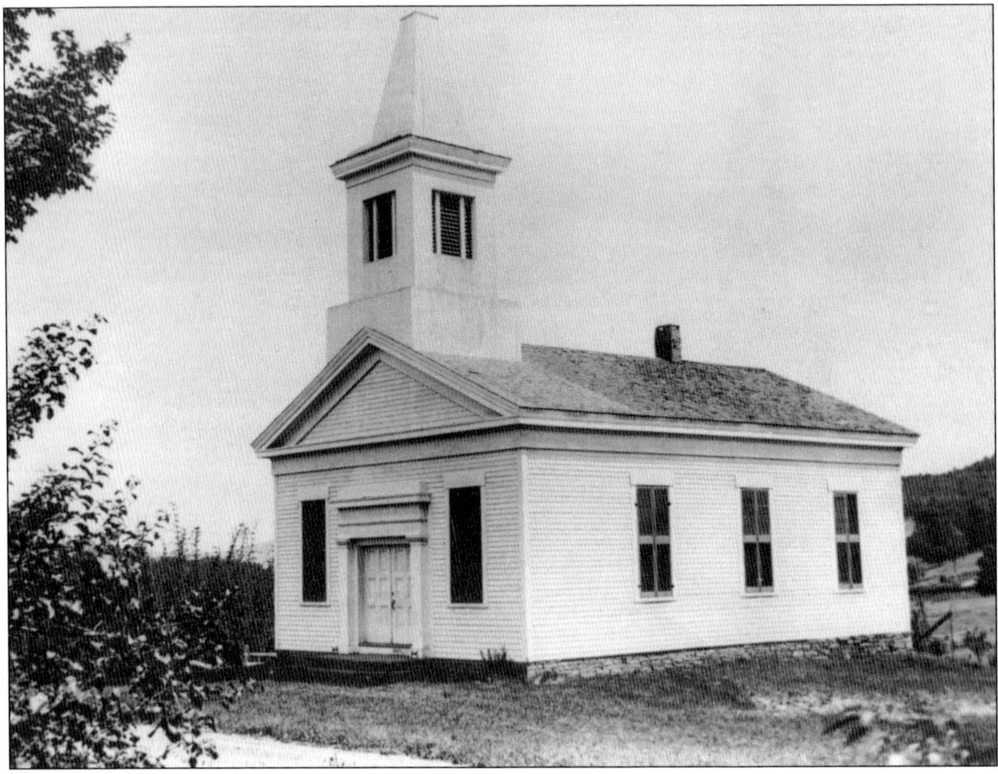

Christian Church of Otsego and Hartwick, one of the first Christian churches in New York State and the first in Hartwick Township, organized in January 1814. Known as Christian Hill Church because of its location, members met first in homes or at the schoolhouse. An 1830 stone building preceded the church pictured here and was dedicated in 1843. By 1905, with declining membership and as others joined the Hartwick hamlet parish, this church became extinct.

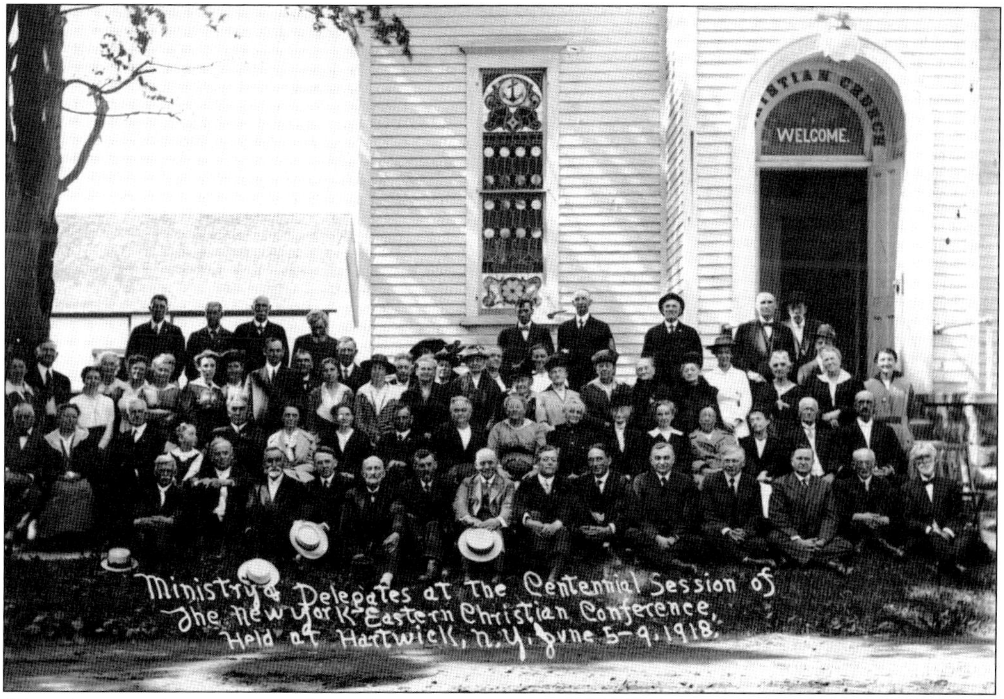

Churches were/are meeting places for traditional worship and teaching as well as locations for music concerts, special speakers, conferences, and community-organization dinners. This view shows delegates at a regional Christian Conference held at Hartwick Christian Church in 1918. Worship services and community events have continued since the erection of the church building in 1853.

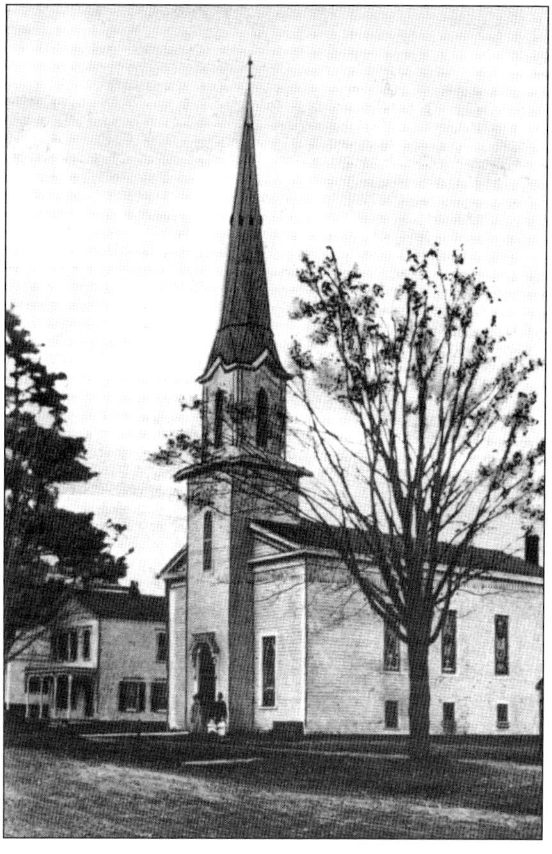

A second Hartwick hamlet church is Hartwick United Methodist Church, pictured here in 1907. Services, with Methodist circuit rider preachers, were first held in family homes, then for a time in the stone schoolhouse on South Street. The new church building seen here was erected about 1840. Records show an active Ladies Aid Society in 1898 and a Sunday school since 1864, with many Bible schools, picnics, ice-cream socials, and other events held throughout the years. (RF.)

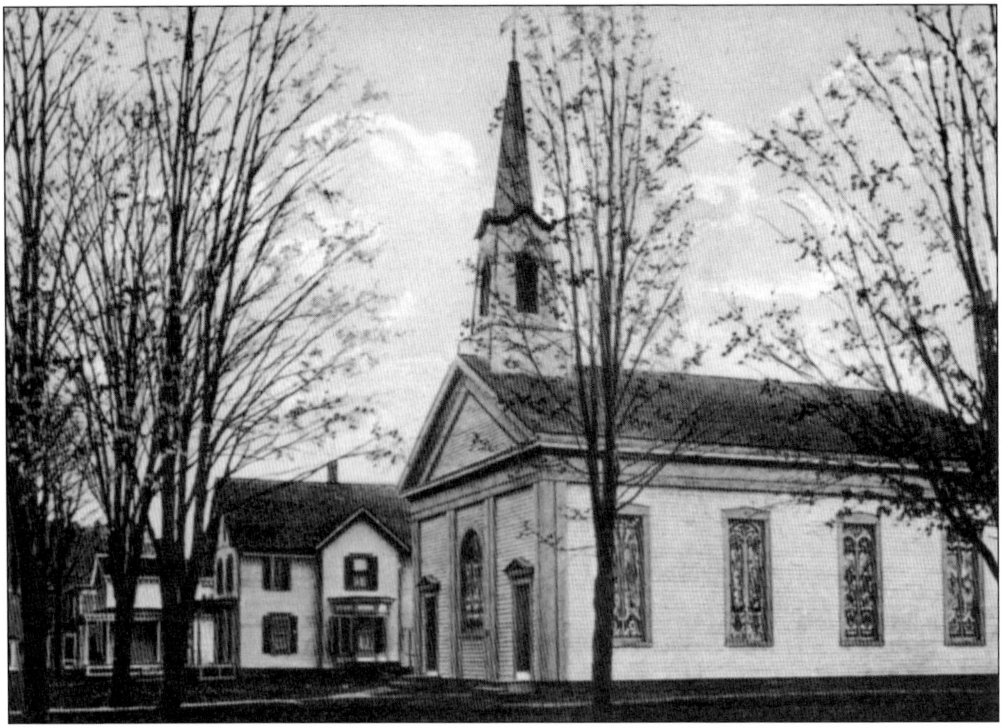

One of the oldest churches in the county, Hartwick Baptist Church was organized in 1795 with 12 charter members. The church first occupied a building to the west on Main Street (site of the present Hartwick Day Treatment Center) before completion of the present building in 1854. Located at the corner of Main and South Streets, the church has continued with an active ministry in the community since that time. (RF.)

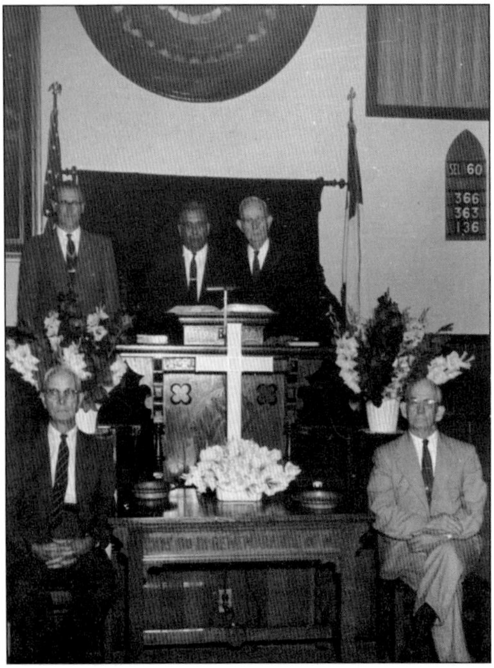

Marcus Wells, a local businessman, lawyer, inventor, and active member of Hartwick Baptist Church, composed the well-known hymn "Holy Spirit, Faithful Guide" in 1858. The large stained-glass window on the front of the church depicting the first two lines of the famous hymn is a memorial to Wells. This photograph shows some church members 100 years later as they celebrate Marcus Wells Day. Seated are O.A. Smith (left) and James Ainslie, and standing are, from left to right, Eugene Ward, Rev. Walter Miller, and Reverend Dickenson.

Every community in the township had at least one district school, with an increase from 7 in 1810 to 18 by 1868. Families in each district provided the building with all physical necessities, as well as provisions for a teacher. A copy of Lynn Maynes 1910 teacher's contract with the trustees of Maples School No. 13 is seen here.

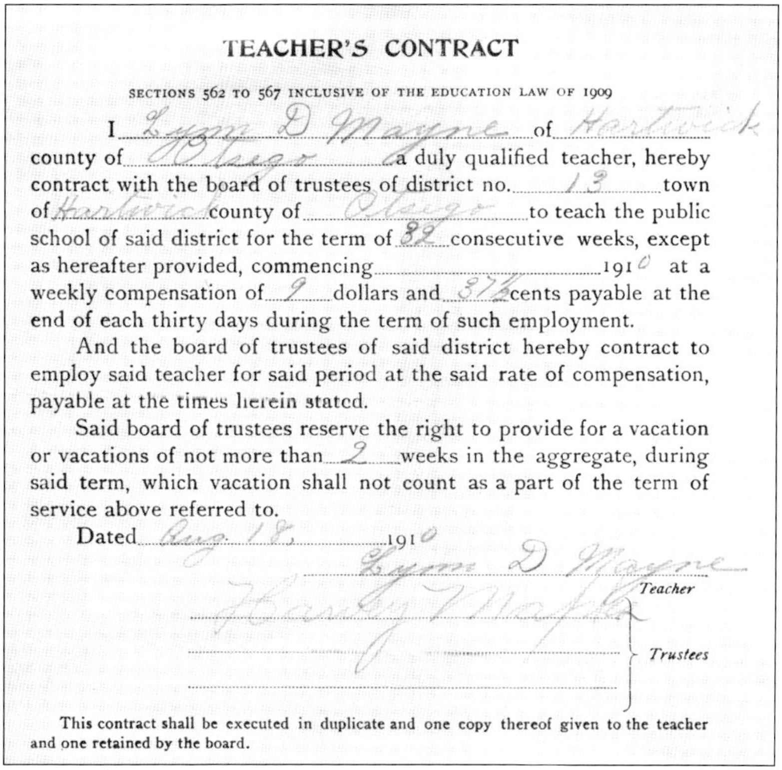

TEACHER'S CONTRACT

SECTIONS 562 TO 567 INCLUSIVE OF THE EDUCATION LAW OF 1909

I Lynn D Mayne of Hartwick county of Otsego a duly qualified teacher, hereby contract with the board of trustees of district no. 13 town of Hartwick county of Otsego to teach the public school of said district for the term of 32 consecutive weeks, except as hereafter provided, commencing .... 1910 at a weekly compensation of 9 dollars and 37½ cents payable at the end of each thirty days during the term of such employment.

And the board of trustees of said district hereby contract to employ said teacher for said period at the said rate of compensation, payable at the times herein stated.

Said board of trustees reserve the right to provide for a vacation or vacations of not more than 2 weeks in the aggregate, during said term, which vacation shall not count as a part of the term of service above referred to.

Dated Aug. 18 1910

Lynn D Mayne Teacher

Harvey Maples Trustees

This contract shall be executed in duplicate and one copy thereof given to the teacher and one retained by the board.

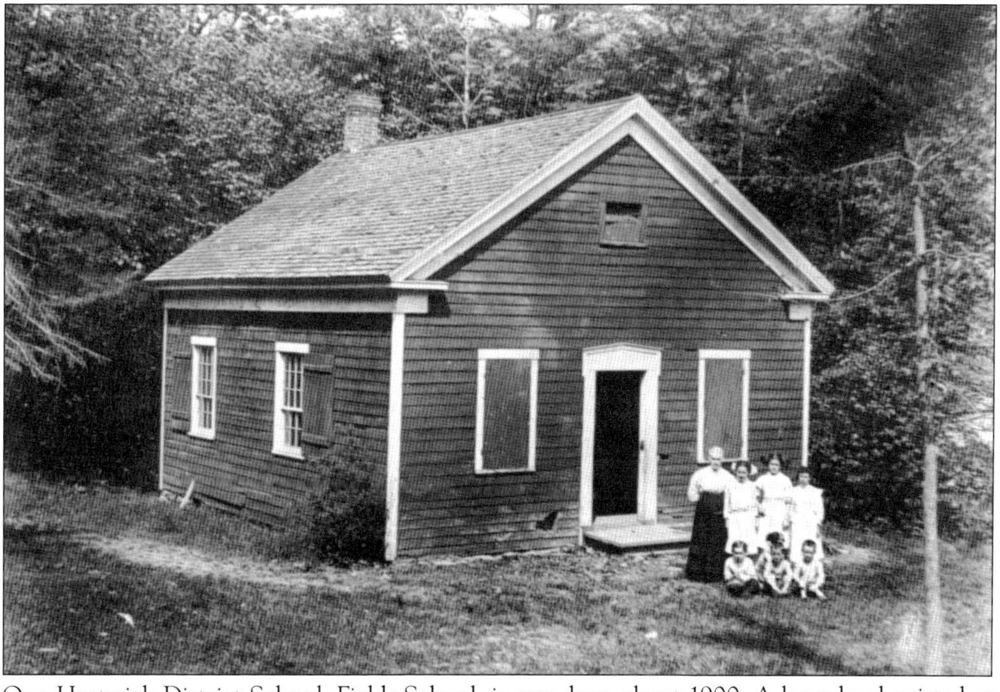

One Hartwick District School, Fields School, is seen here about 1900. A log school existed at this location first in 1802 on land belonging to early settler William Field. The teacher posing with her students is Mrs. Jennie Joslin. (DP.)

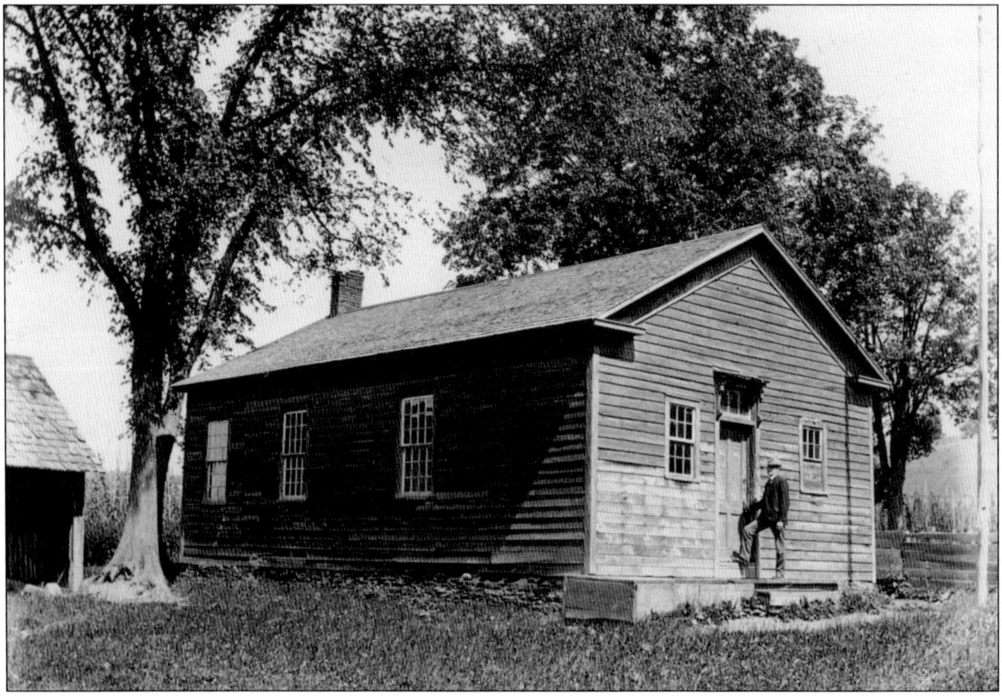

Hinman Hollow District School No. 12 (earlier changed from No. 18) is seen here about 1900. When first built, as early as 1862, the building front faced the road. Used for church services, funerals, and weddings, after closing as the neighborhood school, the building is now owned by the Hinman Hollow Grange. (EH.)

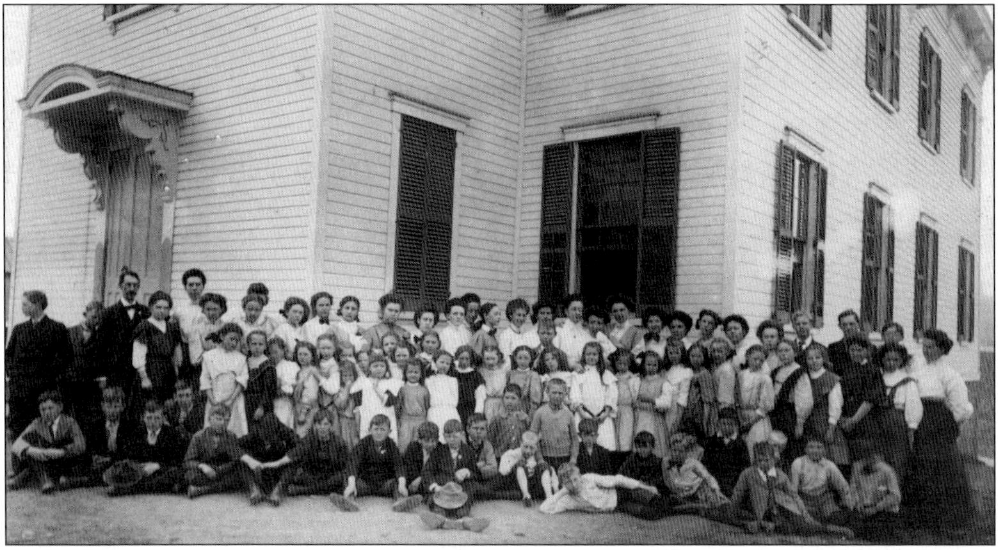

Hartwick School District School No. 4 served the east side of Hartwick hamlet and stood on South Street. The original stone building, erected before 1815, was replaced in 1878 by a large, wood-framed edifice, and the west side of Hartwick ("Brooklyn") District School No. 17 consolidated with it. Around 1900, this school became Hartwick Union School and Academy, with improved academic courses and the addition of students from smaller districts outside of the hamlet. This view shows the faculty and student body at that time.

A larger school meant more extracurricular clubs and athletics. Hartwick's first basketball team poses here. From left to right are (first row) Carl Thomas, George Porter, and H.L. Harrington; (second row) Blain Talbot; (third row) Ben Talbot, coach Lynn Sill, and Chauncey Beach.

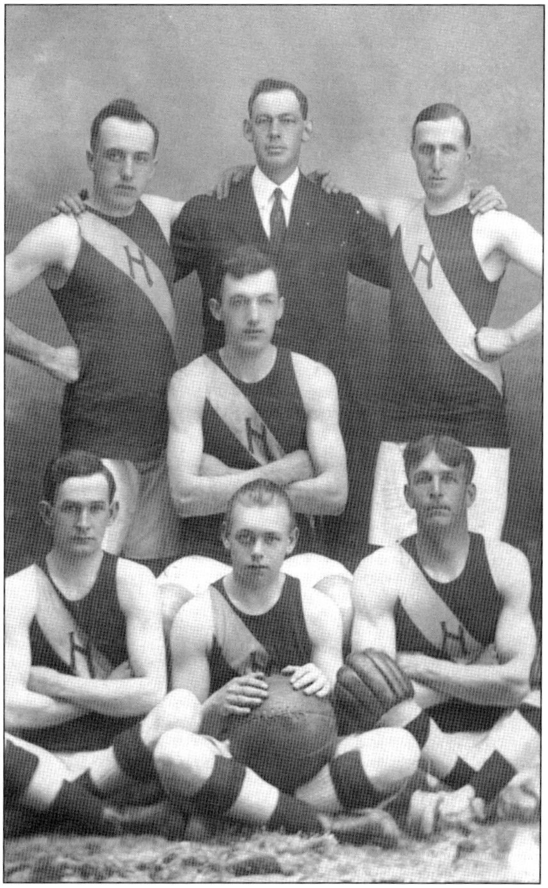

The Union School girls had a basketball team as well, and they are pictured here in 1910. From left to right are Angela Cortright, Elsa Wood, Katherine Burlingham, Harriet Burnum, Maude Simmons, Mildred McEwen, and Mabel Gruby. (DP.)

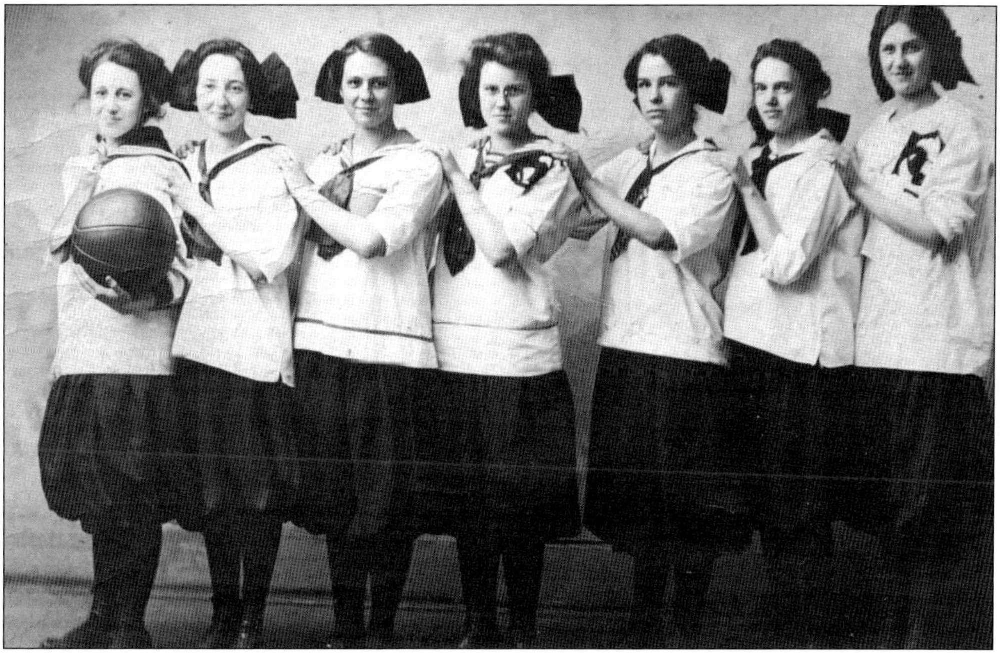

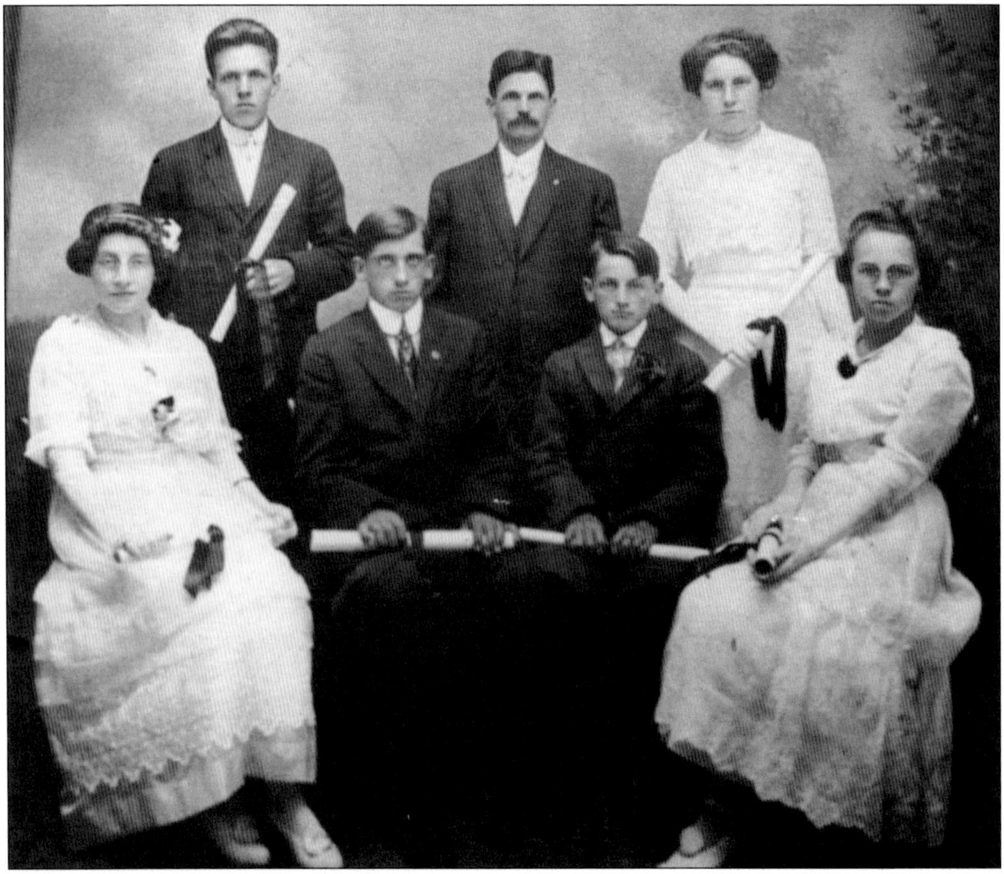

Records of graduates were not accurately kept at first. This 1914 image shows an early Union School graduating class. Identified in the first row, third from left, is Milton Bunn.

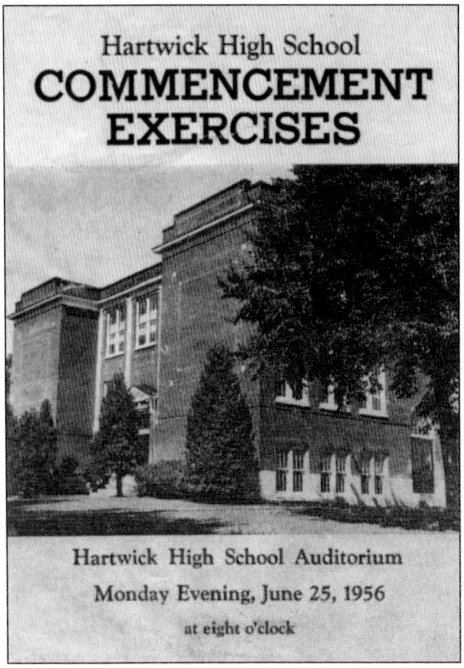

The Union School building outlived its usefulness after 40 years and was replaced in the fall of 1921 by a larger brick high school at the cost of $60,000. In 1934, there was a faculty of nine, and 100 pupils were enrolled from kindergarten through 12th grade. The school ranked high academically, and students won many prizes and scholarships. The school is pictured here on the front of the June 1956 commencement program.

Sports of all types were important, along with academics, and were enjoyed by both girls and boys. An unidentified girls' basketball team from 1928–1929 is pictured here.

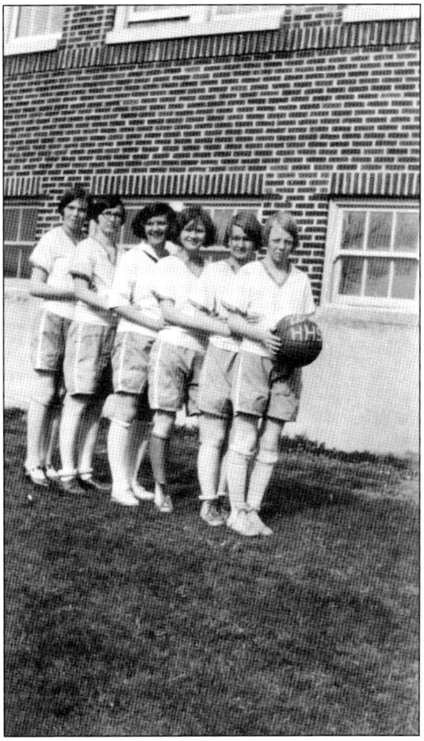

Hartwick High School became well known for championship athletic teams. The first undefeated Hartwick High School football team to win a Tri-Valley League Championship is this 1952 team. Pictured are, from left to right, (first row) Leland Beach, Michael Gregory, Francis Schweitzer, Raymond Polulech, Frank McGrath, and Charles Hadley; (second row) John Polulech, William Bresee, John Henningson, Earl Roberts, James Hurtubise, Richard Mistretta and coach William Dalrymple; (third row) manager Herbert Schweitzer, Richard Conklin, William Davis, James Campbell, and manager James McGrath.

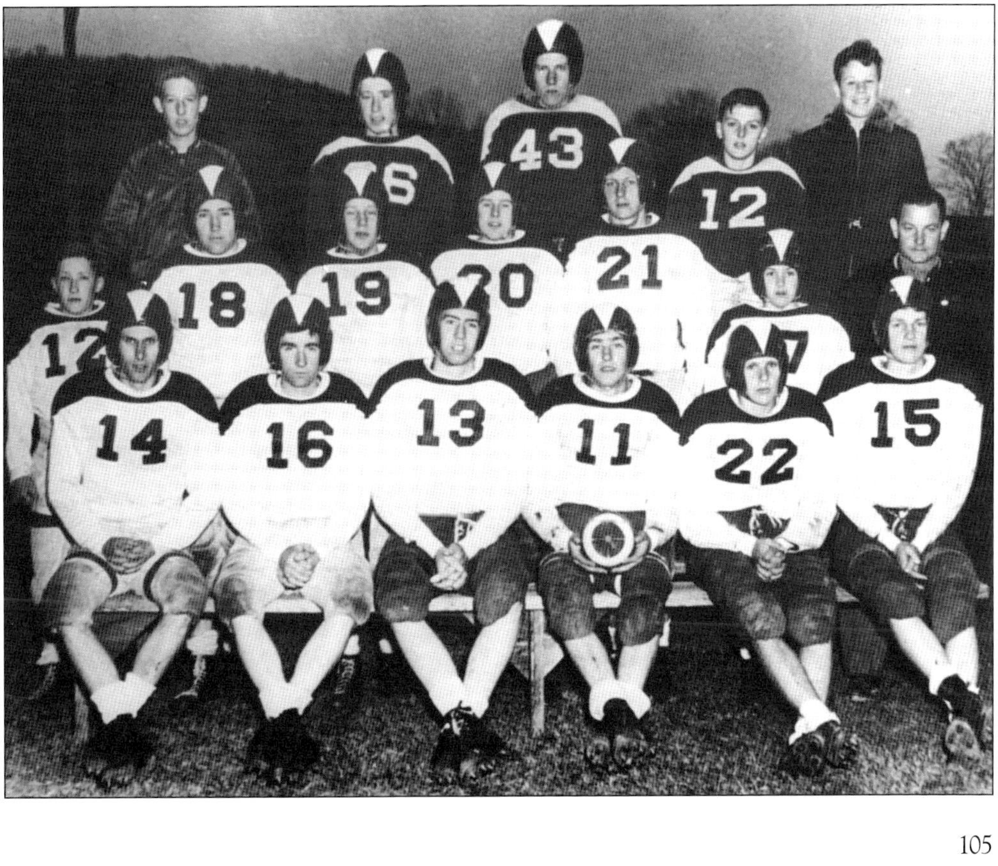

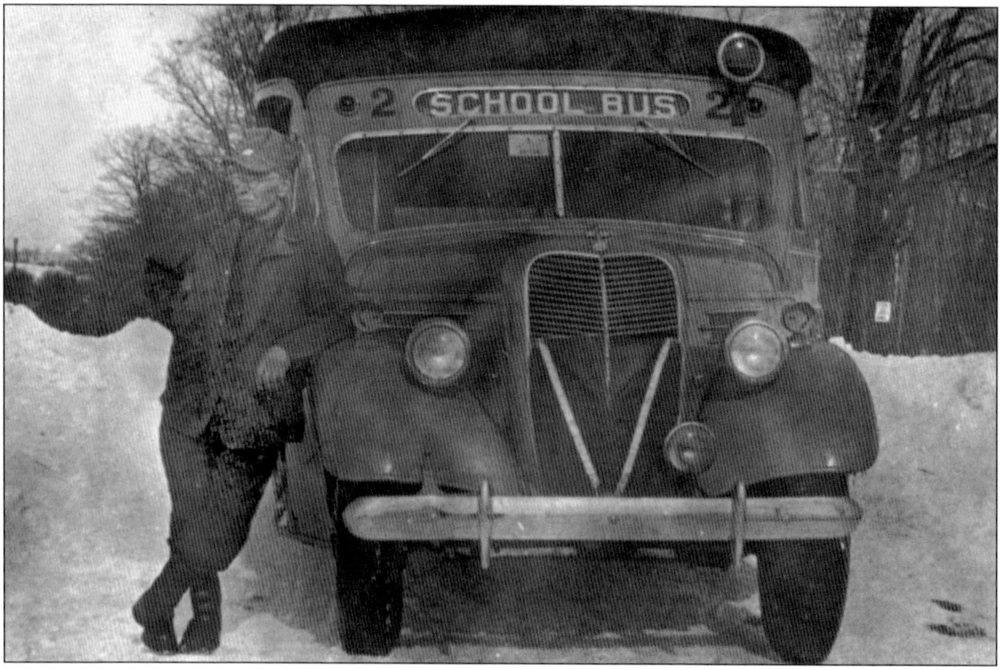

Students were transported in from rural neighborhoods to Hartwick hamlet's central school by contracted drivers in private automobiles and in a small fleet of school buses. Bus driver Harry Perry stands by school bus No. 2 in this 1940s view.

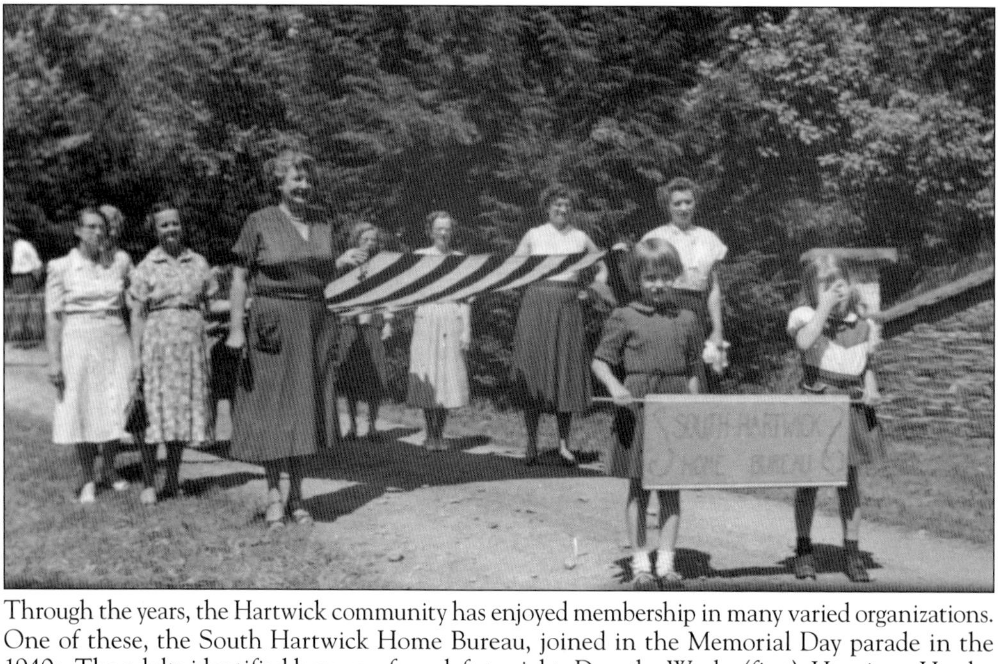

Through the years, the Hartwick community has enjoyed membership in many varied organizations. One of these, the South Hartwick Home Bureau, joined in the Memorial Day parade in the 1940s. The adults identified here are, from left to right, Dorothy Weeks (first), Henrietta Hetzler (fourth), Mary Skubitz (fifth), Elizabeth Bunn (sixth), and Lily Mae Wright; in front, the young girl on the left may be Mary Chamberlain.

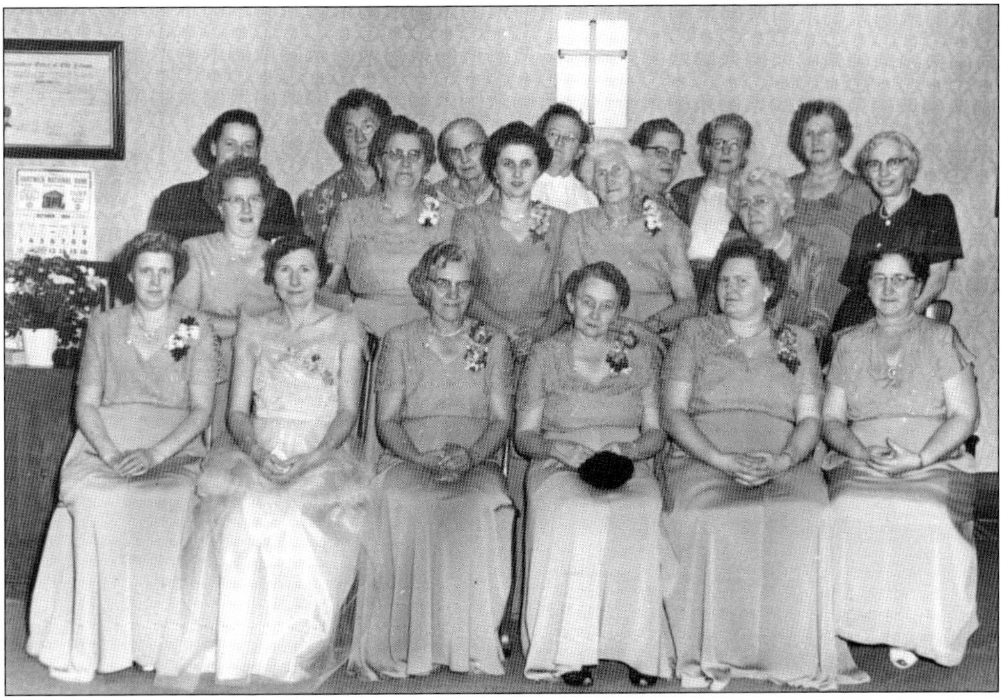

The Rebekahs, a women's auxiliary of the local lodge of Independent Order of the Odd Fellows (IOOF), started the Otego Valley Lodge No. 460 in 1911 in Hartwick hamlet. As a group, they supported the IOOF, looked after the needy, and held public dinners, dances, bake sales, and programs. By 1928, there were more than 100 members. Pictured here is a smaller group of local ladies in the 1940s.

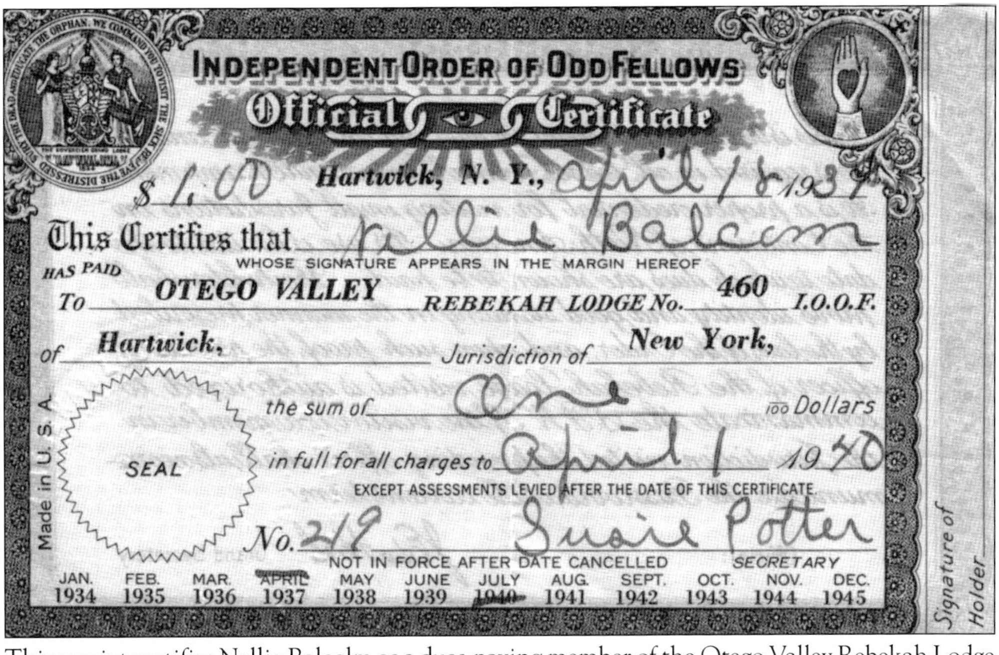

INDEPENDENT ORDER OF ODD FELLOWS

Official Certificate

$1.00 Hartwick, N. Y., April 18 1939

This Certifies that Nellie Balcom

HAS PAID WHOSE SIGNATURE APPEARS IN THE MARGIN HEREOF

To OTEGO VALLEY REBEKAH LODGE No. 460 I.O.O.F.

of Hartwick, Jurisdiction of New York,

the sum of One 100 Dollars

in full for all charges to April 1 1940

EXCEPT ASSESSMENTS LEVIED AFTER THE DATE OF THIS CERTIFICATE.

SEAL

No. 219 Susie Potter

NOT IN FORCE AFTER DATE CANCELLED SECRETARY

JAN. 1934 FEB. 1935 MAR. 1936 APRIL 1937 MAY 1938 JUNE 1939 JULY 1940 AUG. 1941 SEPT. 1942 OCT. 1943 NOV. 1944 DEC. 1945

Made in U. S. A.

Signature of Holder

This receipt certifies Nellie Balcolm as a dues-paying member of the Otego Valley Rebekah Lodge of Hartwick, with all membership and visitation rights/privileges in associated Rebekah lodges.

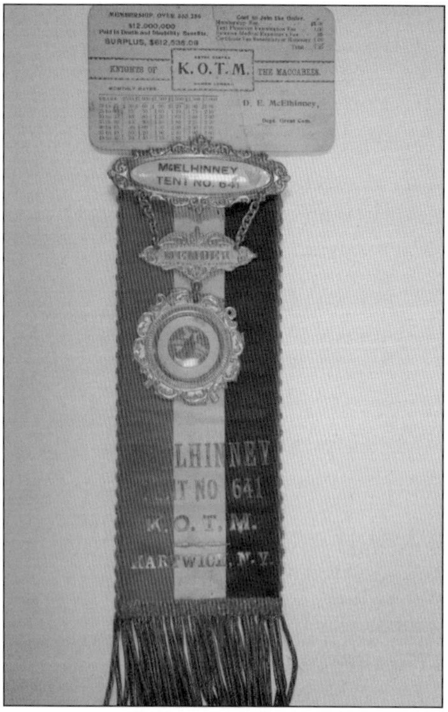

Knights of the Maccabees, a secret beneficiary society, organized in Hartwick around 1901 through the efforts of Misses McElhinney and Eldred of Cooperstown. Well known for excellent "home and relief" insurance policies, the Maccabees were also active socially, hosting ice cream socials, suppers, and picnics. (GW.)

Chapter No. 617 of the Order of the Eastern Star (OES) was formed in 1918 by 36 Hartwick-area members demitted from the Fly Creek chapter. A social, benevolent organization directly linked to the Masonic fraternal order, the OES has provided charitable assistance to needy members, military veterans, and elderly sisters and brothers, first as a Hartwick chapter and since 1988 in combination as the Otsego-Hartwick chapter. This image shows the Hartwick chapter officers in 1961. From left to right are (first row) Mary Hoose, Geraldine Croft, and Mildred Gregory; (second row) Anita Harrison, David Skellie, and Wilma Skellie Dodge.

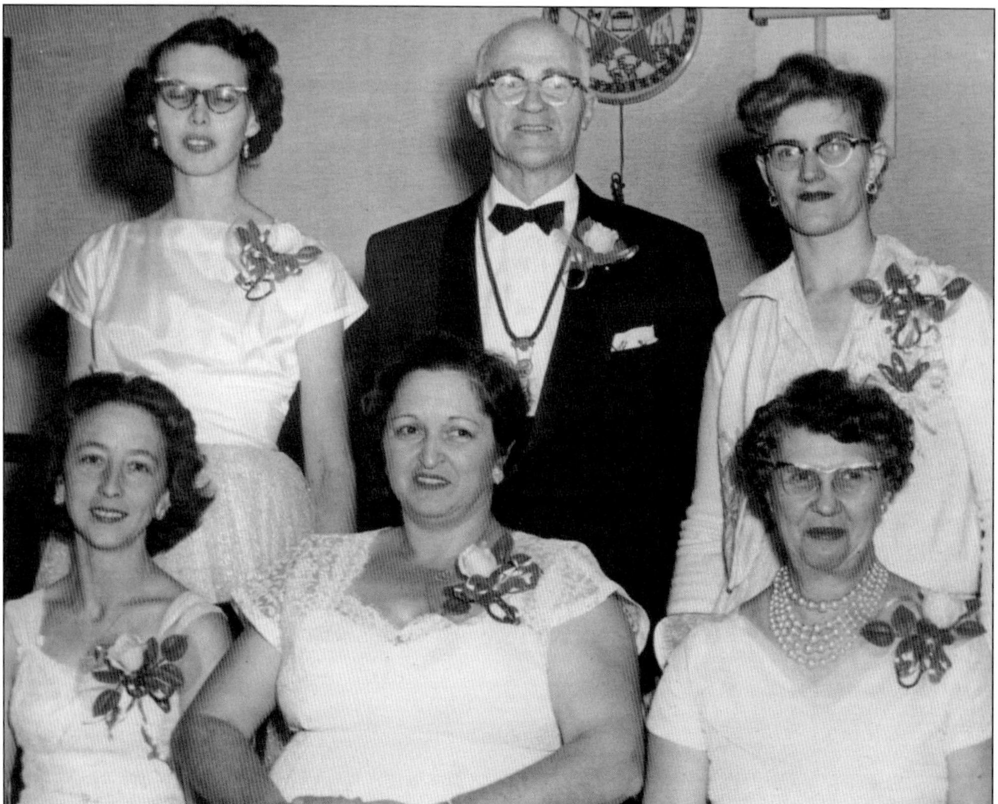

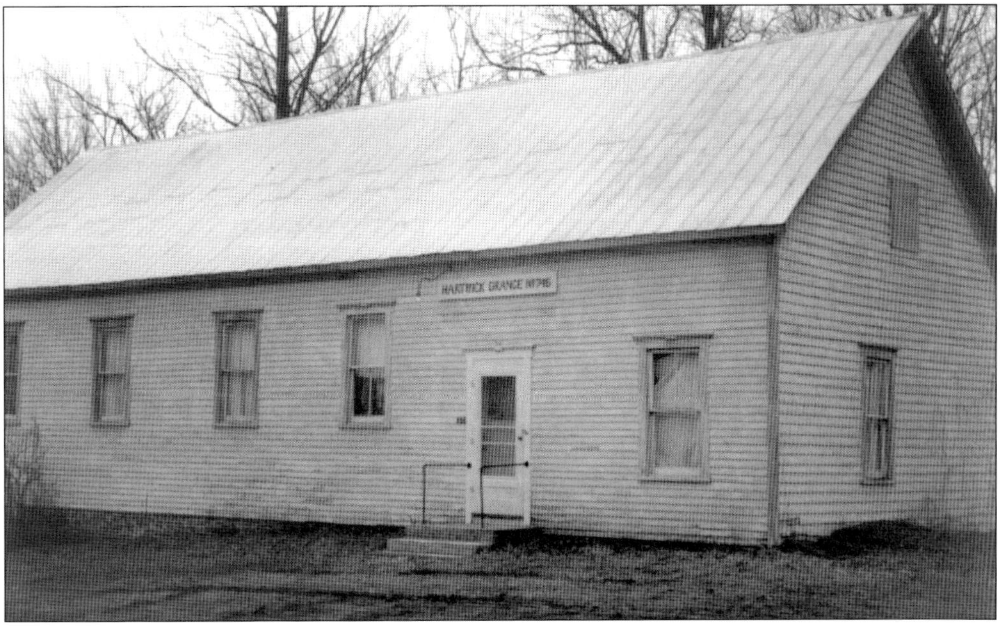

The Grange, a nationwide organization officially named Patrons of Husbandry, was an important association for rural farm families of Hartwick. Through group community membership, agricultural and economic interests were promoted. Cooperatives, sponsored by the Grange with other organizations, gave farmers buying power and some price control for their products. The original building of the Hartwick Grange on Christian Hill (organized in 1891) was replaced by the "new" building after a fire in April 1922. (EH.)

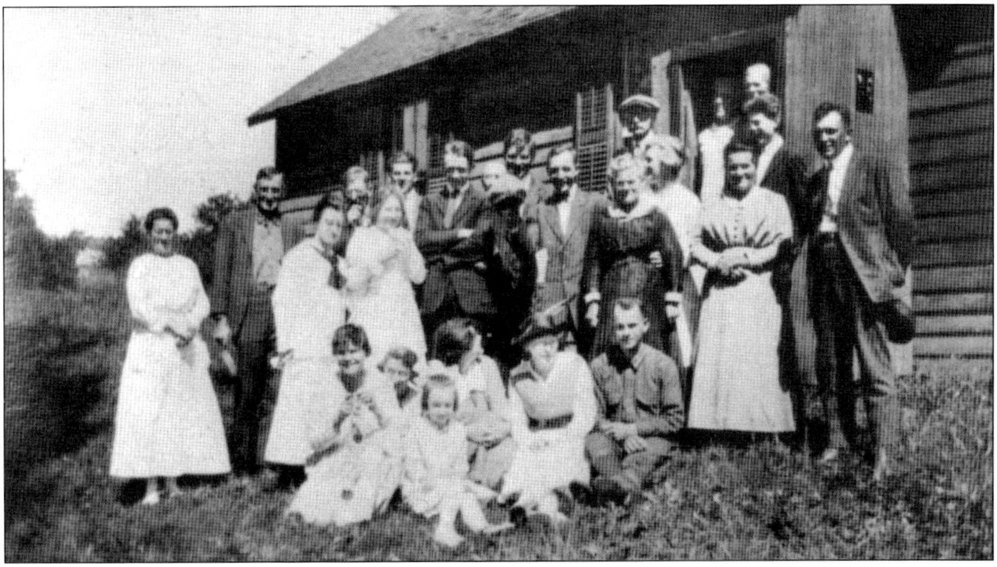

The Hinman Hollow Grange building shown here was purchased in 1914 from George Smith. After becoming dormant in 1928, the Grange reorganized in 1938 and has remained active since. Grange meetings also meant enjoyable social times with dinners and square dances to follow. The Otsego County Fair was organized as a Grange fair in this hall on October 10, 1945. Identified are Lillian Aunger (first row, fourth from the left), Charles Schidzick (first row, fifth from the left), and Henrietta Schidzick (second row, fifth from the left). (EH.)

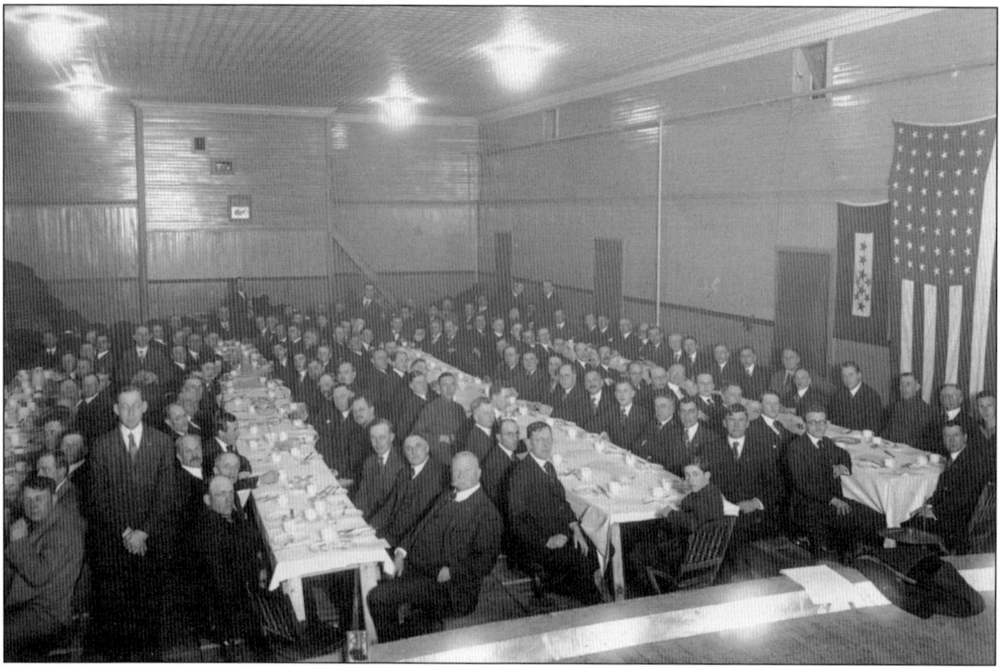

When the Otsego & Herkimer Railway (trolley) offices were moved from Hartwick to Cooperstown in 1912, the former office building known as Tammany Hall was donated for employee use as a social hall. After much planning, the 40-foot-by-90-foot structure was moved by many men and teams of horses across town to a site on Main Street, near the depot. The Employees Mutual Benefit Association (EMBA) Hall was the location for many banquets, dances, and social affairs, including weekly silent movie showings, in the 1920s. The wide stage provided space for plays, lyceum courses, and vaudeville acts. Pictured here during the annual EMBA banquet in 1919 is the original stage before it was damaged by fire. The building today remains in use as a gymnasium and Hartwick Community Center.

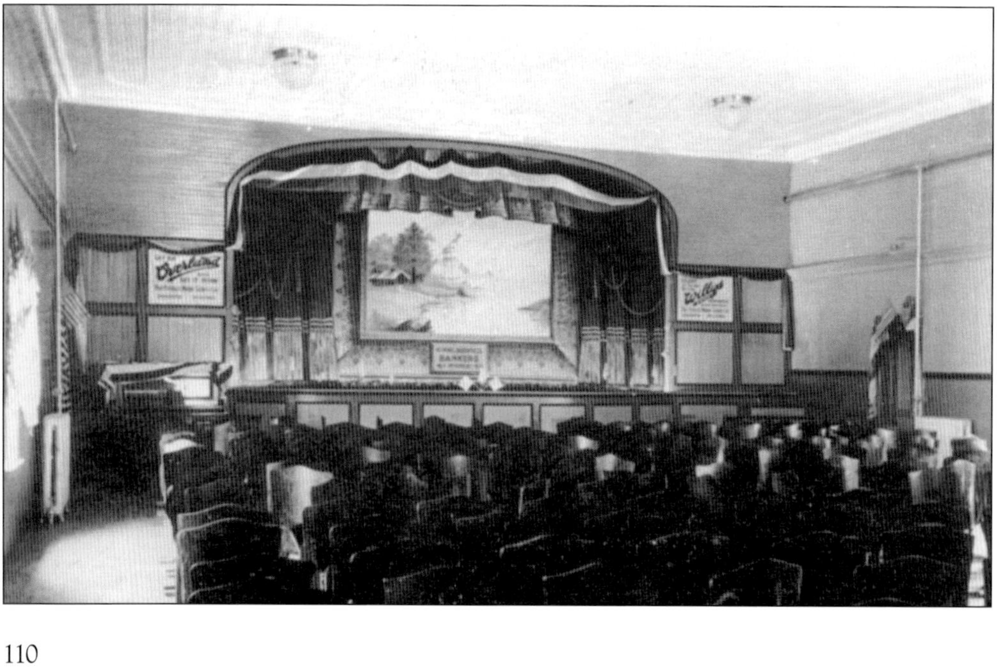

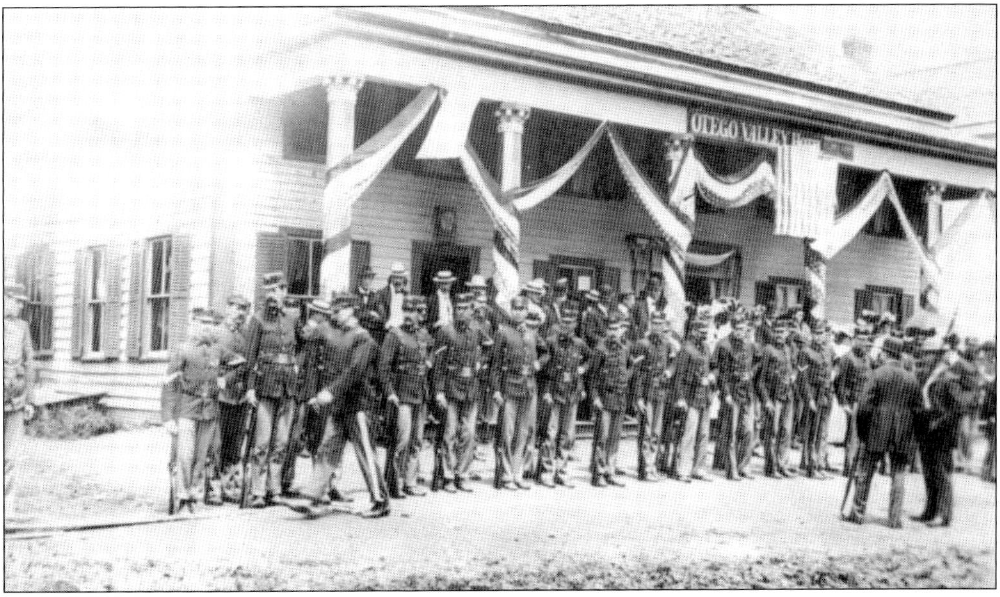

Union Civil War veterans from Hartwick's Grand Army of the Republic (GAR) Horatio N. Duro Post 653 (in existence from 1811 to 1911) assembled here by the Otego Valley Hotel before joining a Fourth of July or Decoration Day (Memorial Day) parade through Hartwick hamlet. The occasion may have been the large July 4, 1902, Hartwick centennial celebration.

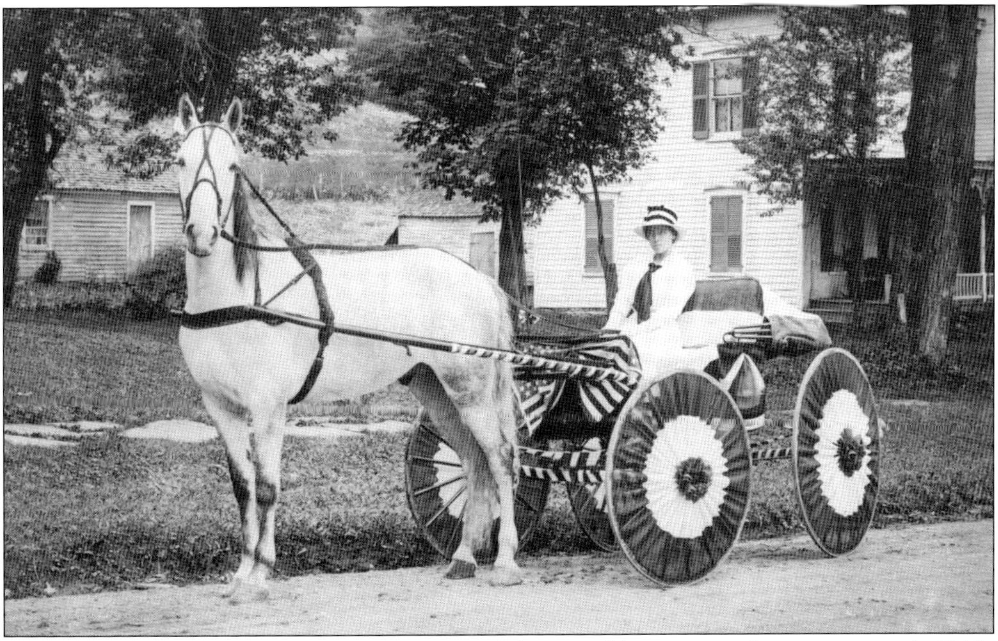

Ruth Joslin of West Main Street, with horse and decorated buggy, is ready to join an early-1900s Hartwick parade. (DP.)

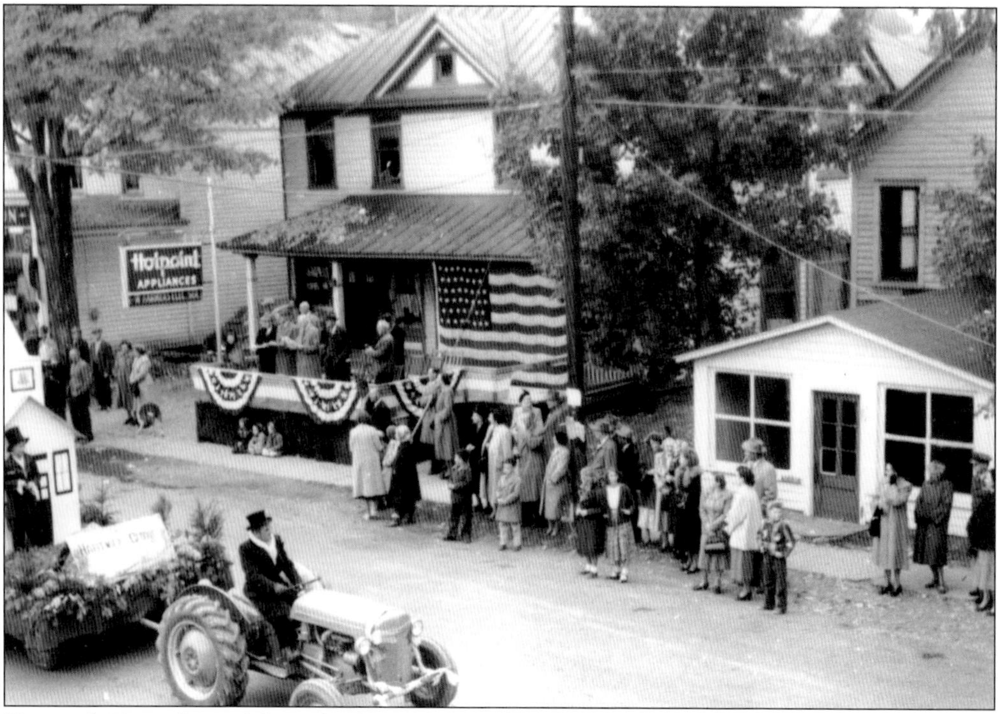

Hartwick Township celebrated 150 years as an organized town in 1952 with community-wide events, including a float-filled parade. The sesquicentennial parade viewing stand, pictured here, stood along Main Street in front of the R.W. Farmer Electrical Service Store building, dedicated in 1958 as the American Legion Hall. Active members of this veterans' organization continue today with military, community memorial activities, public dinners, and fundraising benefits for individuals and families in need.

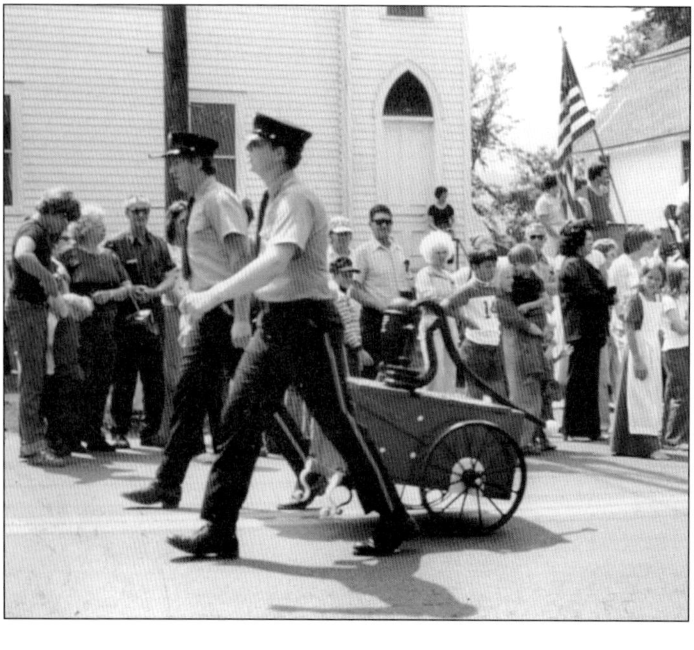

With wood-burning stoves and wooden structures, fire was a real and frequent threat to the Hartwick community. Before construction of a central hamlet fire station, early fire equipment was kept by the Neptune Hose Company in a Brooklyn House shed and by Hose Company No. 1 at the Porter Block (later Risley) Store. Two separate township volunteer fire departments now provide vital protection. Pictured here in a local parade is the early hand-powered fire pump.

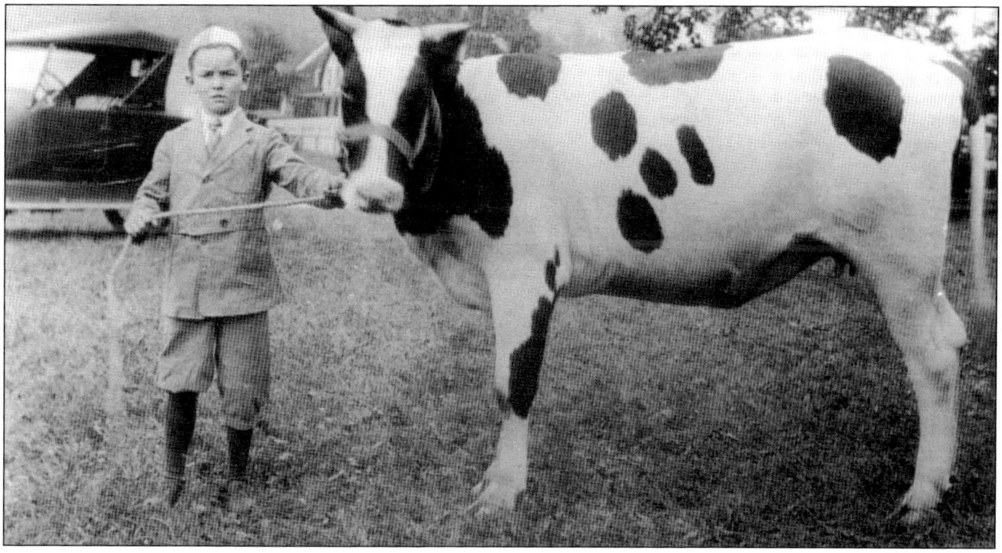

Many Hartwick-area young people ages 10 to 20 have had active years in 4H as members and leaders since clubs first organized here in the 1920s. Members learned practical life skills in agriculture and homemaking and then exhibited projects or competed at shows and fairs. Fun social times and friendships were shared with club members from local to national levels. John Mott is pictured here about 1920 with his first 4H project, a Holstein calf shown at the Otsego County Fair. (CG.)

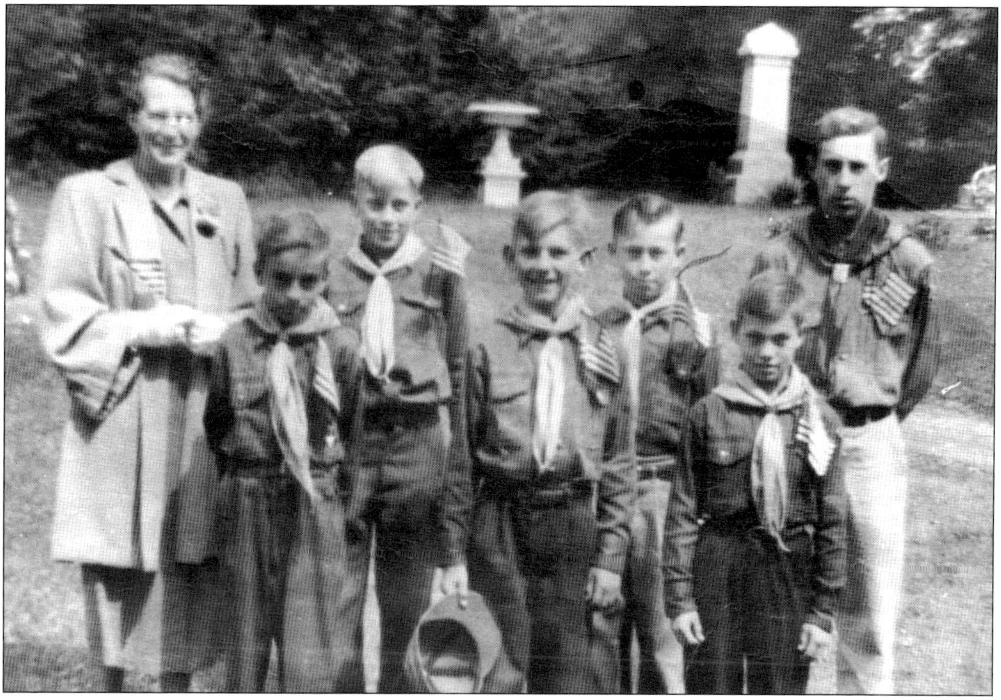

Scouting in Hartwick began in the mid-1940s with 10 boys and an adult leader. Later, Cub Scout Pack 72 grew from a group of 5 younger boys with their parents to a total of 40. Boys of all ages have learned scouting and character-building skills and participated in community events. In this late-1950s Cub Scout photograph are, from left to right, den mother Mrs. Henningsen, Roger Hull, John Henningsen, Lyn Larsen, Richard Conklin, Edwin Carvin, and Boy Scout leader John McGrath.

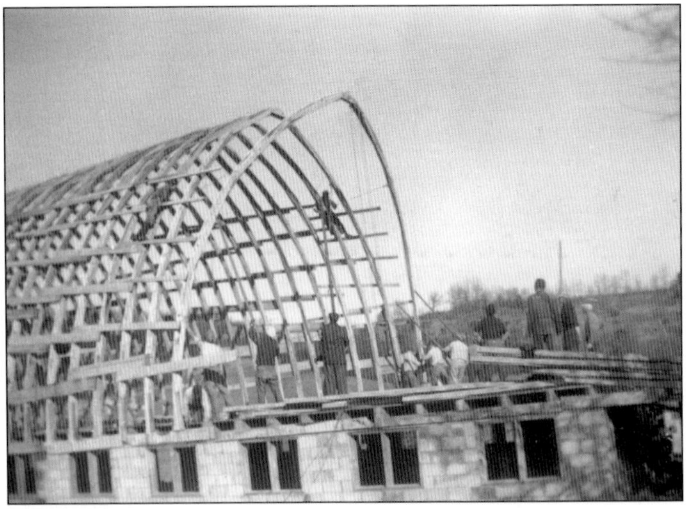

Neighbors helped neighbors with farmwork and housework "bees" (such as husking and quilting) by rotating shared equipment and labor at harvest time and also aided with major building projects such as barn raising. Food, card playing, and dancing would often be enjoyed in the evening after a long day's work. William Powers's Hinman Hollow barn is being raised in this view. (EH.)

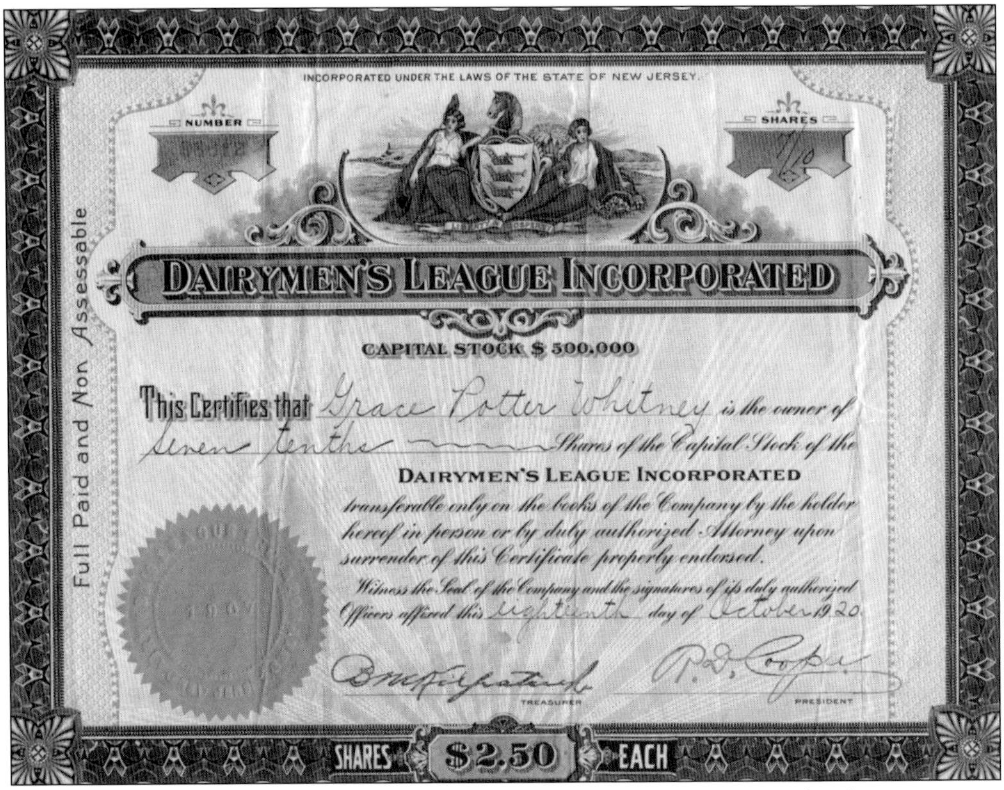

INCORPORATED UNDER THE LAWS OF THE STATE OF NEW JERSEY.

NUMBER

SHARES 7/10

Full Paid and Non Assessable

DAIRYMEN'S LEAGUE INCORPORATED

CAPITAL STOCK $ 500,000

This Certifies that Grace Potter Whitney is the owner of Seven tenths Shares of the Capital Stock of the

DAIRYMEN'S LEAGUE INCORPORATED

transferable only on the books of the Company by the holder hereof in person or by duly authorized Attorney upon surrender of this Certificate properly endorsed.

Witness the Seal of the Company and the signatures of its duly authorized Officers affixed this eighteenth day of October 1920.

TREASURER

PRESIDENT

SHARES $2.50 EACH

Like the Grange, the Dairymen's League Cooperative was an important membership association for dairy farmers of Hartwick Township, whose livelihood depended on stable, fair pricing of marketed milk. Hartwick District No. 7 gave small producers a shared stake and unity in statewide bargaining power. There was also a social element, with district and county meetings, a home department for ladies, and shared dinners, picnics, and other entertainment. A 1920 copy of a Dairymen's League membership stock share for Grace Whitney Potter is pictured here.

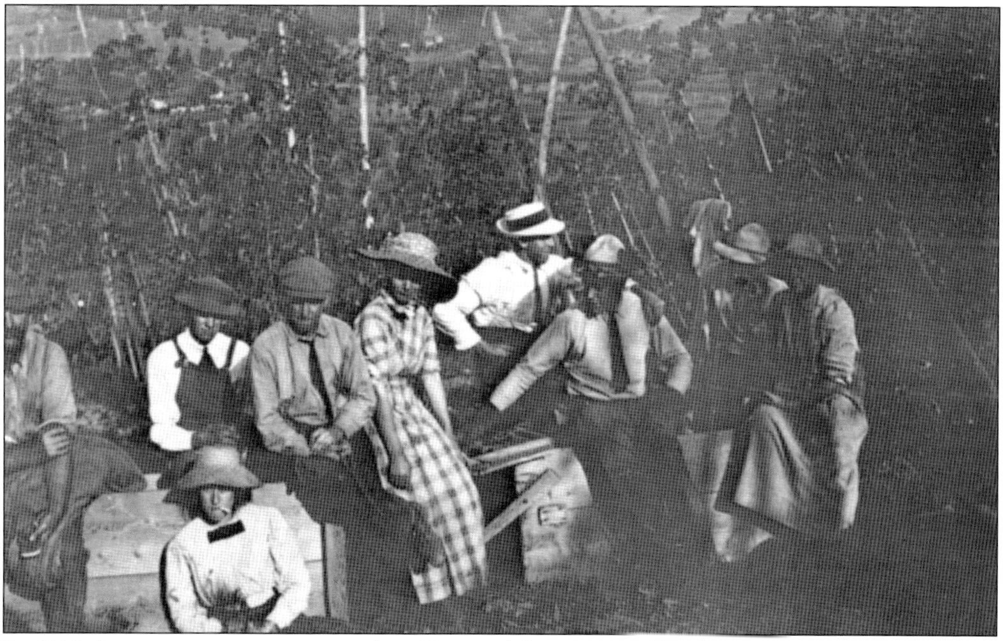

By 1910, farm communities surrounding Hartwick became worldwide centers for hop production. Hops became the main cash crop in Hartwick, and harvest season was, according to Otis D. Mott in an article by his son John A. Mott, "one time—to earn a little spending money." Friends, neighbors, and relatives helped each other at harvest, and many couples met or courted during hop-picking time between shared work, meals, and social evenings. Jesse and Lulu Bishop Wells are third and fifth from the left, respectively, in this view of Christian Hill hop pickers. (DP.)

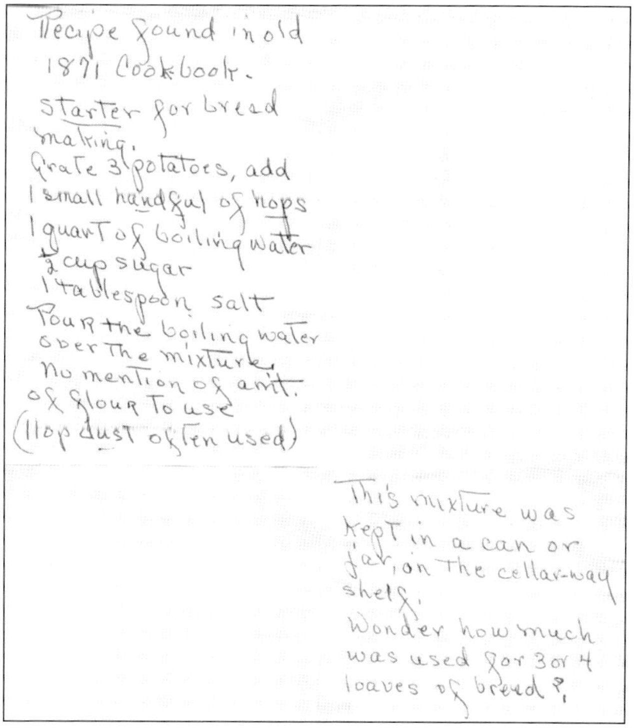

Recipe found in old
1871 Cookbook.
Starter for bread
making.
Grate 3 potatoes, add
1 small handful of hops
1 quart of boiling water
½ cup sugar
1 tablespoon salt
Pour the boiling water
over the mixture.
No mention of amt.
of flour to use
(Hop dust often used)

This mixture was
kept in a can or
jar, on the cellar-way
shelf.
Wonder how much
was used for 3 or 4
loaves of bread?

Hops had many uses beyond flavoring and preserving malt of beer and ale. Bine and leaves could be using for tanning or fertilizer, dried hops could be placed in pillows or used in powder form as a narcotic for sleep, hop syrups could be used for fevers and other medical disorders, and young shoots could be cooked much like asparagus. Many hop recipes survive, including this one for a bread-making starter from an 1871 cookbook.

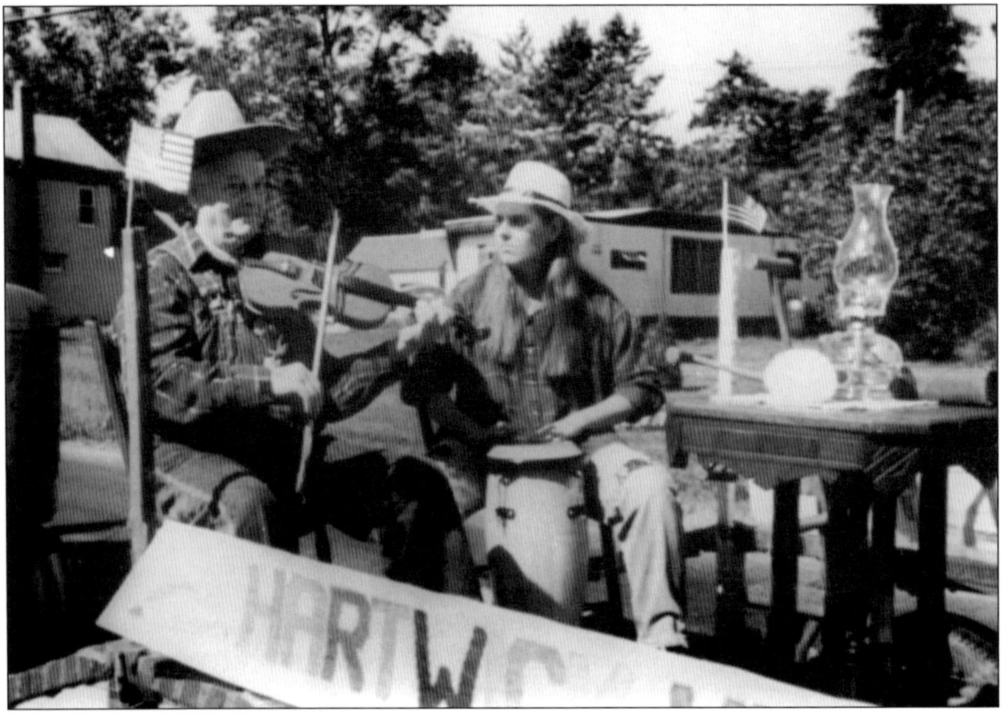

Music and dancing of all kinds provided popular Hartwick entertainment. Among others, the Hartwick Band started after World War I with local musicians, who practiced weekly and gave concerts at community events. Family square-dance parties were frequent, with rugs rolled up, furniture pushed back, and a piano and fiddler to provide the music. William Powers, pictured here on a 1952 sesquicentennial float with his fiddle, had a square-dance band of three who played for years at Grange halls and other area locations.

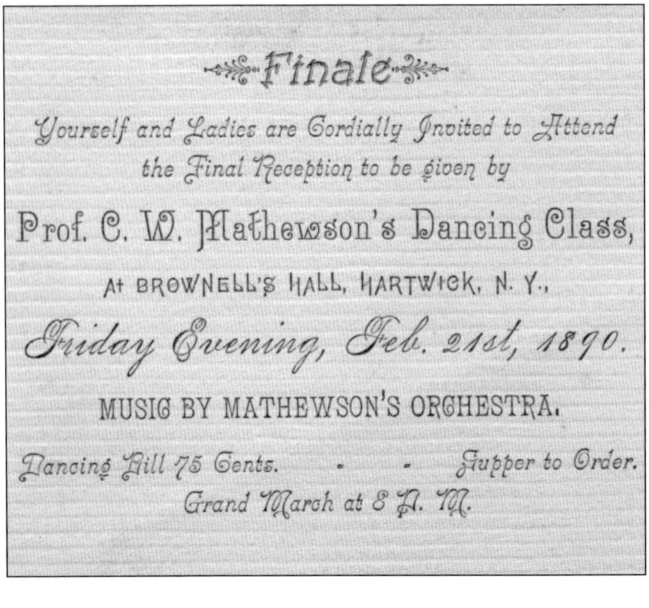

Finale

Yourself and Ladies are Cordially Invited to Attend
the Final Reception to be given by

Prof. C. W. Mathewson's Dancing Class,

At BROWNELL'S HALL, HARTWICK, N. Y.,

Friday Evening, Feb. 21st, 1890.

MUSIC BY MATHEWSON'S ORCHESTRA.

Dancing Bill 75 Cents. - - Supper to Order.
Grand March at 8 P. M.

Dances have always been held in Hartwick, sometimes as fundraisers but often just for pure entertainment or special holidays. The Otego Valley Hotel had a ballroom, as did the Brooklyn House on the west side of town. The EMBA Hall was spacious enough for dramatic programs as well as railroad/trolley dances, and the third floor of the Cottage Hotel held weekly Saturday-night dances. There was even a dancing class with Prof. W.C. Mathewson, as this class-finale invitation shows.

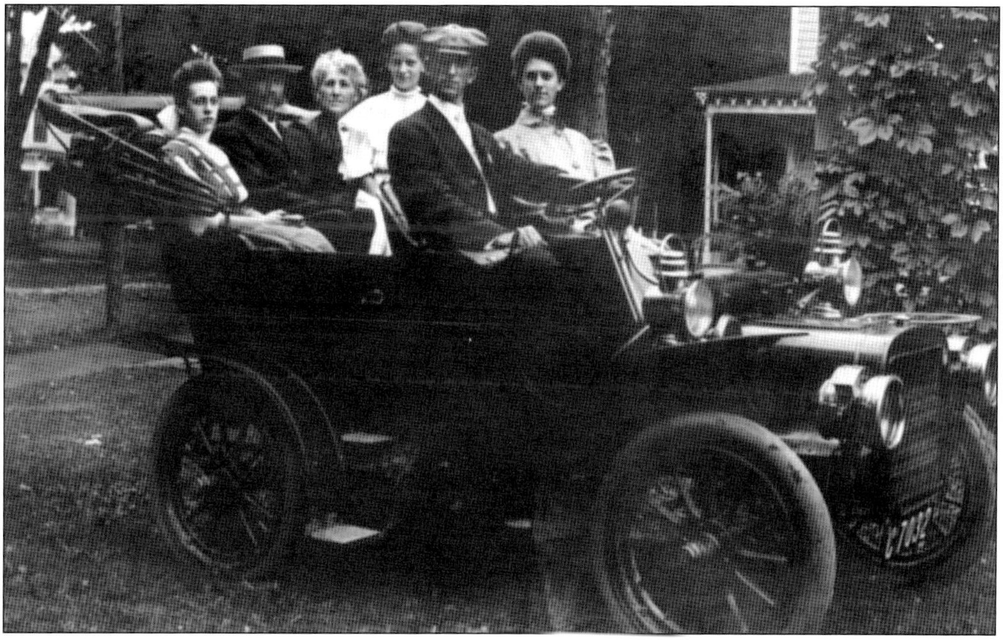

Hartwick had other diversions, as this 1908 view shows. Reverend Booth, pastor of Hartwick Baptist Church from 1905 to 1909, and his family are ready to experience a drive in one of Hartwick's first automobiles. (RF.)

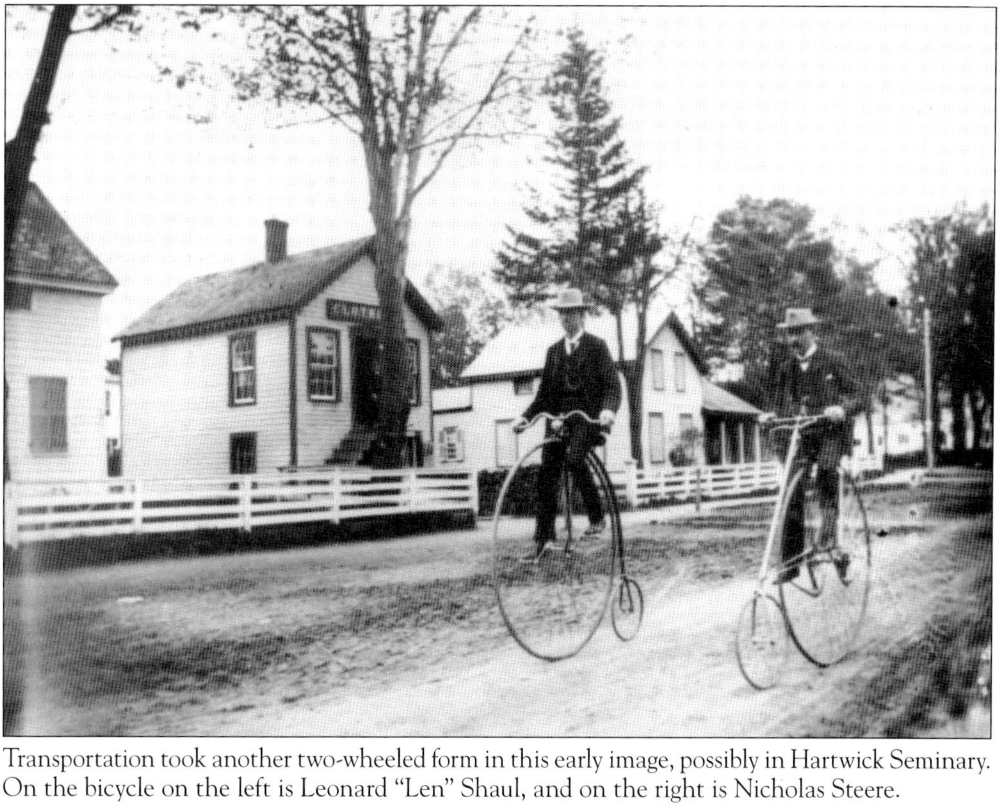

Transportation took another two-wheeled form in this early image, possibly in Hartwick Seminary. On the bicycle on the left is Leonard "Len" Shaul, and on the right is Nicholas Steere.

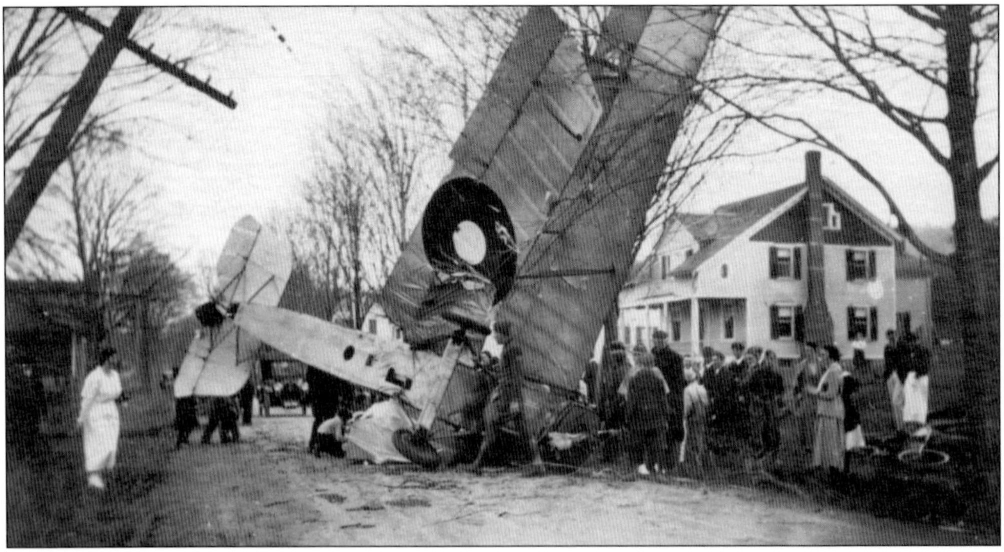

Arnold Lake camp owner and pilot Maurice Harrison flew a small airplane in the 1940s, often landing on the lake. Other pilots are known to have given airplanes rides in Hartwick hamlet during the 1930s and 1940s, with landings on the field across Main Street from the depot. One unidentified pilot was not so successful, as this photograph shows of an airplane crash in Hartwick Seminary.

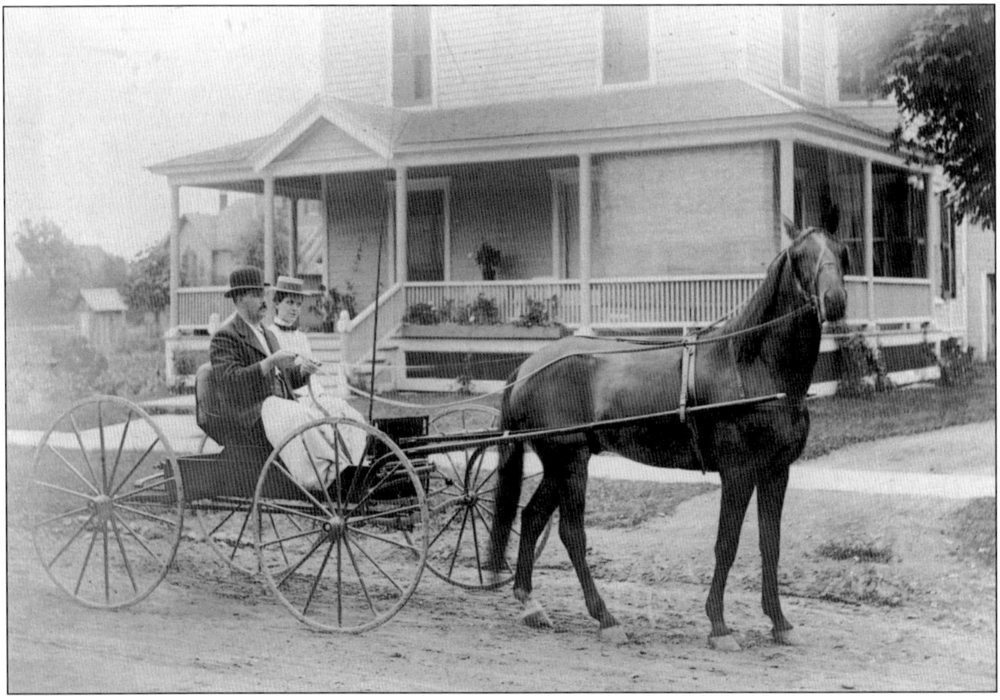

Leonard Proctor and Mr. Avery had a racetrack on the site of the North Street Hartwick hamlet cemetery with the judge's stand located near the present vault. A fairground is identified on an 1868 map to the east of the racetracks, and a man named Backus was known to own and race horses. This undated Main Street image may show one of those horses; its partial notation reads, "14 year old record 224 ¼ has paced 1/8 of a mile in 15 seconds; a two minute gait as an 8 year old."

Seven

Some People around Hartwick

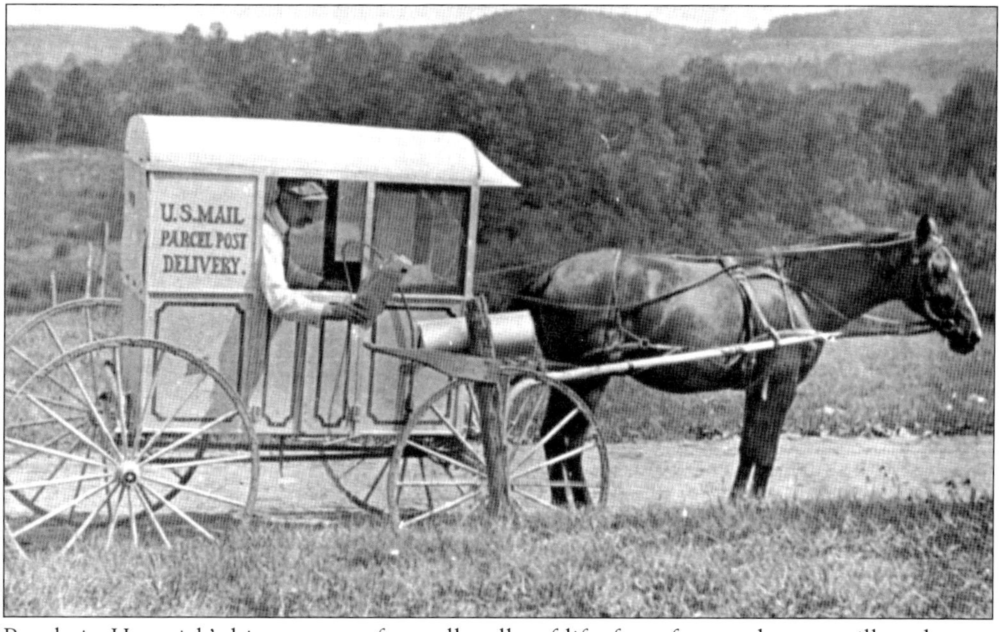

People in Hartwick's history came from all walks of life, from farmworkers or mill workers to tradesmen, professional men and women, businessmen, and political leaders. Some are still well remembered, while others have faded into the past, but all had their part in creating the Hartwick of today. One local man, now gone, who provided an important daily service was Hartwick's first rural delivery mailman, Everett Pope.

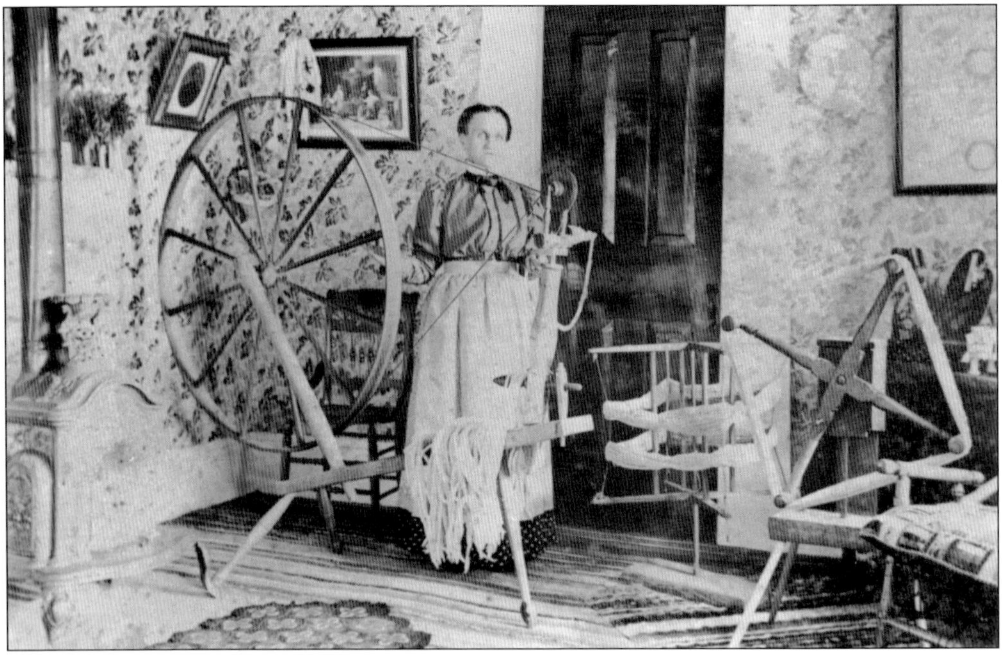

Women as well as men worked hard to meet basic family needs. Along with completing regular housekeeping chores, homemakers grew and preserved food and made all family clothing from farm-raised sheep and flax. In this view, an unidentified Hartwick homemaker on the Fuller farm works with her spinning wheel to prepare yarn for the weaving process. (DP.)

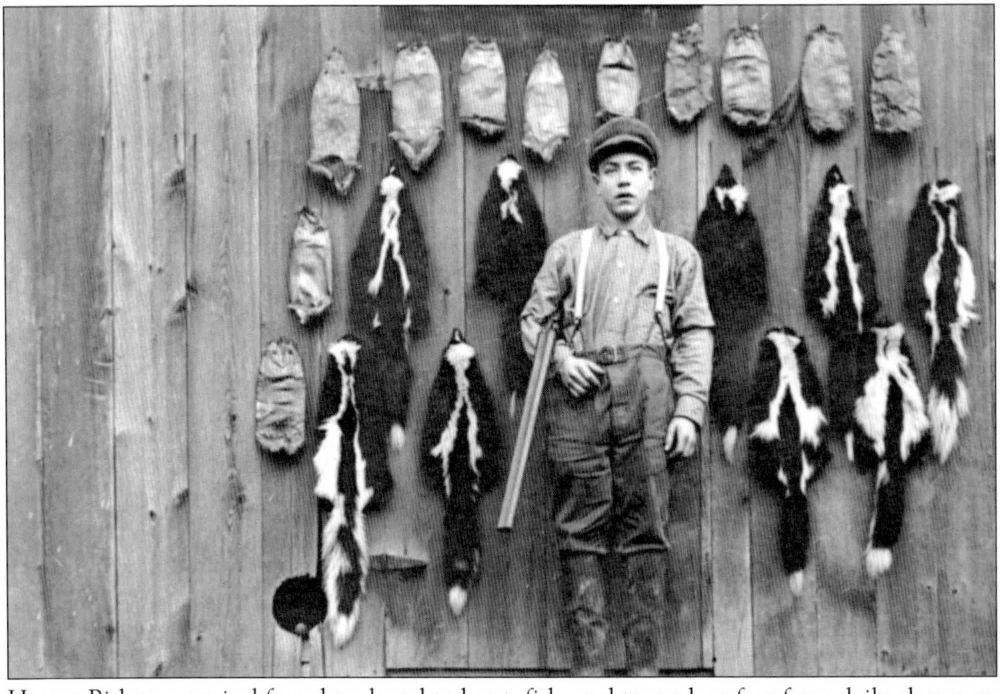

Homer Bishop, a typical farm boy, loved to hunt, fish, and trap when free from daily chores on the family farm in the White House area. This image shows some of his trapping and hunting trophies on the Bishop barn wall in the 1920s. (DP.)

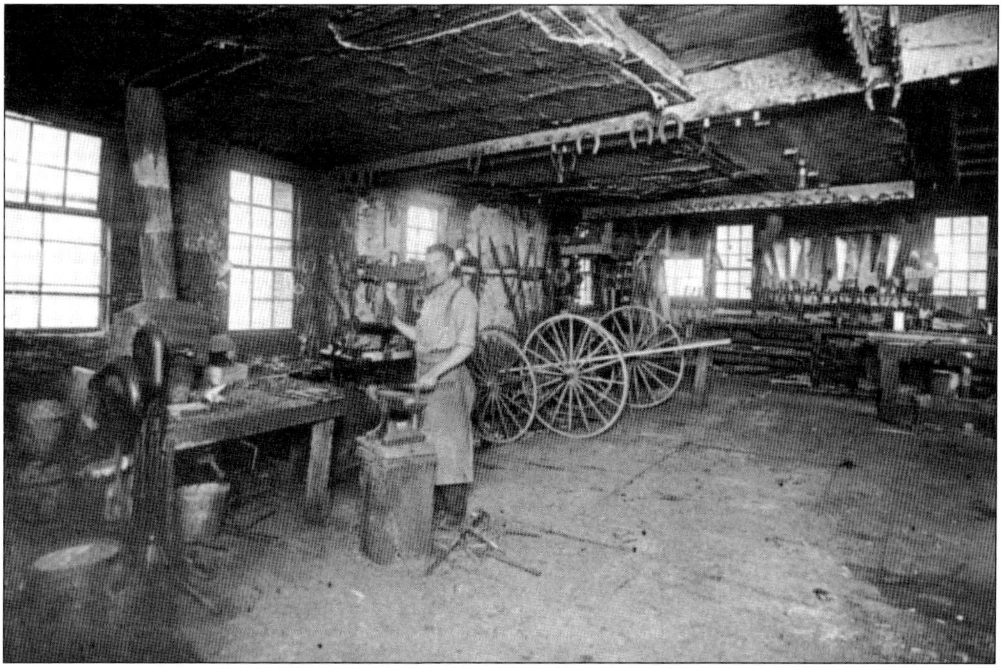

Blacksmiths, as essential craftsmen and in high demand, provided shoes for work animals and all types of iron articles for homes, farms, and mills. Every community had multiple blacksmith shops, with 12 listed for the township in 1872. This unidentified blacksmith provided wagon and blacksmith services around 1900 in the Hartwick hamlet at a shop located on the site of the former Williams Foundry west of Otego Creek.

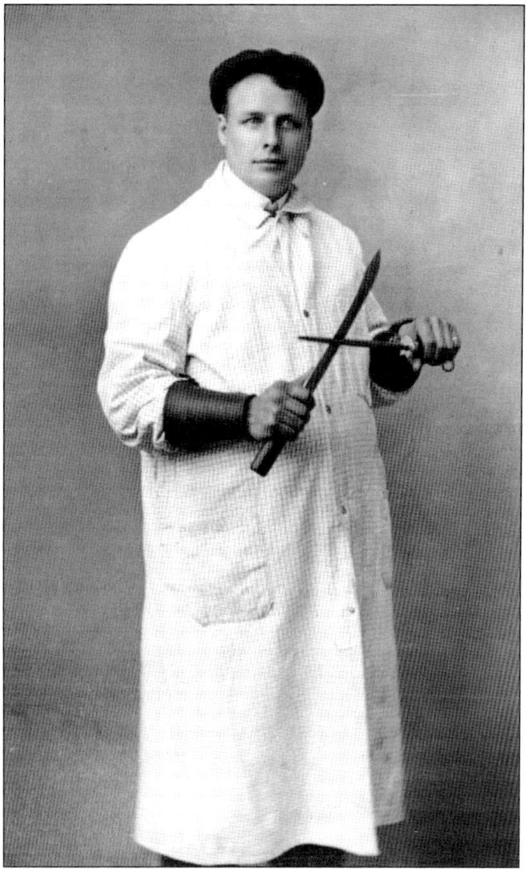

Farmers raised their own meat for family use, while hamlet town residents could buy fresh meat at local groceries or meat markets. In 1907, Hartwick hamlet had three meat markets, including one operated by Earl DeMett on central Main Street. Owner and butcher Earl DeMett is pictured here in 1913. (ST at FAM.)

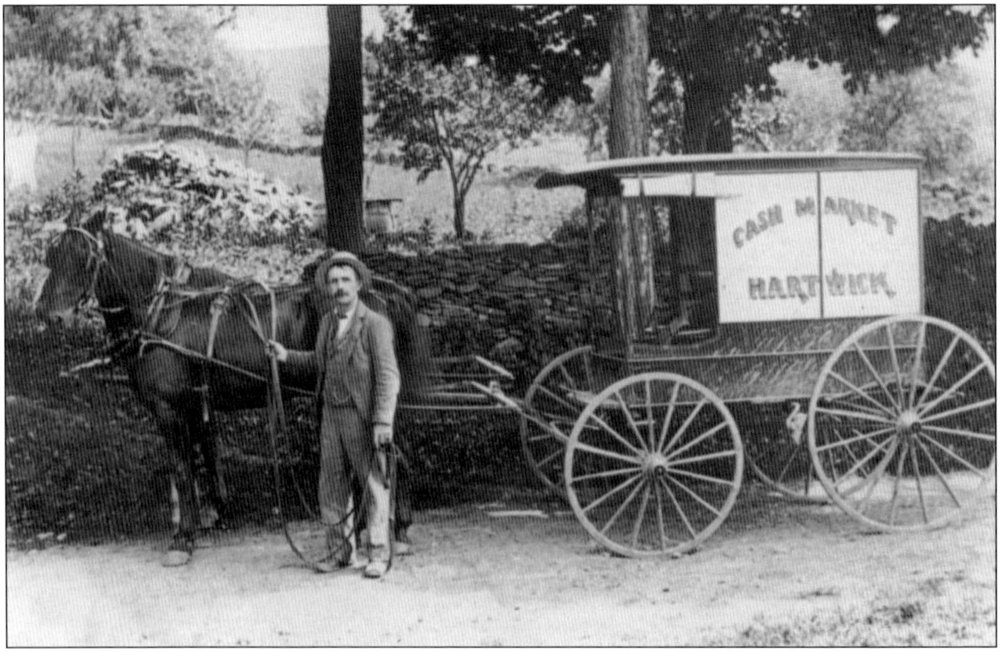

Township communities had many varied small businesses through the years, with frequent changes of owners and locations. Men competed for business with the addition of delivery services. James Telfer and family delivered meat and milk locally, and Delos Harrington, pictured here around 1900, operated a successful meat-delivery route.

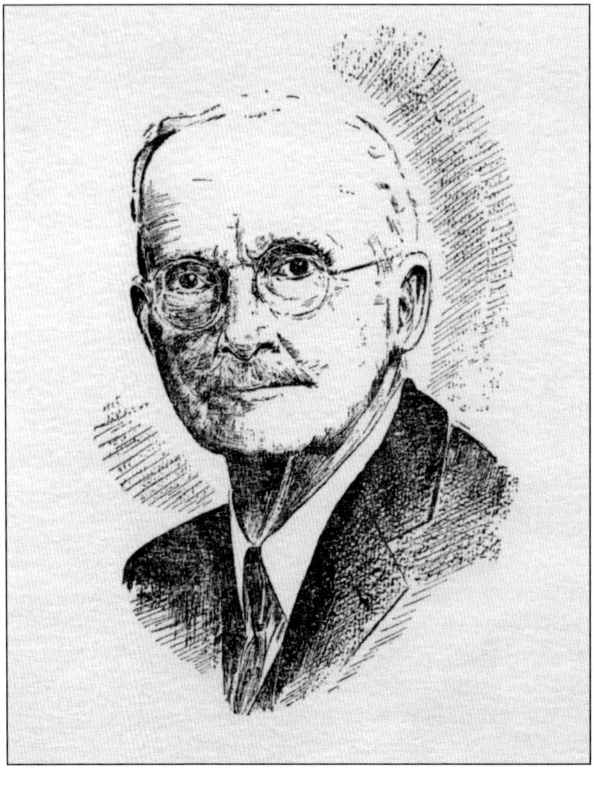

As a young boy in 1882, Frank Bresee began his business career by peddling small notions door to door to local homemakers. From this small beginning, he went on to start a mercantile store in South Hartwick, then to operate a busy corner store in Hartwick hamlet, and finally in 1899 to found the Oneonta Department Store, which grew by the 1930s into "the largest department store in central New York," according to an article in a local newspaper celebrating the store's anniversary.

Jehiel Todd and family came from Connecticut in 1796 to purchase the southern half of Tubbs Patent from Judge Cooper. The land spanned Oaks Creek, the border between Otsego and Hartwick Townships. The Todd family, represented here by son Zerah, harnessed the creek's waterpower to create Todds Mills (Toddsville), a thriving manufacturing mill town with grist, lumber, paper, cotton, and woolen mills.

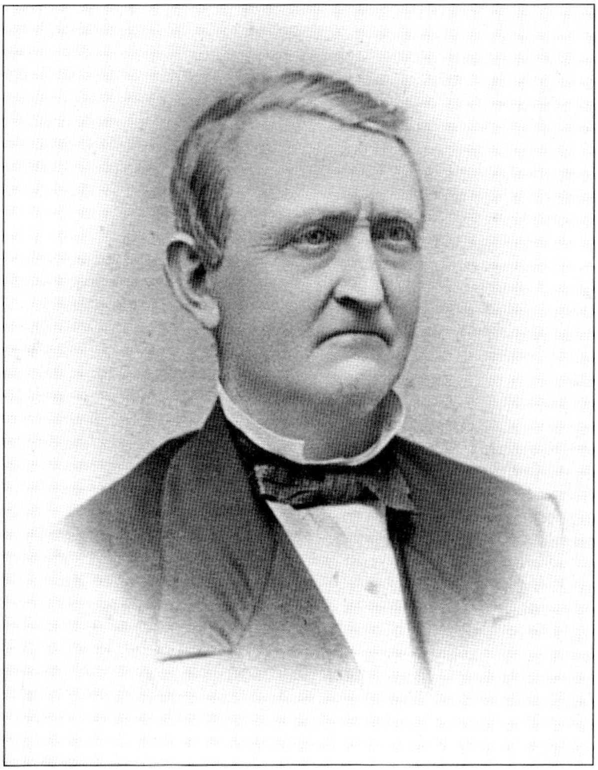

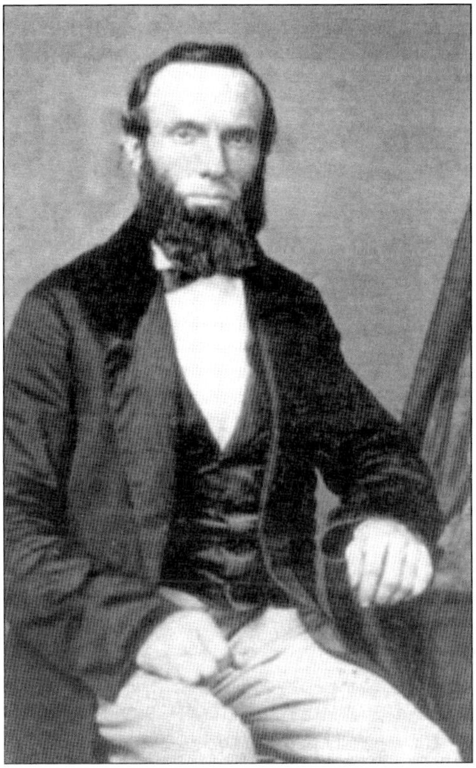

Chester Rockwell came from Connecticut to South Hartwick in 1813, purchased Lippitt Mills, and constructed a dyke to harness the waterpower of Otego Creek. Water, and later steam, ran the grist and sawmill but primarily a large woolen mill. The Rockwells (father and sons Erastus and Chester W.) were large property owners, operating mills in several locations. Chester W. is pictured here. South Hartwick, with the Rockwells, prospered until the woolen mill burned in 1861.

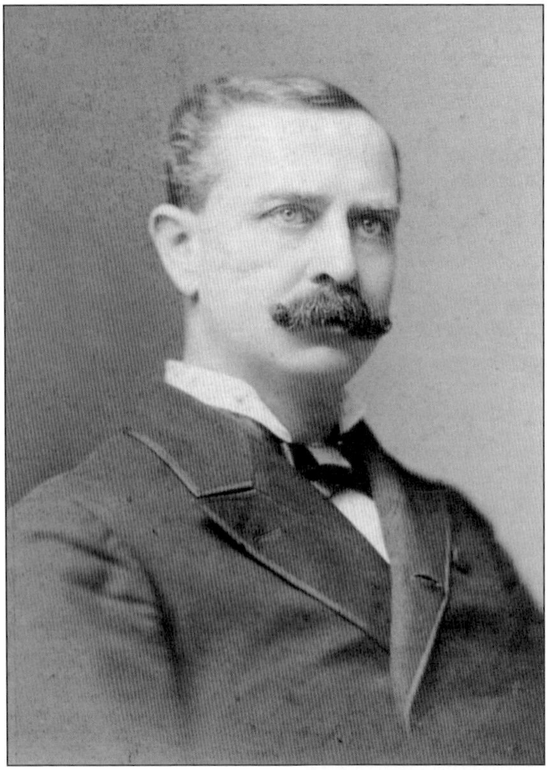

At least 17 doctors are known to have served in Hartwick throughout its history. One of the more recent was Dr. George Schoolcraft. After training at Albany Medical School and practicing in Albany, he came to Hartwick in 1897. Dr. Schoolcraft was active in community organizations and, along with having some eccentric mannerisms, was known as a friend and well-respected country doctor (who made house calls) for over 45 years.

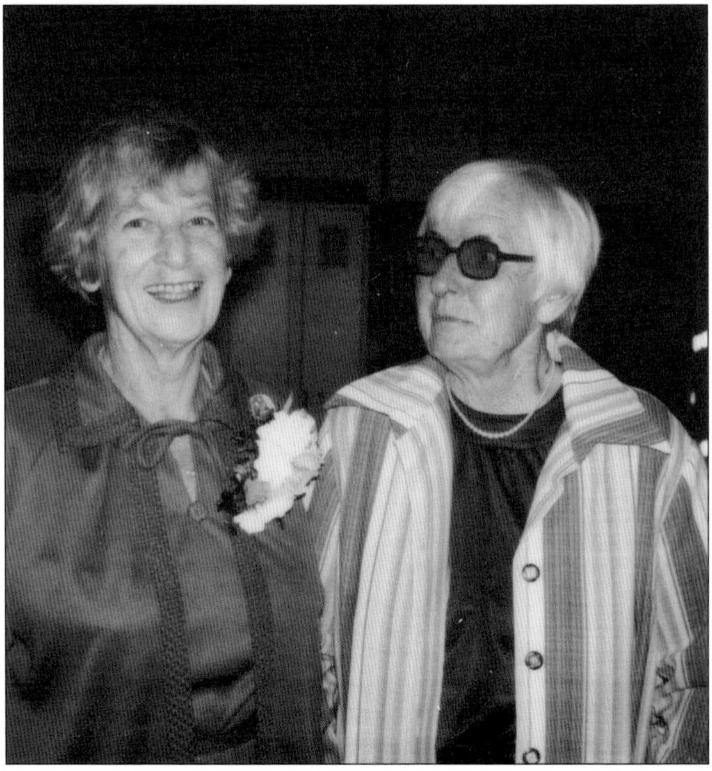

Dr. Steffie Baker (Pullis) was born and first trained in Germany, then practiced medicine in remote Bolivia, South America, before coming to the United States in 1948. Well known as an excellent diagnostician and beloved family doctor, she practiced medicine here for over 30 years before retirement. Seen here (left) with close friend Mary Telfer, Dr. Baker was honored at a large community-wide reception in 1978.

At age 93 in 1952, Arthur J. "Putt" Telfer was the "nation's oldest active commercial photographer." While born in Cooperstown and operating a photography business there for over 60 years, his family ties and first studio (opened at the four corners in 1878) were in Hartwick, where he owned a home and a studio on North Street before moving to St. Johnsville and then to Cooperstown in 1887. "Putt," known for a former pastime of "putt-putting" around Otsego Lake in a motorboat, produced a prolific photographic record (estimated already at 300,000 by his 81st birthday in 1936) of all aspects of community life in Hartwick and the Otsego County area. As seen below in a Hartwick parade, he was a familiar sight motoring about in his 1915 Ford roadster.

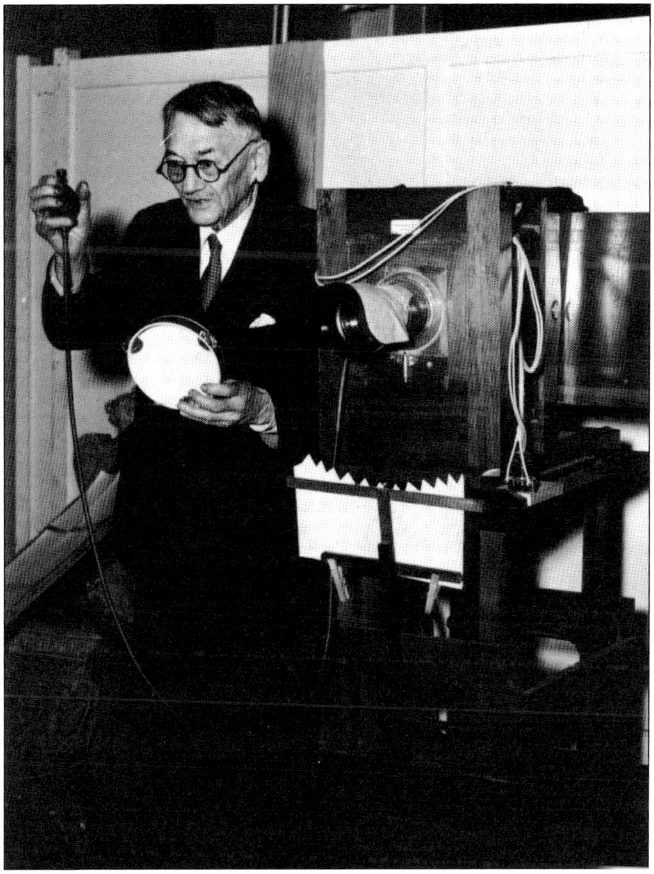

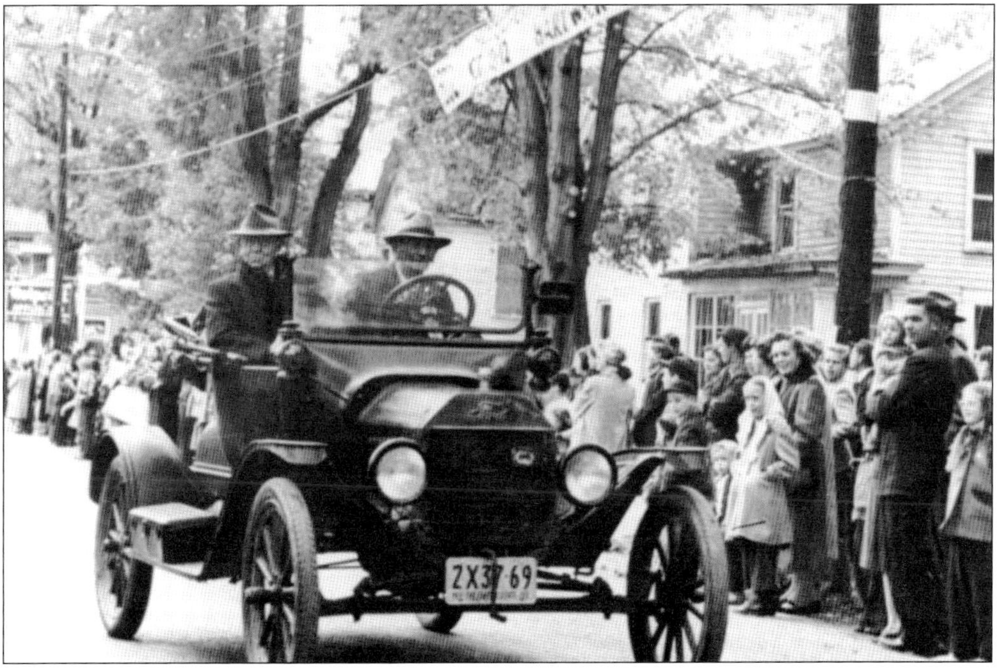

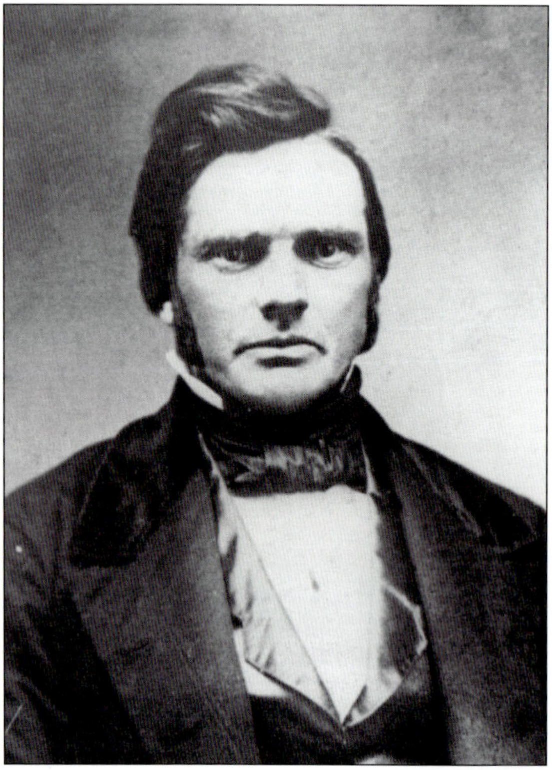

Marcus Wells was born in 1815 to a Christian Hill farm couple. At the age of 12, when his father died, Marcus apprenticed and then worked as a carpenter to help support his family. Later, he became a farmer, inventor, businessman, lawyer, and devout church member, but he is best known as composer of the well-known hymn "Holy Spirit, Faithful Guide." This hymn has been translated into more than 16 different languages.

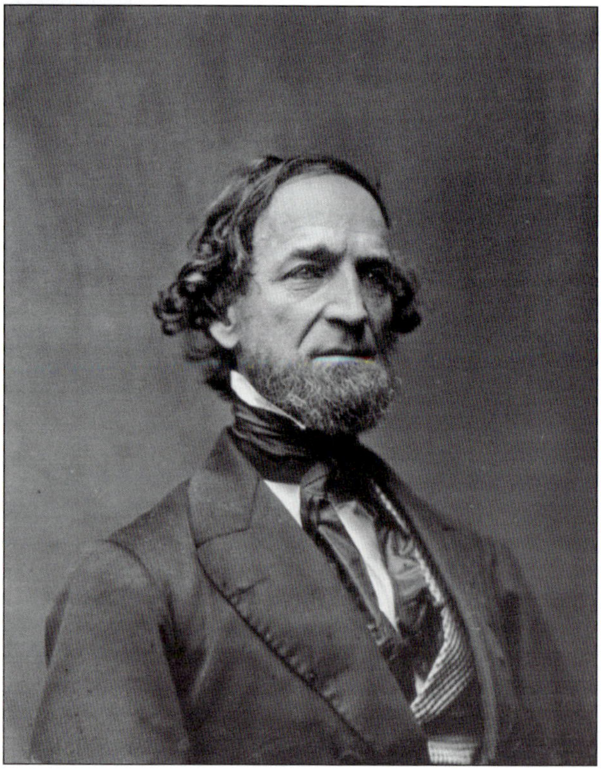

Isaac Newton Arnold, an 1831 graduate of Hartwick Seminary and Academy, rose to prominence as a close political friend of Pres. Abraham Lincoln. As the congressman from Illinois, Arnold became the "eyes and ears on Capitol Hill for President Lincoln" and in 1864 introduced a resolution calling for a constitutional amendment to end slavery in the United States. This led to passage of the 13th Amendment in 1865.

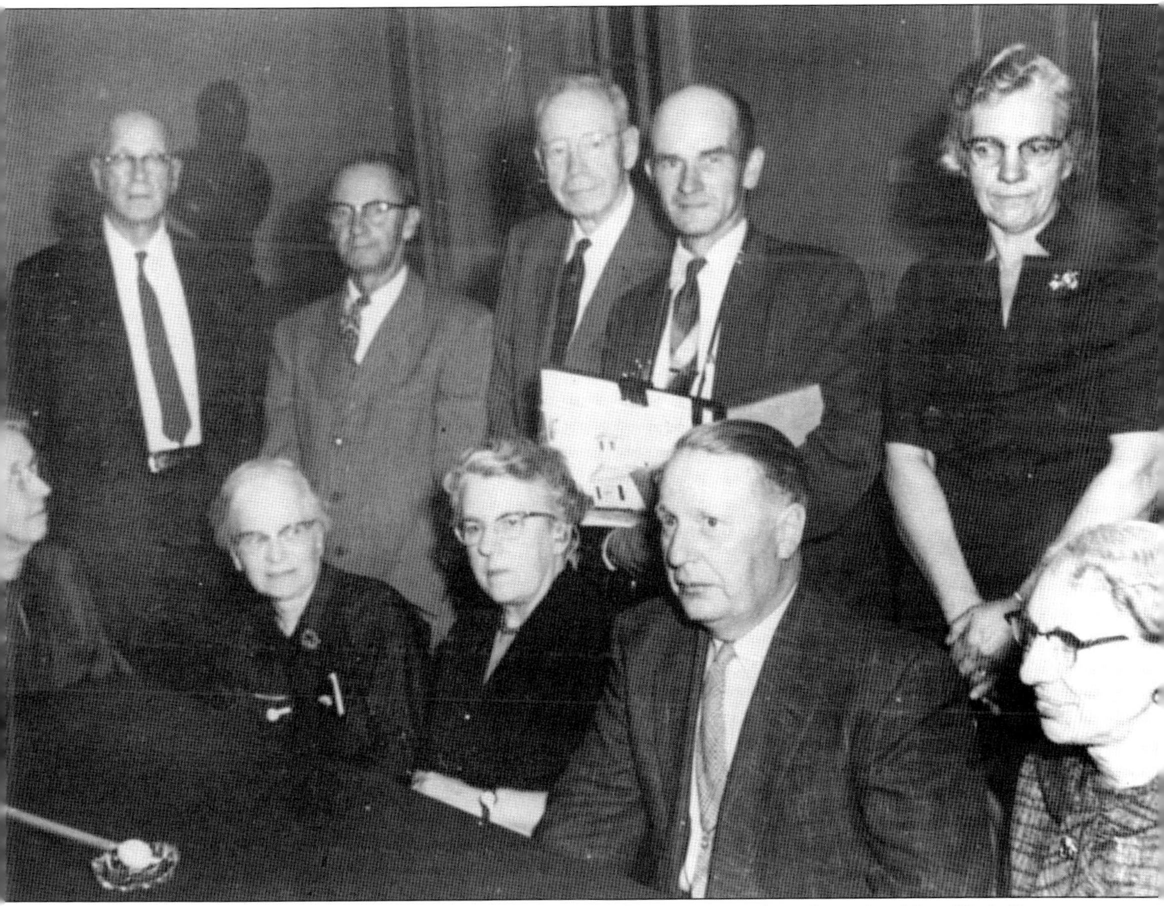

In the early 1960s, a panel of local history enthusiasts from Hartwick gathered at New York State Historical Association's Fenimore House in Cooperstown to present a Town of Hartwick history program to the community. Each panel member shared history of a selected township community. This same group of history lovers later formed the nucleus of the Hartwick Historical Society, which formally organized in 1969. The panelists pictured here and their topics are, from left to right, (first row) Naomi Bilderbeck (Hartwick hamlet), Esther Backus (Hartwick Seminary), Martha Hollister (Toddsville), Kenneth Augur (Hinman Hollow), and Pearl Weeks (town historian); (second row) Dr. Roy Butterfield (moderator and county historian), Ramon Chase (Chase), Harry Bilderbeck (Hartwick hamlet), John A. Mott (White House), and Nellie Balcom (South Hartwick).

Discover Thousands of Local History Books Featuring Millions of Vintage Images

Arcadia Publishing, the leading local history publisher in the United States, is committed to making history accessible and meaningful through publishing books that celebrate and preserve the heritage of America's people and places.

Find more books like this at
www.arcadiapublishing.com

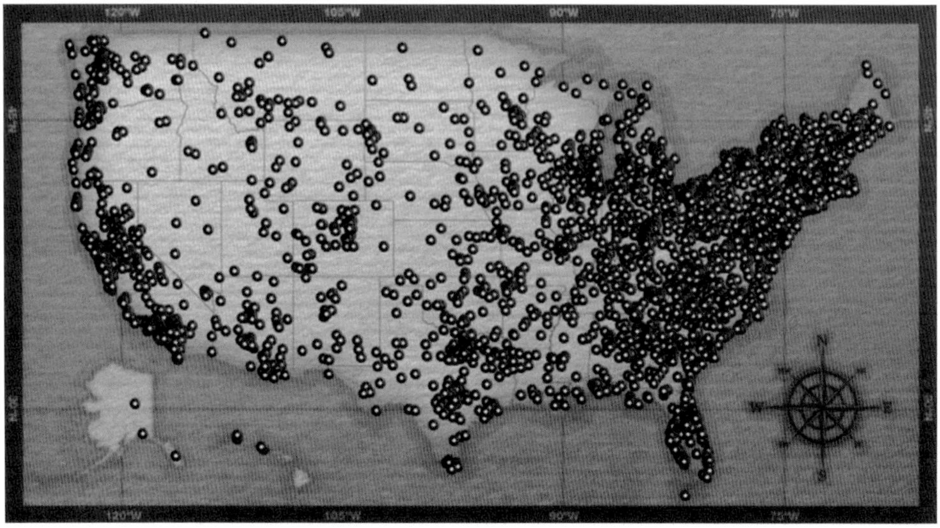

Search for your hometown history, your old stomping grounds, and even your favorite sports team.

Consistent with our mission to preserve history on a local level, this book was printed in South Carolina on American-made paper and manufactured entirely in the United States. Products carrying the accredited Forest Stewardship Council (FSC) label are printed on 100 percent FSC-certified paper.

MADE IN THE USA